WEISER ☿ CLASSICS

THE WEISER CLASSICS SERIES offers essential works
from renowned authors and spiritual teachers, foundational
texts, as well as introductory guides on an array of topics. The
series represents the full range of subjects and genres that have
been part of Weiser's over sixty-year-long publishing program—
from divination and magick to alchemy and occult philosophy.
Each volume in the series will whenever possible include new
material from its author or a contributor and other valuable
additions and will be printed and produced using acid-free
paper in a durable paperback binding.

Predictive Astrology

Tools to Forecast Your Life & Create Your Brightest Future

BERNADETTE BRADY

Foreword by Theresa Reed

WEISER
BOOKS

This edition first published in 2022 by Weiser Books, an imprint of
Red Wheel/Weiser, LLC
With offices at:
65 Parker Street, Suite 7
Newburyport, MA 01950
www.redwheelweiser.com

ISBN: 978-1-57863-767-6
Library of Congress Cataloging-in-Publication Data available upon request.

Series Editors
Mike Conlon, Production Director, Red Wheel/Weiser Books
Judika Illes, Editor-at-Large, Weiser Books
Peter Turner, Associate Publisher, Weiser Books
Series Design
Kathryn Sky-Peck, Creative Director, Red Wheel/Weiser

Interior diagrams © Red Wheel/Weiser
Typeset in Arno Pro

Printed in the United States of America
IBI

10 9 8 7 6 5 4 3 2 1

To my father
who gave me the Eagle . . .
and my mother
who gave me the Lark.

Contents

List of Charts

Foreword

When I was a young girl growing up in a rural area, I felt like an alien. I didn't fit in with my community—or my family, for that matter. Much of my time was spent trying to figure out who I was and why I was stuck in this environment. Unfortunately, no one seemed to have a satisfactory answer to my questions. That is until fate brought astrology into my world.

I was introduced to the wonders of my natal chart in my mid-teens through a fellow misfit's mother. She painstakingly drew little symbols and numbers by hand on a circle divided into twelve sections like a pecan pie. It looked like a cryptic code or strange piece of art. What did it mean—and what might it reveal about me?

I soon found out exactly what those odd markings meant as she began sharing her findings. Suddenly, everything started to make sense. I felt like I finally had the answers I desperately needed and could understand who I really was.

My astrology studies began in earnest that day, which wasn't easy since there weren't many resources available, especially in that neck of the woods. I had to hunt for the information like a tireless detective or rely on my friend's mother's books, which were falling apart at the seams. (She gifted me one of her astrology books before she died. It's one of my most prized possessions, wrapped in plastic and tucked away on my bookshelf.)

I think many astrologers start out the same way—we want to figure out our purpose. But soon, there are other questions to explore and many astrological rabbit holes to go down.

Once I understood what I was all about, I became curious about where my future might lead. Unfortunately, while a few of my books covered the transits, I had a hard time finding anything that explained predictive astrology in a way that made sense to me. That is until I got my hands on Bernadette Brady's *Predictive Astrology: The Eagle and the Lark.*

The book begins with a story of the lark who wanted to sing to the gods. But he was too small, and his wings were not strong enough to take him as high as he needed to go. Along came an eagle, who had the power to lift him up to the heavens. The lark got on the eagle's back, and, sure enough, he was able to reach the gods and deliver his sweet song. This is an analogy of how predictive astrology works—a strong foundation (eagle) supports you. At the same time, your intuition (the lark) helps to make the information "sing."

Suddenly all of the pieces began to fall into place. Like the lark in the fable, I wanted to soar higher, view the grand picture, and be able to see my story or the life story of my clients unfold in an intuitive yet precise way. I needed the back of the eagle to carry me to the next level. The techniques in this groundbreaking book helped me—and it will help you, too.

Brady weaves solid astrological techniques, such as transits, secondary progressions, and eclipses, along with sound advice on troubleshooting your mistakes, trusting your intuition, and using other systems when the ones you count on don't deliver the results.

One of the things I found most helpful in this book was the latter part. Sometimes I would make an astrological prediction only to have it go completely sideways. I can assure you this is enough to shake even the most experienced astrologer! Brady encourages the reader not to give up but instead to dig in and explore other methods, which might reveal something that slipped by.

An example she gives involves a man who got in a lot of trouble on a trip and was not happy that Brady had not predicted it. This led her to rip apart every aspect, transit, progression, and more until she peered into his solar return—and there it was. A simple answer. This story illustrates the dogged work an astrologer must be ready and willing to do when delving into predictive astrology.

For folks who want to see the future via astrology, it can be overwhelming at the beginning. There is so much detailed information to consider, and I think I can speak for most astrologers when I say it can lead to analysis paralysis. Where do you begin? Information overload can be a real problem. But Bernadette Brady breaks everything down to the bones with techniques that will help every astrologer, from budding to adept, deliver helpful, precise readings without the astrobabble. She provides a workable foundation, solid as an eagle's back with wings that will take your astrological readings to the next level.

Soon you'll have the confidence and vision to see where you're going—and that's when the intuition begins to sing along.

This book is a valuable resource, one I keep near my desk to refer to when I feel stuck. It has served as a faithful guide in my understanding of predictive astrology.

Predictive Astrology is a timeless masterpiece that every astrologer will want by their side as they deepen their astrological studies. The best way to learn is through practice, trial, and error, with a good teacher at the helm. Bernadette Brady is one of the best in the field. With this book by your side, you're getting a master class in understanding what goes into predictive astrology. Perhaps this can help you, the reader, understand fate's role in your life—and how to make it work for you.

To your bright future,

—Theresa Reed
Astrology for Real Life: A No B.S. Guide for the Astro-Curious

Acknowledgments

To write a book takes a large amount of support, encouragement, and patience. For providing this, as well as endless editing, my deep thanks go to Darrelyn Gunzburg.

For the making of gallons of tea, while endlessly proofreading, my thanks go to Ysha De Donna.

And thanks to my white-haired old friend Robert.

The Fable of the Eagle and the Lark

Once upon a time there was a lark who was renowned for her beautiful singing. Her song was judged by all who heard her to be the sweetest sound on earth. From dawn to dusk she would sing her song and as she sang, the beginnings of a desire grew. The desire was to sing for the gods.

She realized that if she could fly high enough the gods would be able to hear her. So the lark leapt into the air and flew as high as she could, but her wings tired and although she sang, she knew that the gods could not hear her. Determined now more than ever, she decided that she would climb the highest mountain and then fly from the peak. But even this could not get her high enough to be heard in heaven.

One day she saw an eagle soaring high in the sky, far higher than she had ever flown, and she knew with unbounded certainty that if she could fly as high as the eagle, the gods would hear her beautiful song. So she watched the eagle and when he landed, she approached the huge bird. The small but brave lark explained her dilemma to the great eagle and asked if he would carry her on his back so that, together, they could entertain the gods.

Now the eagle was aware of the gods because he could fly in their domain and yet, ashamed of his raucous voice, he never had the courage to contact them. Eagerly he agreed to carry the tiny lark.

Tentatively she climbed onto his back and with a stretch and a flap of his mighty wings, he set aloft. Higher and higher they soared. The lark was almost too scared to look down and yet onward still they flew. The lark had never been this high. She could see the whole world spread out beneath her. And then, all of a sudden, they were there. The tiny lark knew that now it was her turn, the eagle having done his part. Firmly she stood up on the eagle's back and, filling her lungs with air, began to sing. Heaven was filled with her glorious music. The gods were astonished at the power of the eagle and enthralled by the beauty of the lark's song. The eagle was no longer ashamed and the lark was filled with joy. Together, as a team, they had brought music to the gods.

Since time began, the human race has quested the future. Whether it be the knowledge of a successful hunt, the weather patterns, the movement of the enemy, or the outcome of a journey, to know the future was to have an advantage. This need was so great that every tribe or clan had its own seer, sage, shaman, or priest. This person's role was to explain the unexplainable and give meanings and patterns to seemingly random events, thereby reducing fear and creating greater stability. If the tribe's seer died, then the tribe would "find" or project these skills onto another individual.

The human race has come a long way since those first early scratchings on cave walls. But the need for the seer has not changed. In our modern world, there are still the unexplained, the uncertain future, and the need in the community for some individuals to "see" ahead of time. So the modern community seeks out individuals who, willingly or unwillingly, will take on the role of the seer.

There are many pathways that lend themselves to the ancient projection of seership. Scientists predicting outcomes, the bureau of meteorology predicting weather, election forecasters predicting results, and the economists predicting the economy are seers on the side of the establishment. Clairvoyants, psychics, tarot readers, numerologists, tea-leaf readers, and astrologers are, in the public's eye, the seers of the non-establishment.

Thus as we decide to study astrology to fulfill our own needs, all too often, within a few weeks of commencing study, the student's friends will not only want to know about themselves but also want the student to be their seer. The student's personal quest for truth and meaning in life thus becomes burdened by the community's ancient longing for a seer.

Predictive work in astrology is also enmeshed with the collective's need for mystery, wonder, and spirituality. So as astrologers we find that the pathway to predictive astrology, which begins as a personal quest for knowledge, turns into this minefield of other people's expectations. In order to negotiate a clearer path through this minefield, astrologers have put a great deal of energy into developing new predictive techniques, and in a striving to fulfill the needs of the community, we keep trying to build a better, and therefore safer, wheel.

But herein lies the paradox: for if predictive astrology is a quest, then it will unconsciously be considered unreachable, for it is in the nature of a quest that it should not be achieved too easily. In addition, the projection of seer can also be so overpowering that no sane individual would want to carry it. So astrologers can, like Jason of Argonaut fame, constantly seek, without recognizing what they have already achieved, and place predictive astrology so high above them that, no matter how hard they try, it cannot possibly be obtained.

Thus the first point to be made in pursuit of reliable predictive astrology is: recognize that you can already predict using astrology and how impressive this is to a layperson. For example, if you know that a person is going to have transiting Pluto conjunct the natal ascendant at a given time, then as an astrologer, you would expect some event to occur in that person's life. If you know no more than that, your prediction to the layperson seems amazing. In addition, provided the birth time is correct, you can do this with a high level of accuracy.

Acknowledgement of such simple feats in astrology, considered awe-inspiring by the general public, allows predictive work to be taken down from its pedestal. By recognizing the simplicity of these skills and how easily they can be taught to another, the minefield of projection becomes a little less dangerous. However, this minefield can still exist, and, faced with this difficulty, astrologers have three possible paths that they can follow: the first is to abandon the whole issue and firmly announce that predictive work cannot be done. This is not really an option but an external appearance adopted to push back the community's need for a seer.

The second approach is through new methods and techniques such as high-powered computing, micro-aspecting, and employing the ultimate in precision calculations. Reams of data are produced with this approach, and astrologers are swamped by the numerous echoes of the same information rearranged in an infinite number of mathematical ways. The average astrologer, confronted by this approach, perceives that the journey lies through a mathematical maze of confusion.

The third approach is one of intuition. These astrologers abandon mathematical techniques and, without any real understanding of the tools that they are using, leap into the deep end and "go by what feels right." The difficulty with this approach is that it cannot be taught, explained, or repeated, and students following this example can find themselves in an empty void of vagueness and disillusion.

Neither of the last two approaches is in error. The problem occurs when they are used exclusively. For astrology is both an art and a science and has to have both components in balance for the best possible results. So an astrologer's intuition is like the tiny lark in the fable, and the techniques and methodology of an astrologer's craft, the mighty eagle. Separately they are both valid and valuable. Together they can achieve results before unreachable.

The next step is to recognize when and how to use intuition. What is the point of intuitively draining your metaphysical batteries to reach a conclusion that could have been logically derived? Far better to sing with your intuition after logic has gone as far as it can go.

The boundaries between eagle and lark must be observed and each one used in its proper time and place. Too often one sees eagles balancing on the backs of squashed larks as astrologers derive immense volumes of data from confused or misunderstood origins. Similarly, if astrologers are not clear on what they have predicted via techniques and what they have predicted via intuitive leaps, then it is very difficult to know where they may have gone wrong and how to correct it.

This book is about the eagle, its strength and weakness, and where he can go wrong. It is about the lark and when to let her sing.

The first step in the successful use of the eagle is to understand the nature of the beast. Thus it is important to acknowledge that the origins of astrology are in the world of science. Indeed it is the original science, and its metaphysical doorways are reached through corridors of mathematics and astronomy. In other words, an understanding of number-crunching and the logic of the techniques used are needed by the astrologer. It is easy in this computerized world to push a few buttons, get a horoscope printed out, and let intuition flow, bypassing all the problems of learning how to calculate charts, progressions, returns, and so on. What flows, of course, is the song of the lark, and if the song is beautiful, what a shame that it's sung from the ground rather than from the back of an eagle.

There is an old rule and a valid one: "You only get out of something what you put in." Astrology is based on science and calculations, and it seems, from my experience, that unless you are prepared to "do your apprenticeship" and learn the basis of the craft, the doors that astrology can open remain closed. The lark may sing, but it has no way of reaching the gods.

The First Step—Fate, the Raw Material of Astrology

Once you sort out the values of, and boundaries between, technique and intuition, you will be taking the first step towards predictive astrology. Then, with eagle under one arm and lark under the other, you will find yourself looking straight into the face of fate.

If we can read the dynamic patterns of a birth chart to give the timing and descriptions of future events, then we must not only acknowledge some "master plan" to which the individual is subject but also realize it is the very raw material with which we are working. For as astrologers we work with fate, just as a cobbler works with leather and a blacksmith works with metals.

Therefore, like any other trade or craft, we need to understand the raw materials of our trade in order to produce results. A blacksmith, in making a horseshoe, does not expect to produce a pound of butter for the simple reason that it is not within the capabilities of the raw material.

So what are the limitations of our raw material? What can it do? What can't it do? How much of a person's life is dictated by fate? Just as the blacksmith has to know the metal's limitations, the astrologer needs to know about fate's limitations. These "how much," "how often," type questions do not have easy answers, but for the predictive astrologer, they cannot be avoided.

Astrologers can only work with the part of an individual that is subject to fate. Thus the accuracy of any prediction is limited by the amount of involvement the individual has with fate.

So how much is a person's life dictated by fate? If the answer were "all of it," then predictive work would be easy, with nothing being left to chance. Astrology would be able to accurately and consistently predict every event of a person's life. It would become a science belonging to the world of that which could be measured, weighed, tasted, and tested, with human beings being equal to a well-designed robot. News broadcasts would tell us what was going to happen, rather than what had happened.

If, on the other hand, the answer is "none of it," then astrologers for the last 5,000 years have been barking up the wrong tree. Since I also find this difficult to believe, the only answer left is that some of a person's life is influenced by this master plan or fate.

If this question was not difficult enough, there is another one. Does the effect of fate on a given individual's life vary from childhood to adulthood, from situation to situation, or not at all?

We are now sailing into very deep seas, and indeed many students faced with these questions might throw up their hands and walk away. But serious predictive astrologers must be concerned with defining the raw material of the craft and need working answers before the quest of predictive astrology can be achieved.

An approach, therefore, to the above unanswerable questions is to consider that there are two major forces at work: one called fate—the raw material of astrologers—and the other called life or free will—the element that is not contained in a chart. The hypothesis that we as astrologers believe is that fate is life's demand for wholeness, or, put more simply, it is our role as a human being to strive for wholeness.

This fated struggle for wholeness that life experiences via a person is represented by the journeys, stories, and problems contained in the birth chart. Fate strives to teach by placing obstacles in the pathway of life, a little like lessons being set for a pupil. We can then make a choice: we can choose to learn quickly and accurately within the parameters of the lessons, or we can continually fail. This is the choice that we have, and fate could well have been the first to say: "You can lead a horse to water . . ."

If we pass the test, then fate will move on to the next set of lessons, like a pupil graduating to a higher class, but the lessons will not cease.

So in this model, and it is only a model, fate at a particular time presents the individual with an option, or lesson, arranged in a variety of ways, a little like a multiple-choice list. The individual, being fated by the quest for wholeness, selects one or more options on the list, either consciously or unconsciously. We would like to think an option is selected based on the individual's desire for maximum personal growth, but an individual has free will in these matters. So the individual's ability to choose an option is assigned to free will, and allocated to fate are the nature and timing of the multiple-choice list.

Thus astrology can predict the timing and style of the forthcoming events, but it is the human part—the part not shown in a chart—that chooses the exact expression of the event.

This model for the marriage of fate and free will may seem simple, but it does allow predictive astrology to take on some shape and boundaries.

Since astrology works with fate, we can expect to be able to predict the timing and nature of the options fate is going to present to the individual, while at the same time recognizing that the options on the list are also going to vary, depending on how well the individual has "learnt lessons" beforehand.

Defining and predicting the exact option may be possible but not necessarily probable. This type of prediction—picking the exact event—would fall into the realm of the lark or intuition, because the actual choice made by the individual, according to our model of fate and free will, belongs to the free-will part.

This model is by no means complete. Indeed no model or answers to the questions that have been raised will be totally satisfactory. But the dilemma of predictive astrology is that a model has to be created. The advantage of the above model, or indeed any model, is that you will know what you can and can't predict, when to use your intuition, and when your astrological logic will be sufficient.

For example, you could look at a client's transiting Uranus conjunct the natal Sun, define the timing of the transit, give an understanding to the client of the types of events that could occur within the timing, and then change gears into the intuitive mode and, using your knowledge of the client and of life itself, indicate the option that will be the most likely.

If you find that you are wrong, then it is an easy matter to see if your astrological logic was at fault. A case of a faulty eagle. Or was it your intuition? The lark needing a bit of work?

The real value of such a system is that the feedback on predictive work can be used constructively.

Predictive astrology is a series of decisions that eventually lead to conclusions. If the conclusions are incorrect, then knowledge of the decisions made along the way is an invaluable aid to improving the results. But one of the first decisions that you have to make as a predictive astrologer is to define a model of your understanding of fate.

Chapter One

The Alphabet

Every language has an alphabet, and predictive astrology is no different. What the astrologer is trying to do in formulating a prediction is to take the language of the Cosmos and translate that information into the conscious world of the client. The way in which we produce this information from the Cosmos is via the predictive system we use, i.e., transits, progressions, and so on. However, no matter what system you use, there is one common thread, and that is the definition of the basic units or alphabet with which the language or data is written.

The alphabet of astrology is made up of the planets, aspects, houses, and signs. With these basic components, the Cosmos can spin a million or so stories. In a natal chart, the stories are magical and mysterious, involving mythology and the history of a person's race. In such a world, the language creates very complex messages, for people have their whole lives to "tinker" with the particular coded messages termed a natal chart.

However, in the world of predictive astrology, the information is present for only a short period of time, and there is no time to explore the concept being presented. There is just time to hear the basic message and to act on it before the next signal comes in. So although the language may be undiscovered Shakespeare, the perception is of a simple dialogue.

Whatever the method of dynamic predictive astrology used, by its very definition it must be a temporary connection to the natal chart. The dynamic planet (progressed or transiting) makes itself felt by way of an aspect and thus connects to the chart; it then symbolically transmits information or energy and, finally, disconnects. It is not there forever, like a natal aspect. It is transient—a tourist traveling through an unknown country.

Thus the dynamic planet comes onto the stage of clients' lives like an invader or intruder, the pragmatist in the plot. The rest of the actors (natal planets) on stage have to deal with this energy, which is seen as raw, young, and not integrated into the system. For this reason, the dynamic planets and aspects, unlike their natal cousins, do not have time to grow and mature in their expression and consequently take on slightly different and considerably simpler meanings.

For example, say Jane has Saturn opposing the Sun in her natal chart. She has her whole life to work with it, grow it, develop it, mature it. The inferiority complex in youth that this aspect can indicate would most likely convert to an achievement drive in adulthood. Granted this achievement drive could be spurred on by a fear of failure fueled by feelings of inadequacy, but Jane has worked with this aspect and can thus get better results from it. This is an aspect that is part of her, that over the years has gained rapport with other facets of herself. On the other hand, if having transiting Saturn opposing her natal Sun, restrictions and commitment suddenly come thundering into her life, with none of the subtleties of the above mentioned natal aspect. Before she has time to "turn the tables on it" and mature it, the transit is gone.

So in working with predictive astrology, the key issue is to recognize this simplicity. The language of astrology is rich and beautiful, but in predictive work, its rich symbolism is put into simple packages. The symbols do not lose their beauty, they are simply less complex in their expression. This concept can be encapsulated by the KISS principle—Keep It Simple, Sweetheart—which indeed is a golden rule of predictive astrology. So with simplicity as the Rosetta Stone of prediction, let's look at the alphabet of our language.

Planets in Predictive Work

The following are some keywords, which are by no means absolute, for the luminaries and planets when they are involved in dynamic astrology.

SUN

Key Principle: life, vitality, the very being, self.

Rate of travel through the zodiac: about 1° per day.

Time to travel through a chart: 1 year.

Use in predictive work: receives transits and makes and receives progressions.

Figures: father, authority figures of any type, a famous person, a superior person.

The Sun is the foundation stone of the human being. In a natal chart, it represents the life journey and story that will be undertaken by the individual seeking awareness. Thus the Sun sign is important, for it reveals the myth or story that the individual follows through life. Transits and progressions to or from this luminary indicate events in the journey of life and a reassessment of personal identity. The person may experience this as life-threatening or life-supporting. Either way, it is like turning the page in the story of life and getting on to the next "adventure."

MOON

Key Principle: mother, feminine, nurturing, children, body or kinesthetic responses to world (i.e., emotions).

Rate of travel though the zodiac: about 12° per day.

Time to travel through a chart: 27½ days.

Use in predictive work: receives transits and makes and receives progressions.

Figures: mother, children, loved ones that you nurture, people who need physical help.

Dynamic contacts to the Moon will color emotional processes. You experience changes in emotional responses, changes in eating habits, changes in body rhythms. Things that are dear to you, things that are part of your security system, could change. The Moon, more than any other planet or luminary, takes on a very strong bias from the sign that it occupies, and this should always be considered when dealing with this luminary.

MERCURY

Key Principle: methods of information-collecting, processing, and distributing.

Rate of travel through the zodiac: up to 2° 30′ per day.

Time to travel through a chart: about 1 year.

Use in predictive work: receives transits and makes and receives progressions.

Figures: young people, or people who deal with information or stationery.

Dynamic contacts to Mercury herald events concerning paperwork, study, writing, talking, short journeys, and a great deal of movement. New ways of gaining information may be encountered by a spectrum of methods, from finding a new bookshop to having prophetic visions.

VENUS

Key Principle: relating, relationships, resources.

Rate of travel through the zodiac: up to 1° 15′ per day.

Time to travel through a chart: about 1 year.

Use in predictive work: receives transits and makes and receives progressions.

Figures: young women, artists, lovers, or money-handlers.

Dynamic contacts to Venus will emphasize your relationship to the world or to an individual. You could find yourself changing your attitude to a group of friends or falling in or out of love. Your sense of worth is questioned; the value of things, such as friendships or relationships, is examined. You become aware of resources—emotional, spiritual, or financial—and this is a time when these resources can be stretched.

MARS

Key Principle: focused action, directed motivation, drive.

Rate of travel through the zodiac: up to 0° 40′ per day.

Time to travel through a chart: about 2½ years.

Use in predictive work: mostly for receiving transits, and for progressions. Only used for making transits indicating acute days, or days of great activity. It also has some value as it transits through the houses, showing where the current motivation is at the moment. Also used for making or receiving progressions.

Figures: young, rough, strong, motivated, sexual, angry, or coarse males or females.

When a chart is receiving a Mars contact, it will indicate that anger, motivation, or drive is being activated. The reason is enthused with an idea or feeling. This idea may plunge the reason into physical activities, to experience strong sexual motivation, encounter angry people, or even cause the person to be part of an accident.

JUPITER

Key Principle: expansion of the worldview, growth, movement.

Rate of travel through the zodiac: about 30° a year.

Time to travel through a chart: 12 years.

Use in predictive work: mainly for its ability to make transits and receive progressions.

Figures: grandfather, teacher, guru, traveler, adventurer.

When Jupiter is being emphasized by dynamic astrology, there are going to be changes to your worldview. What you are learning, what you are mastering, what you believe in are all areas that can be affected. Jupiter is the energy of expansiveness, whether you like it or not. It takes joy in the big picture and will influence life by the desire to expand the individual's world. The outward effect of this can be to bring study (mental expansion) or travel (physical expansion of the worldview) into your life. If it is impossible for the world to expand due to the life circumstance, then Jupiter will simply change the life circumstance so that an expansion can occur. This may not be a joyful event.

In addition, it would seem that people with a strong natal Jupiter (or who have a large dollop of Sagittarius in the chart) find that transits from or progressions to Jupiter are too excessive, leading to obsessive, manic types of overreactions that generally leave them exhausted at the end of the period.

SATURN

Key Principle: structure, responsibility, commitment, authority, building; to take shape and form; consolidation of one's position in life.

Rate of movement through the zodiac: about 12° per year.

Time to travel through a chart: about 29 years.

Use in predictive work: in both giving and receiving transits as well as receiving progressions.

Figures: any person or group who can wield authority over you. Individuals who intimate. Individuals or groups for which you are responsible.

Saturn is the planet of material form. Its issues are about being here now, being a physical human being in a physical body coping with our physical needs and dealing with the consequences of previous physical actions. It would seem at times that Saturn is the nemesis of the human race. For, if there is going to be productive or useful growth (Jupiter), there must be a time of pause and consolidation—a time of restraint, a time of testing. Since all life as we know it is subject to this pulse of expansion, contraction, then the indicator of the times of contraction—Saturn—becomes a very important planet in the astrologer's toolbox.

Thus whether it is giving or receiving, in predictive work, it is always strongly felt. When Saturn is making a contact to the personal planets, it suggests periods of having to accept the consequences of one's actions. In its interaction with the outer planets, Saturn produces landmarks in the map of a person's life, showing the times and ways that the individual will struggle against the weight of the physical world and its needs in the search for awareness.

When people are young (pre-Saturn return), Saturn contacts are usually experienced as limiting and restricting, even possibly intimidating. The Saturnian figures, symbolically father, the law, teacher, or boss, come to the surface during the contact to enable the person to be exposed to restrictions in order to learn lessons of responsibility and containment. These same contacts may yield welcome increases in responsibility (job promotion) or stability in the life for a mature individual. Whatever the stage in life, a Saturn transit will have a common theme of work, *hard* work. Under a Saturn contact, a person is held to account, for better or for worse. The following is a guideline to the transits of Saturn:

Saturn-Sun: increase of responsibility or being "under the thumb."

Saturn-Moon: loneliness, isolation, feeling unsupported; needing to consolidate resources.

Saturn-Mercury: serious decisions, burdensome paperwork, study.

Saturn-Venus: making or breaking commitments in relationships; restrictions upon financial affairs.

Saturn-Mars: arthritis, physical restraint, physical injury, being exhausted, hard labor.

Saturn-Jupiter: controlled expansion.

Saturn-Saturn: major life phase (see cycles).

Saturn-Uranus: frustration, slow progress in achieving new goals. Doing something that is groundbreaking.

Saturn-Neptune: illness, tiredness, depletion of resources, despair, to be without hope. This is the major signifier of health problems in predictive astrology.

Saturn-Pluto: blocked energy leading to outbursts that could be violent; melancholy, darkness of feelings; being in a "black hole."

Saturn-North Node: taking responsibility with a group; taking on a fated commitment that is part of the life journey.

Saturn-South Node: increase in responsibilities to do with family or "tribe"; fated, karmic bonds being changed in such a way that the person has to carry a greater load.

Saturn-Ascendant: taking on greater responsibilities; being seen as capable of handling authority; being given authority.

Saturn-Descendant: reviewing and changing commitments in relationships, either business or personal. Being realistic about the nature of a relationship or business partnership.

Saturn-MC: greater responsibility in the career; being seen to stand on one's own feet.

Saturn-IC: family commitments that tie a person to the home; possible problems with the father figure.

Saturn-Vertex/Anti-vertex: encountering authority figures, or encountering a long-awaited responsibility.

The three outer planets (Uranus, Neptune, and Pluto) tend to belong more to the collective rather than to the individual. Particularly with transits, they take on a generational flavor. For example, natal Neptune receiving a conjunction from transiting Pluto will be occurring to everybody born within a twelve-month period. Everyone may have the transit, but few would be aware of it. Even a Mars transit squaring natal Pluto will be affecting *your* generation. Watch for the expression of the energy in the world of fashion, on the nightly news, or in the papers, but don't look for it in an individual's chart unless that individual is a world leader in fashion or politics, and so on.

However, when the outer planets form relationships to the inner natal planets, they all challenge, in some manner, the Saturn structure that exists in that area of the person's life.

Saturn and Jupiter can be seen as a harbor mouth; inside the harbor, we can control the sea, breakwaters, piers, docks, and so on. However, beyond the harbor the ship is exposed to the uncontrollable open sea. Jupiter beckons us out of the harbor, Saturn tells us to be well prepared for the journey, and Uranus, Neptune, and Pluto are the open sea—the collective. No matter how well prepared the vessel, events can and will occur.

URANUS

Key Principle: fast unexpected change; a turnaround, an awakening. Freedom. The sudden storm at sea.

Rate of travel through the zodiac: about 4° per year.

Time to travel through a chart: about 84 years.

Use in predictive work: generally used for its ability to make transits and receive progressions.

Figures: any person who is considered to be unconventional, independent, chaotic, eccentric, or rebellious. In addition, the exciting person, the person who brings change. Intellectual and/ or non-committed.

Uranus is about change, unexpected, seemingly without pattern. The desire to break patterns of responsibility. Not necessarily to be free of the responsibility but rather just to be free. The wild card, electric, weird, fast, non-emotional, life-in-the-fast-lane. The energy of this planet is chaos. This may be welcomed or may be feared. Spontaneous change by way of a general non-emotional reaction, because the individual does not have the luxury of time between events to brood or ponder. A ship in a storm does not have time to meditate on the problem.

When Saturn has our life firmly in its grasp via order, routine, habits, and lifestyle, Uranus will come thundering into our world, to alter, change, or confront us with the vulnerability of our "nice, safe, secure systems."

The energy of Uranus seems to radiate out of a person when it is strongly transiting a chart. Lightbulbs can pop, electrical failures and computer hiccups seem to trail behind us like unwanted guests! The following are simple guidelines to the types of expressions of Uranus in transit.

Uranus-Sun: the sudden desire for freedom and re-classification of the self.

Uranus-Moon: release from personal emotions; events happening so fast that the person does not have time to emotionally react; freedom from emotions. Release from the conventional view of mother/child.

Uranus-Mercury: sudden ideas, changes in speech, encountering a foreign language, new books, and so on.

Uranus-Venus: changes to socializing patterns; falling in or out of love; changes in financial situation.

Uranus-Mars: haste, accidents, anger, sexual energy, passion.

Uranus-Jupiter: when we have transiting Uranus conjunct transiting Jupiter, the community expresses explosive energy—brush fires and the like. On the personal level, this combination can be exciting but not too life-changing.

Uranus-Saturn: see Saturn.

Uranus-Uranus: see cycles.

Uranus-Neptune: very little manifestation on the personal level; signifies inspiration, change for the better, a flash of enlightenment on the collective generational level. A hopeless case with no apparent solution can become resolved.

Uranus-Pluto: another generational transit that may have little effect on the individual.

Uranus-North Node: sudden encounters with groups or people that expand our world, bringing changes that redirect us on our life path.

Uranus-South Node: changing the "tribal" structure; an old issue can surface and be cleared.

Uranus-Ascendant: sudden changes to the person's life; immense drive for change/freedom; change of name, changes to the physical body.

Uranus-Descendant: rapid change to relationship patterns: new type or style of relationship, sudden forming or breaking of a relationship; an awaking to one's true needs in relationship.

Uranus-MC: sudden change of job or career, changes to social status, for better or for worse.

Uranus-IC: changes in the family or where the person is living; changes to the physical home.

Uranus-Vertex/Anti-vertex: encountering people who instigate change; this change can be welcomed or feared.

NEPTUNE

Key Principle: loss, confusion, the world dissolving, boundaries disappearing. Lost at sea.

Rate of movement through the zodiac: about 1° to 2° per year.

Time to travel through a chart: about 165 years.

Use in predictive work: generally for its ability to make transits and receive progressions.

Figures: the grandmother, the wise old women. The victim or martyr. The visionary or spiritual.

The first sign of a Neptune contact is a sense of loss, despair, hopelessness, or confusion. Many people instinctively use this as a time to travel, a time to live on the surface of cultures, to escape from their own world and drift through someone else's. For others, there can be times of indecision instead of decisiveness, confusion and dreams instead of clarity and logic. This may or may not be a difficult experience.

The dream world can become more vivid and intuition can be highly tuned. This is a time when the boundaries of Saturn are once again challenged, not by the frontal attack of Uranus but rather by slow erosion. The structure crumbles—not because of weakness but because of a massive failure of the foundation. Methods of coping (Saturn) no longer work; people are usually faced, in this time, with inactivity. They can take no action to solve their problem; they must wait for the problem to dissolve.

The following are some guidelines to the transits of Neptune:

Neptune-Sun: confusion about one's role in the world; desire to escape, travel, or recluse while one reconsiders—possibly on an unconscious level—the way in which one exists in the world.

Neptune-Moon: a visionary, drug-sensitive, spiritual time during which the individual experiences the dissolving of emotional responses. Time out from the world to unconsciously reorganize one's emotional reality.

Neptune-Mercury: awaking to the metaphysical. Art, poetry, spiritual ideas. Daydreaming. Inability to carry on with study, loss of paperwork, disconnecting from the world of paperwork, and so on. Being deceived.

Neptune-Venus: illusions in love relationships; romantic love that may be wonderful or may leave the individual to deal with cold realities after the contact has finished. Confusion in financial matters; being conned.

Neptune-Mars: loss of motivating energy; energy draining away; loss of libido. Normal focus energy becoming unfocused.

Neptune-Jupiter: idealism, seeking the guru that has the answer to everything.

Neptune-Saturn: see Saturn.

Neptune-Uranus: see Uranus.

Neptune-Neptune: see cycles.

Neptune-Pluto: a large generational combination that should not be delineated on a personal level, as a few million other people will be having the same combination at the same time. Look for this transit's expression via the media.

Neptune-North Node: finding one's spiritual path, finding a group or "tribe" with a basis in the arts; healing; drug abuse; the metaphysical that propels one into a new life direction.

Neptune-South Node: loss in the "tribe" of an old wise woman; a restructuring within the tribe of the spiritual leader, or the visionary one in the family; meeting a person from the past with whom you feel a spiritual connection.

Neptune-Ascendant: dissolving the image that a person presents to the world; change of personality, as seen from outside. These changes can be catalyzed by despair, or through the escapism of travel.

Neptune-Descendant: dissolving relationships. Loss, being separated from one's parents when young; new type of relationship needs surfacing in the individual.

Neptune-MC: letting go of a career drive; loss of social status, redirecting social status into a more Neptunian field. When young, it can also imply the loss of a parent or grandmother.

Neptune-IC: confusion about one's role in the family. Moving from the home in a way that brings loss of family, relatives, or close friends; e.g., moving to another country, moving from the city to the country, or vice versa. Also, events concerning the grandmother's role in the family.

Neptune-Vertex/Anti-vertex: encountering a spiritual, creative, healing, or victim-type of person who repels or attracts you.

PLUTO

Key Principle: transformation via the catalyst of deep emotional reactions. A storm in the harbor.

Rate of movement through the zodiac: about 1° per year.

Time to travel through a chart: about 248 years.

Use in predictive work: for its ability to make transits to a chart and receive progressions.

Figures: mother figures, loved ones, family members. People connected with death and dying.

Pluto contacts carry the flavor of instinctive emotions such as grief, lust, protection of loved ones, and so on. These contacts are the instruments the Cosmos uses for changing the redundant patterns that Saturn has set up in your life. Feeling is the essence of the contact. Change will come about via intense feelings that cannot be rationalized away or forgotten. So Pluto contacts are big. They bring into the life the gut-gnawing emotions that we know only time will resolve. It is the storm in the harbor. That which was safe, home, or inner is violated, torn down, pulled apart. The harbor has to be rebuilt.

At rare times, the transit can also bring in unexpected success if the person is dealing with groups of people. However, there will still be emotionally churning events in the private life. The following are just simple guidelines for the effects of dynamic Pluto on a chart:

Pluto-Sun: a threat to the sense of self; life-challenging.

Pluto-Moon: emotional distress; issues with mother or mothering; issues with groups of women; stress on the emotional bonds that bind lovers/family together.

Pluto-Mercury: obsession with an idea; tunnel vision; putting all your energy into a project.

Pluto-Venus: intense, fated connections with an intimate relationship; forming a relationship that is "bigger than the two of you." The sudden and emotionally packed ending of a relationship. Matters involving large sums of money.

Pluto-Mars: anger and possibly violence; great physical exertion; large projects that take a great deal of energy.

Pluto-Jupiter: desire for greater power, a greater field of influence. This combination, however, is often not that conscious and would be considered secondary to other major contracts.

Pluto-Saturn: see Saturn.

Pluto-Uranus: see Uranus.

Pluto-Neptune: see Neptune.

Pluto-Pluto: see cycles.

Pluto-North Node: meeting a group with which you feel karmically connected.

Pluto-South Node: intense emotional changes to your family or tribe; meeting something or someone from your past that strongly affects you.

Pluto-Ascendant: change, by emotional events, to the personality of the person. The body, the name, the way in which you present yourself to the world can all be altered via a turbulent emotional period.

Pluto-Descendant: emotional restructuring of personal or business relationships; emotionally charged court cases. For a young person, this transit can also be a change to the parent's relationship.

Pluto-MC: the dramatic rearranging of career or social status. The sudden claim to fame, or the emotional shock of an unwanted redefinition.

Pluto-IC: Strong emotional events concerning home and family; issues with mother figure; changing of the tribe by birth or death; moving the home in such a way that there is no going back.

Pluto-Vertex/Anti-vertex: Encountering an individual or place with whom you feel a deep karmic bond.

NORTH NODE

Key Principle: groups, associations, that which the individual is trying to achieve in life.

Rate of movement through the zodiac: about 20° per year retrograde.

Time to travel through a chart: about 18 years.

Use in predictive work: in the receiving of transits and progressions.

The Dragon's head or Caput Draconis is named after the concept of a giant celestial dragon who swallowed the Sun and the Moon during an eclipse.

The nodal axis is entangled with events or people that seem fated. The North Node represents events placed in your future revealed by the passage of transits or progressions. The South Node represents events from your past—not just the past of this conscious life but also the past of your collective memories. The Hindus would say that the Nodes are the Dharma of life, the "truth" of life, the true meaning and pathway of life.

So the North Node is perceived as new things, new groups of people, new friends that have an impact on the individual, the making of memories that will later be held as important. In addition, the individual can become conscious of a required change to the life path as this point receives a transit or progression.

SOUTH NODE

Key Principle: the past, family, inherited material.

Rate of movement through the zodiac: the same as the North Node.

The Dragon's Tail or Cauda Draconis are other names for the South Node.

Since the North and South Nodes form an axis, progressions and transits to the South Node will also be occurring to the North Node. When a planet makes a conjunction to this point, better results are achieved if it is read as conjunction to the South Node rather than an opposition to the North Node.

Issues come from old family history, or things from the past. The past seems to swamp the present, old illness could flare up, friends one has not seen for twenty years suddenly appear. Lost or forgotten photos, paperwork, people, and illness can all come to the surface as this point receives a conjunction from a dynamic planet. *Déjà vu* experiences, meeting of strangers that you feel you have "known before," can also take place.

Angles in Predictive Work

There are the four points in a chart, called angles. Each one, apart from Equal House and M-House systems, governs a house of great importance.* The 1st house, the ascendant, is the house of the persona and the physical appearance. The IC governs the 4th house, the house of home, family, and hearth. The descendant is the cusp of the house, the house of relationships, the anima/animus. And the MC defines the 10th house, which is concerned with the way that a person is viewed, judged, and classified by the community.

All of these areas are of prime importance to a person's life, and therefore planets forming conjunctions to either the IC or the descendant will be considered conjunct these points rather than as oppositions to the MC or the ascendant. In other words, the descendant and the IC should be considered as points in the chart with their own meanings, as are the ascendant and the MC.

---

* The M-House system is a form of Equal House system where the MC is used as the reference point. It defines the 10th house cusp, and all other house cusps are in 30 divisions from this point. Thus the ascendant can be in either the 1st or 12th house.

With all other aspects (apart from the conjunction) the ascendant or MC should be used as the points receiving the contact.

THE ASCENDANT

Key Principle: the self, the environment; your reaction to the world around you; awareness.

The ascendant is the boundary between the 12th house and the 1st house. When it receives a contact, particularly a conjunction, then something that has been hidden comes into the light of the 1st house, awareness is gained, greater consciousness of the situation is achieved. This can be very jolting or very inspiring, depending on the actual planet involved.

With contacts that are not conjunctions, the person feels or senses that the environment, or the way that he or she reacts to the environment, is under pressure to change.

THE DESCENDANT

Key Principle: relationships that are committed.

Any contacts over this point by a conjunction will bring issues of relationship to the forefront of the life, whether it is marriage, a business partner, or a legal pulling together, such as a court case (i.e., Smith vs. Jones is a legal bond between those two people), or a relationship where there is a mutually agreed commitment.

If the person is too young for these types of relationships—although one should not overlook the depth of bonding that can occur with a teddy bear and how its loss can become symbolic of a major grief experience—then the descendant can be projected onto the parents, and their relationship can go through the changes that are being symbolized by the child's dynamic contacts.

THE MC

Key Principle: the person's visible position in the community.

The Midheaven, or Medium Coeli (Latin for "middle of the sky"), is a public point. No transit or progression there can be kept quiet, so to speak. Matters involving the job, career direction, and lifestyle can emerge as this point receives contacts. There are many ways that one's social status can change—marriage/divorce, wealth/bankruptcy, promotion/dismissal, and so on.

When we are young, this point can also symbolize the parent by whom we define our public self. Generally this is the father, since traditionally a person carries the father's surname. However, times are changing, and the MC can symbolize the mother if she is the main public figure in the family.

THE IC

Key Principle: home, family, tribe, the hearth.

The Imum Coeli (Latin for "bottom of the sky") is known as the IC.

Conjunctions to this point bring the issues of the family and hearth to the forefront. These could be experienced as mother problems, becoming a parent, moving house and home, someone moving into your home, a rearrangement of your relationship to your family, a death in the family, or an ending in some way. In addition, it can also be a time of increased awareness of the effect of family-inherited karma or patterns.

VERTEX/ANTI-VERTEX

Key Principle: to encounter.

Planets conjoining this axis (which is the only transit or progression with which I work for this axis) symbolize that you will encounter a person, subject, or an event that will be of interest. You "let it into your life." Think of the hundreds and thousands of people and ideas that you bump into as you travel through life. Only a very small percentage will you allow to enter into your world. Dynamic planets to this point show when these "enterings" occur.

With the anti-vertex, there is a sense of releasing, allowing things to move out of your life. However, as these two types of events can quite often occur simultaneously, it is difficult to split the meanings of the vertex from the anti-vertex.

All of the above are just guidelines, basic sketches that, although simplistic, are a guide to the essence of each of the planets and points in dynamic predictive work. However, be aware that compared to the potential richness of these symbols, any keywords for them are dry, dusty, and without life. These guidelines are not the final statements on the meanings of these symbols, for there can never be a final statement. As long as there is life, symbols change and grow. Indeed, fifty years from now many of these "keywords" may be obsolete.

Planetary Cycles

Another type of planetary combination happens when a planet makes an aspect to its natal position. When this happens, it heralds a new developmental stage for the person. Once you reach your twenties, society considers that you have "grown up," that all of your developmental stages have been completed. However, this is far from the truth, and there are a number of stages that await all of us.*

SATURN RETURN (ABOUT AGE 29)

Let's measure this for realism: ". . . and they lived happily ever after." The classic ending to most fairy stories. The belief sold to us is that if we can make the transition into adulthood, comply, do what is expected, then we too can live happily ever after. The Saturn return is the realization that this is just a fairy story, and if we really want to live happily ever after, then we have to take control and set up our life in a more realistic manner.

The unreal expectations we carry from childhood of our right to a hassle-free marriage, children, career, and so on crumble and hit the cold light of day. Any part of the life that is supported by illusions or other people's projections will undergo the Saturnian measuring stick. The ship sets to sea; if the sails are not ready, the ship will be in difficulties.

This process of being examined by the Cosmos can be rewarding or devastating. For it is a time of taking responsibility on all levels of one's life and letting go of the parents, real or otherwise. This can be a period of recognition and advancement as the individual is given greater responsibilities or a time of being forced to suffer the consequences of previous unrealistic attitudes.

Transiting Saturn will also form squares and oppositions to its natal position and these times will echo similar issues to the Saturn return.

The Saturn waxing square at 7, 36, and 65 are periods of taking action to begin a cycle of different types of commitments and responsibilities, be it school, consolidating one's career or life path, or retirement.

The Saturn oppositions at 14, 43, and 72 are all periods of challenging all that hold authority over you, and the waning squares of 21, 50, and 79 are all times of productive output based on the hard work that one has already done.

---

* For a list of planetary conjunctions from 1900 to 2050 see Appendix 4 on page 261.

URANUS OPPOSITE URANUS (ABOUT AGE 40)

One of the mid-life crisis aspects, this is a time of reflection on what has been achieved with the life since the Saturn return. It's time to re-plot the life course and reevaluate "what you are doing with your life" now that you are an adult. There is also a challenge to that which has limited you in the past. Old beliefs that things can't be done will fall away. This can be liberating, or if you do not want to engage the new, then it can be a time of anger and frustration.

NEPTUNE SQUARE NEPTUNE (ABOUT AGE 40)

Another mid-life crisis aspect. You question your spiritual beliefs. A time for discovering the areas where you can put your creative or spiritual energy. Issues of integrity and boundaries of discrimination are also revised. There can be an active expression of the spiritual belief as these beliefs come into greater conscious. Or, on the other hand, it can be a time to encounter confusion or deceit.

PLUTO SQUARE PLUTO (BETWEEN AGE 35 TO 55)

For the generation of Pluto in Leo and Virgo, this is another mid-life crisis aspect happening in the early 40s. It's time to reassess what is of emotional importance, which deep emotional bonds are valid, and which emotional involvements are really superficial. This is the chance to start to become wise about emotional needs.

SECOND SATURN RETURN (ABOUT AGE 56)

Retiring; accepting that the "young active phase" of the life is complete, assessing what you have done with the first phase and planning the next phase is what happens now. Once again, this can be rewarding—a time of release from some responsibilities—or it can be distressing, with you feeling that you have wasted your life.

NEPTUNE OPPOSITE NEPTUNE (ABOUT AGE 83)
AND THE URANUS RETURN (AGE 84)

It's time to accept your life story as it has unfolded—time for reflection, the need to relive the past to "get it right"—smoothing out the unexplained emotions and questions so that they do not have to be carried past the boundaries of this life. The coming of wisdom is now.

Dynamic Aspects

The next part of the alphabet concerns aspects, for these are the methods that the dynamic planets use to interact with the natal chart. The nature or manner of the aspect is just as critical and important as the planets and points involved.

Dynamic planets are like actors on a stage. If on this stage there were an old woman with a wand, then only by her words and actions (method of interacting with other actors on stage) would we understand that the character is either a fairy godmother or a wicked witch.

Aspects are the avenues through which the planets or points communicate with the chart. They are connections—like the wiring system of a telephone company. Some connections can be difficult; some can be easy. You may be talking to an old friend on the phone, but if the connection is bad, you could have a very frustrating phone call.

The following descriptions look at the meanings of the aspects when being used in *any* form of dynamic astrology. Remember, the meanings are simple and somewhat undeveloped as compared to natal meanings because these aspects are only temporary visitors.

In line with the KISS principle, the set of aspects presented here are the basic 12th and 8th harmonic aspect families. Transiting quintiles to secondary progressed Moons may give some interesting information, but this will most likely be gleaned at the cost of the more obvious and indeed more important events occurring to the individual.

THE CONJUNCTION (0°)

Key Principle: a basic unit of the self or natal chart changes into
something else.

A conjunction is like *Invasion of the Body Snatchers*. The tourist comes in and takes over. The two energies combine as one, with the invading planet being the more dominant. There is a sense of oneness, sameness; the intruder has the upper hand because it is foreign, new to the scene. The chart has no defense against it because it has become one with the chart. The natal chart is thus thrown into imbalance, with the foreign energy being seen as the stronger: Neptune conjunct natal Sun, and the person is all Neptune. The qualities of the natal Sun are swallowed by the transit or progression.

Using the metaphor of the actors on stage, a conjunction enters and replaces a character, assuming the name and role but bringing new words and actions. If the actor were challenged on the change, she would ask: "What change?" The other actors in their confusion will allow the new actor to become the main character.

The conjunction implies that a part of the natal chart experiences direct contact with a different type of energy and reclassifies itself to line up with this new energy. For example, transiting Saturn conjunct natal Sun could well make people appear to have authority or be able to handle responsibility. Transiting Uranus conjunct natal Venus can convert the quite shy Venus into an outgoing, promiscuous type. These people experience that type of Venus not in others around but in themselves. Their friends will see the change, but to them they simply feel different. The conjunction is a very unsettling aspect because these people experience changing behavior patterns without necessarily feeling any real cause. This can lead them to question their very sanity, or wonder if they are heading for a nervous breakdown, and so on.

THE OPPOSITION (180°)

Key Principle: someone, or something, is causing you to make a decision.

The opposition is the direct polarity in meaning to the conjunction. With this aspect, the energy is seen as separate from the self. Someone, or something, is interacting in your life in a way that is contrary to what you want. Someone or something "out there" is *doing* something to you, and furthermore it's *their* fault. They have done it, whatever *it* is.

The theme of an opposition is blame or learning from another's actions. This projection can run the gamut from love to hate and will be placed upon some object, person, or group that is outside of us. The key to working with the opposition is to realize that the projection is coming from within, and the external events are merely a mirror.

In our stage metaphor, an actor comes in and in some way challenges another actor. There is nothing subtle about it; it is the old-fashioned swashbuckling sword fight of the movies. Transiting Uranus opposing natal Venus will place a promiscuous, boisterous person in your way who flirts with you, teases you, and asks you to change in ways you had not previously considered.

With transiting Saturn opposing natal Sun, someone or something restricts you, challenges your authority, tests your commitments, or puts your sense of responsibility under pressure, asking or demanding that you take on greater responsibilities in some way.

There is always choice with an opposition, and this choice places you in the position of having to make decisions. You make this decision because of the actions of another or the actions of a group.

THE SQUARE (90°)

Key Principle: events, that are nobody's fault, are forcing you into a new type of action.

The square is the aspect of action based on tension. It is action born from frustration. An event will occur for which it is impossible to blame anyone but results in you being forced into a mode of action that you have not yet explored.

It forces action in new areas. If your car breaks down and is off the road for a while, you may be forced to use public transport. You may not be familiar with this system of transport and find that you have to learn new information and timetables, have to get out of bed earlier, and encounter a whole new group of people. All these things cause tension. It is impossible to blame anybody effectively, and the results stimulate actions rather than decisions. When something, about which nothing overtly can be done, occurs, and as a result of this you have to take a course of action that is new to you, you are experiencing a square.

With transiting Saturn square the natal Sun, your father could get ill, and as a result you have to stay home and look after him, thereby learning that you can cope with less time for yourself. The Uranus-Venus example when placed through the lens of the square implies that you are placed in a situation in which you have to be more outgoing. You don't just *become* more outgoing, as with the conjunction; neither do you have a *choice* about it as with the opposition, but rather you find yourself being *forced* into the new action.

In the metaphor of the actors, the stage or the set may suddenly fall down or the lights go off due to a power failure. The actors are thereby forced to take action that was not planned. There is nothing they can do to stop the events occurring. There is no one they can blame and no one to approach to "stop doing this thing."

So the square pushes us into corners that we can't avoid. We rarely want to go there, so we are picked up by the scruff of the neck and placed there. We scream, kick, maybe even swear, and after the outburst we realize that the only way out is to do something that we may never have tried before.

The best approach to take with a transiting or progressed square is to roll up your sleeves and take the action being indicated by the events.

THE SEMISQUARE (45°)

Key Principle: frustration of action that leads to a null result.

The semisquare seems to have one purpose in life, and that is to teach patience and persistence. The semisquare in predictive work indicates that a great deal of frustration will occur if action is undertaken.

You encounter an endless array of obstacles and delays. If you try to push through one set of problems, another set will appear. Very little is achieved in that area of the chart while the semisquare is in force. Our actors may experience this energy as hecklers in the audience; the Venus-Uranus example might act out as sexual harassment at the office; the Sun-Saturn combination as the tax department deciding to do an audit.

This aspect is like waiting for the silt to settle in a pond. If you take action and try to pat it down, it gets worse; walk away, give it time, show patience, and the pond will clear. Blocks, holdups, frustrations, delays, and lack of achievement are all symptoms of the aspect. Controlled patience seems to be the only answer, together with not trying to change the world while a semisquare is involved with your chart.

THE SESQUIQUADRATE (135°)

Key Principle: frustration of action that eventually leads to a
delayed achievement.

This aspect is the combination of the square and the semisquare, both mathematically as well as philosophically. This allows the action of the square but only after the considerable frustration of the semisquare, caused either by the individual through procrastination or by the actions of another.

These are the delays that force people into new modes of action— but only after several attempts to proceed in the old direction: With the broken-down car, as in our example for the square, the car would stop but then nearly fire, again and again, forever promising to run smoothly, drawing the person into a greater and greater state of frustration. Eventually, the car would need to be repaired, and the person would have to use public transportation.

There is always a turning point when the energy does start to flow with this aspect. The most suitable approach is to be aware that there will be holdups and delays, and instead of easing up until the aspect is cleared, as with the semisquare, the turning point should be hurried forward by determinedly pushing for the results desired.

In the Saturn-Sun example, we know that you are going to have to make a commitment or take on responsibilities, but procrastination (or desiring to start the job but being delayed) is the essence of the transit. Or with the Venus-Uranus, knowing that you have to mix with a group of people or expand your social set is the issue, but you are unhappy about it and put it off as long as possible. Or, you may find the group you are working with very frustrating, but need to stay with them to achieve the outcome that you want.

THE TRINE (120°)

Key Principle: rapid development of a situation due to the removal of all obstacles.

This is a fascinating aspect in predictive astrology because it represents speed—speed due to lack of friction. All obstacles or deterrents are removed, so life flows quickly upstream or down the drain. The trine is not concerned with the direction of its movement as long as it is moving. It's like being on ice skates. If you have been striving for a result against a restricting force, suddenly that force is removed, and you fly forward on your skates, suddenly achieving the movement that you wanted. On the other hand, you may be striving to stop some trouble occurring, keeping the lid on something or hanging on by the skin of your teeth. The transiting or progressed trine will remove the restraining force you are applying, and suddenly everything collapses.

Rapid achievement or rapid failure—the essence of this aspect is no resistance, the removal of all hindrance. Speed of deterioration in a health problem that could lead to a welcome death for the terminally ill or finally reaching the top of that mountain for which you have been striving. If you are striving for a positive event and a dynamic trine occurs, then the event is achieved. If, on the other hand, you are striving to prevent a negative event from occurring, the dynamic trine rapidly precipitates the problem.

With the Sun-Saturn example, there can be a sudden increase in responsibilities or sudden restrictions placed on the individual, all depending on the bias of the individual at the time of the transit or progression. Similarly with the Venus-Uranus, rapid joy, socializing, or an affair comes to pass, or one's social life or affair comes to a rapid end. It indicates speed—of achievement or of decline.

THE SEXTILE (60°)

Key Principle: encountering a chance that may or may not be used to gain what is needed.

The sextile has two types of expression in its capacity as a traveler. Both expressions contend opportunities, but opportunities can manifest in different ways.

You can create your own opportunities or the world can drop them in your lap. If the sextile is between negative elements or Yin (Earth and Water), then you create the opportunity. Thus something that you do or think of yourself uncovers an opportunity that may or may not be taken up.

If, however, the sextile is between positive or Yang elements (Air and Fire), an opportunity is going to drop into your lap. So you should be on the lookout for something coming into your life that seems promising—quite different from the first in the way you experience it. Both are opportunities. The one problem with this aspect is that if you are not in a position to take up the opportunity, then the sextile can symbolize quite a dramatic event to create the space in your life for the new options.

Sextiles are events, but the events themselves are not important; what is important is that the person needs to look behind the event and ask the question: "What doorways are now open to me that were not open before this event occurred?" These doorways are the opportunities that the Cosmos is offering. These doorways are the dynamic sextiles—energy or gift.

The Sun-Saturn example would indicate that the doors that are opening are allowing for an increase in responsibilities, which could lead to positive results. In the case of Venus-Uranus, the person would be presented with opportunities for greater socializing and/or an affair that he or she has the option to take advantage of or not. It is through the dynamic sextiles that we are given the opportunities to find new pathways in our life.

THE SEMISEXTILE (30°)

Key Principle: timing, being in the right place at the right time.

This aspect does not, in my experience, have a great deal to add to the predictive astrologer's tool kit. It is very subtle in its expression, and if it is going to have an effect, it seems to put the person in the right place at the right time. Some astrologers consider it to be a very stressful aspect, but I feel that this is more relevant to natal astrology. In the field of prediction, I have not found this stress represented.

THE QUINCUNX OR INCONJUNCT (150°)

Key Principle: moving into a new situation; change; release, letting go.

The quincunx causes change and separation in its mode as a traveler. It walks on stage and stops the play, changes the plot, or moves everybody to a new theater. Change and separation can be expressed in many ways, starting with the ultimate separation of death, traveling, illness, moving house and home, or maybe just isolating yourself because you are studying.

From changing an opinion to breaking up a relationship, the quincunx wants to move you into a new situation whether you are ready for it or not. Sometimes this is very stressful; at other times, it may be joyful.

The Sun-Saturn quincunx is a statement about the releasing or letting go of a set of responsibilities; leaving a very structured situation. A prisoner being released from prison is experiencing a Sun-Saturn quincunx type event. It could indicate a person retiring from work, someone stepping down from a position of authority; a mother may have this aspect as a child leaves home, and so on. The Venus-Uranus example would be talking about the ending of a socializing time, the ending of an affair, the completion of a time of high social activity, the end of a vacation, or going back to work or school.

Houses in Predictive Astrology

The principle of houses and house systems has gone through some very difficult times in the history of astrology, for often they have been belittled, argued about, denied, ignored, and, at times, even condemned. For the last two thousand years, there have been many disputes about house systems, and, indeed, some branches of astrology have stopped using houses altogether.

So what is this thing called a house, with such a checkered past?

In simple terms, a house is used as a quick method of defining a planet's position within its diurnal orbit. The four phases of planetary movements in a relationship to its diurnal orbit are divided into semi-arcs. See figure 1.

Planets rise in the east over the ascendant, and when they culminate around the midheaven, they have finished their diurnal rising semi-arc. They then proceed to move westerly toward the descendant. As they reach the descendant, they have completed their diurnal setting semi-arc.

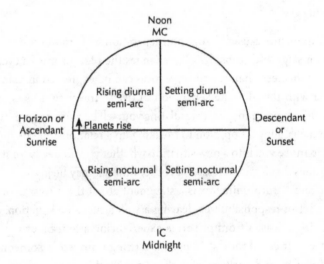

Figure 1. Semi-arcs

The planets continue to drop in the chart as they move closer to the IC and, upon reaching the IC, they have completed their nocturnal setting semi-arc. The final phase is when the planets rise toward the ascendant, traveling through their nocturnal rising semi-arc.

Astrologers who work with house systems believe that the position of a planet in a particular semi-arc alters the way the planet is experienced by the individual. Instead of expressing a planet's position as being halfway through its rising nocturnal semi-arc, an easier method is to say that the planet is in the 2nd house. Instead of saying that a planet has currently traveled 85 percent of its rising diurnal semi-arc, we can simply say the planet is in the 10th house. So the house numbers are a convenient way of expressing the diurnal information.

If two people are born at precisely the same instant in time but at different places on the globe, their planetary patterns will be absolutely identical. However, the house position of the planets will be quite different because the sign rising in one place may well be setting in another.

It is the location on the Earth at any particular time that dictates the position of a planet in its particular semi-arc or house. Therefore it is the planetary positions within the houses and the zodiacal orientation around the twelve houses that personalize the planets, separating them from all other planetary patterns or events happening at the same time but in different parts of the globe.

The cross formed in a chart by the intersection of the ascendant/descendant and the MC/IC axis is called the "Cross of Matter," and through the zodiac signs on the four points of the cross, the astrologer gains information concerning the nature of the struggle that the spiritual being has in dealing with the physical world.

In the world of symbols, the cross represents the physical and dealings with the physical world. In symbolic language, the circle implies wholeness or spirituality. Therefore, a cross in a circle (see figure 2) is a symbolic statement of spiritual essence placed into the physical world, or physical essence striving for spiritual wholeness.

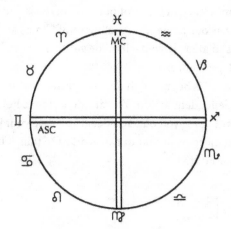

Figure 2. The Cross of Matter

When a person is born, the contribution of the physical world is the Cross of Matter, formed by the geometry of the person's location. The planets, representing the Cosmos, are the universal or spiritual contribution and are "captured" and placed on the physical map. Since the houses are derived from a need to understand a planet's orientation to the Cross of Matter, the houses are about the physical world in which your spiritual/cosmic/planetary energy finds itself.

Since predictive astrology is very involved with matters of the physical world and how the spiritual energy, the human being, is going to cope with physical events in the physical world, then the houses play a large role in the astrologer's predictive tool kit.

The following guide to the meanings of the houses in predictive astrology will help students become familiar with the concepts. Like the aspects, the meanings of the houses should be kept very simple. The houses are defined through the lens of predictive work and therefore are seen purely as areas where events can unfold. They are also defined by the way they could be emphasized by the transit grids discussed later in the transit section.

THE 1ST HOUSE

Key area of life: the self, the physical body, and appearance; independently taking action.

The 1st house is the area of the persona and, as a result, governs not only physical appearance in terms of our style of dress, but also the physical body and even our name. It is the house of "I am" and is concerned with your efforts to identify yourself in the world in which you live. It also defines your independence.

When this house is being emphasized, it shows that you will be most likely to take independent action. You decide to move house rather than having the landlord force you out. You decide to leave your job rather than to have circumstances push you out of work. Or things happen to you physically, to your body.

Transit Grids

If the 1st house is found:

In the top row of a grid, it implies that independent action seemingly causes the events to manifest. Because you want to do something, events will occur in another area.*

In the middle row of a grid, it implies that the area with which you are most concerned is the physical body, your appearance, or your independence. Accidents or name changing can occur with this placement. One of the features of this placement is that you will feel in control of the situation. In other words, you will be aware that it is your personal actions that are pulling the strings of the event.

In the bottom row of the grid, the ruler of the first house is receiving or producing a transit. This planet is strongly connected with your independence and personal action. Thus the consequences of the event affects the physical body or appearance as well as your independence. Therefore the client can be advised to take personal action because it is a time of personal strength.

THE 2ND HOUSE

Key area of life: personal resources—material, mental, spiritual; security.

The 2nd house is the midpoint of the rising nocturnal semi-arc and is a combination of the meaning of the 1st (the persona, the individual) and the 4th (the home, family, tribe). In astrology, we translate this midpoint to mean that which you personally can claim as your own; that is, personal property.

Personal property is not just the physical objects around you; it is also the personal resources and talents that you have at your disposal—self-esteem, value systems, attitude toward security.

When being emphasized by predictive work, the issues are resources, self-esteem, and security in terms of money, mental attitude, or spiritual support.

Transit Grids

If the 2nd house is found:

In the top row of a grid, it implies that, due to your situation or attitude to your physical, mental, or spiritual security, events are going to occur. You

---

* Transit Grids are explained on pages 45–87.

may be short of money, or just have come into some money. You may just have become more emotionally secure, which leads you in a new direction.

In the middle row of a grid, the events that are going to occur will focus on issues of security—mental, physical, or spiritual. The focus is now on getting the money, or finding emotional security, or dealing with issues of self-esteem.

In the bottom row of a grid, the ruler of the 2nd house is receiving or producing a transit. This planet is very concerned with issues of security. Thus the consequences of the events will affect mental and/or physical, spiritual security: loss or gain of money, gain or loss of emotional support as a result of the event, greater self-confidence as a result of how you handle the event, and so on.

THE 3RD HOUSE

Key area of life: information coming from, and into, familiar areas—such as siblings—or areas considered as local.

This is traditionally the house of thinking patterns, short journeys, transport, siblings, early education, communication, paperwork, and the local neighborhood. Everything about this house is familiar. When it is being emphasized by predictive work, it is an indication that there are no surprises, and the events are pertaining to "your own backyard," so to speak.

The definition of the backyard will vary from individual to individual. If you travel extensively, you may consider the entire country in which you live as a local area. On the other hand, if you have never left the hills where you were born, you could have massive culture shock by just traveling to the nearest city. For the hillbilly, the journey to town would be a 9th house statement rather than the 3rd house event that a suburbanite would call it.

Transit Grids

If the 3rd house is found:

In the top row of a grid, it talks of issues arising due to familiar things in the environment. Siblings, the family car, daily paperwork. Things that you know about, things you take for granted. It is because these things are so familiar that you are not aware of possible difficulties or events about to come from this area of life.

In the middle row of a grid, it shows that the familiar areas described previously are now the major causes of concern or effort: paperwork that should be routine is now having to be focused upon, hassles or joys with siblings, car breakdowns causing you to change your route to work, learning, or starting a study course.

In the bottom row of a grid, the ruler of the 3rd house is receiving or producing a transit; thus the consequences of the events affect the familiar environment of learning, siblings, etc. Familiar patterns are changed as a result of events and new things are learned. The backyard boundaries are moved around a little.

THE 4TH HOUSE

Key area of life: the physical abode, the family, the end of an issue.

The 4th house is an angular house and is situated around the Nadir, the lowest point on the Cross of Matter. This is the hearthstone, the point of warmth and nurturing in our lives. In predictive astrology, we can define it as the home, the family, the physical abode as well as the unconditional parent—mother or father.

Any matters to do with real estate, alterations to the abode, members of the family leaving home, people moving into the family home, or family heritage matters belong to the 4th house.

Transit Grids

If the 4th house is found:

In the top row of a grid, it implies that a situation that has been happening to the family or at home caused events to manifest in another area of the life. For example, you may decide to build a room onto your house and as a result of that decision, you take a course in carpentry.

In the middle row of a grid, the events are happening in the home or family area and your main concerns are issues of home and family: troubles at home or moving home, changes in the family—births or deaths—children leaving home, and so on.

In the bottom row of a grid, the ruler of the 4th house is receiving or producing a transit; thus consequences of events cause changes in the home or family. In addition, there is also an implication of a finalization of the situation. The home situation is now not the central issue, but is changed as a result of the central issue. For example, you may change jobs and, as a result of that, have to relocate to another city. The main issue is the job, but the consequence of this issue is that you had to change residences.

THE 5TH HOUSE

Key area of life: creative recreation and its results; children, lovers, and artistic pursuits.

Halfway between the family and home (4th house) and the point of personal relationships (7th house) is the area of the 5th house. In this area you learn to take the childhood conditioning and create a new set of behavior patterns or expectations by bouncing them off the wall of personal relationships.

This area is versatile and, therefore, not tied to old habit patterns. It encompasses play and recreation, for this is the way that creativity is learned. Children are the ultimate ball game between the 4th house and the 7th, and fit into this house as the personal creations of the parents.

In predictive work, this house implies children, pregnancy, the teaching of young children, recreation, productive creativity, and—not to be forgotten—romantic love.

Transit Grids

If the 5th house is found:

In the top row of a grid, it implies that because of a child, one of your personal creations, or the desire for more creativity, events manifest in other areas of life. Because of a pregnancy, you leave work; or you may have a desire to paint, so you change your life situation to create more time for this activity.

In the middle row of a grid, it implies that the main area of your concern is either children, lovers, or that which is your personal creative expression.

In the bottom row of the grid, the ruler of the 5th house is receiving or producing a transit. In Hindu astrology, the ruler of the 5th house yields positive events and results, and although we use a different zodiac, I have found this to hold true in Western astrology even if the ruler is Pluto. Thus the outcomes will be positive, and, as a result of the events, the client can become more creative or involved with children or encounter a lover.

THE 6TH HOUSE

Key area of life: the daily domestic routine; health and diet; breaking habit patterns; duty and service.

In ancient Babylonian astrology, this is the house of slavery, but now it reflects our attitudes to service. When you wake up in the morning and start to make a list of daily chores, that list is your 6th house. The daily routine—the daily "humdrum"—is the 6th house. Whatever this routine is—skydiving, housework, shopping, business mergers, and so on—it belongs to the 6th house. Habit patterns of the domestic life, whatever that lifestyle may be, belong to this house.

The 6th house also refers to matters of health and diet, for the physical body has its own cycles, rhythms, and habit patterns.

Transit Grids

If the 6th house is found:

In the top row of a grid, issues that are part of your daily routine may cause events to occur in another area of life. These issues could be health issues or issues of service and duty. Some event may happen at work.

In the middle row of a grid, the daily domestic life—the daily routine, the daily work—is under stress. It is the area where you feel changes, such as job, health, or habit patterns.

In the bottom row of a grid, the ruler of the 6th house is receiving or producing a transit; therefore, the effects of these events will be felt in the area of daily domestic routines. As a consequence, you can expect changes in your daily patterns. You also find yourself having to take on greater burdens in your daily life.

THE 7TH HOUSE

Key area of life: personal relationships; business partnerships and court cases.

Traditionally, this house represents the area of personal relationships and can reveal your needs, desires, and expectations in a relationship. This house reveals the nature of possible projections in relationships. When you are young, it defines the nature of your parents' relationship.

This house refers to all that is open. There are no secrets with the 7th house. It symbolizes open enemies, court cases, and business partnerships, as these are legal relationships between two or more people. In addition, the 7th house is also involved if you make a union with a divine or religious concept, for this is marriage in a different form.

Transit Grids

If the 7th house is found:

In the top row of a grid, it indicates that, as a result of an attitude to a relationship, events occur in other areas of life. Because of a business partnership, you may travel overseas; as a result of marriage, a woman may get pregnant; and so on.

In the middle row of a grid, events are going to take place in the relationship, through a court case, or via the parents' relationship. These will be the areas of concern. Marriage, divorce, or setting up a business partnership all may be likely events at this time.

In the bottom row of a grid, the ruler of the 7th house is receiving or producing a transit; thus there is an indication that a relationship will be formed or broken up because of ongoing events. The main event may be a trip overseas but, as a result of this trip, you meet someone with whom you form a relationship.

THE 8TH HOUSE

Key area of life: transformation, beginnings or endings, death and birth; money.

The 8th house is the midpoint between social classification (the 10th house) and personal relationships (the 7th house) and can be translated as the house where a person encounters and uses other people's resources. These resources can be emotional, physical, or financial.

This house encompasses a cyclic nature and also talks of the recycling of all things—including life itself. Thus, our attitudes to birth, death, sex, and the resources of those around us fall into the domain of the 8th house.

In predictive work, it also takes on the flavor of intense, irrevocable change—an ending, a completion, a transformation—so that it becomes impossible to return to the old system.

Transit Grids

If the 8th house is found:

In the top row of a grid, it implies that, due to a death, birth, or the desire for change, events will start to unfold in another area.

In the middle row of a grid, issues of birth, death, money, and so on are the main areas of focus. It is not unusual for a pregnancy to be shown as an 8th house placement in this part of a grid. Whatever the expression, you are going to be dealing with the "stuff" of life.

In the bottom row of a grid, it means that the ruler of the 8th house is receiving or producing a transit. This planet in the natal chart will tend to function in intense or extreme ways, even if it is Venus. Thus the ongoing events cause transformation. Situations being described by the rest of the grid tend to come to an end with this placement. This is an important placement as it implies irrevocable change or an ending due to the events that are happening.

If a client asks: "Will my marriage end?" with the 8th house in this position, the answer will be that it will change so much that it will either be finished or so altered that she would not recognize it.

THE 9TH HOUSE

Key area of life: travel and that which is alien; study and places of education; books and publishing.

The 9th house in predictive work is that which is alien, that which will cause culture shock—by physical journeys to other places or through education about things that are not common knowledge in your own group. The house also encompasses the concept of books, since that is the way the human race consciously stores its knowledge. The 9th house, like the 7th, is a very conscious house with nothing hidden.

The hillbilly, in the 3rd house example, would classify the trip to town as a 9th house event. However, once used to the town, the experience would fall into the domain of the 3rd house.

Travel, study, foreigners, flying saucers, publishing, books, unexpected news from afar are all in the realm of the 9th house in predictive work.

Transit Grids

If the 9th house is found:

In the top row of a grid, it indicates that due to the person's desire to study or travel, and so on, events are stimulated in other areas of the life.

In the middle row of a grid, the study, travel, or encounters with alien people or things becomes the main area of concern or interest for the individual. When the client is going to take a trip overseas or start some form of higher education or is simply having trouble with a pen pal, the astrologer can expect to see the 9th house in such a position.

In the bottom row of a grid, the ruler of the 9th house is receiving or producing a transit. Like the ruler of the 5th, this planet in the natal chart will always yield expansion in a constructive way. There may be a bit of luck involved in the outcome of the transit, and you can push for the results that you would like. Thus the events that have occurred result in one traveling, studying, or in some way broadening one's horizons. Culture shock is going to occur but in a way that broadens the mind, not terrifies it.

THE 10TH HOUSE

Key area of life: social status, career, and how the community classifies you; the Path with a Heart—the life activity that brings personal fulfillment.

The 10th house is how you are judged by the group, for society classifies you by occupation, by marital status, and, at times, whether you are a parent or not. The 10th house is also the parent from whom you gain your social identity. If you have a famous mother, then it would be your mother. If, on the other hand, you carry the family name and are viewed as the "daughter of her father," then the 10th will be your father. Any changes to this structure will be a 10th house event.

The 10th house is also a public house, for once again nothing is hidden and the emphasis of this house implies that you are rearranging the manner in which you are seen publicly.

Transit Grids

If the 10th house is found:

In the top row of a grid, issues of career or social status will light the spark that causes events to occur in other parts of life.

In the middle row of a grid, the way that society sees you is the main area of action in your life. It may be your career, getting married, divorced, becoming a parent, or anything else that will affect your status.

In the bottom row of a grid, the ruler of the 10th house is receiving or producing a transit; thus events that have occurred will lead to changes in your social standing: a new job, finding what you want to do with your life, change of relationship to the 10th house parent.

THE 11TH HOUSE

Key area of life: groups, friends, counseling.

Halfway between your social standing of the 10th and your public face of the 1st house lies the 11th house, representing the meeting of these two points. This is the area of social contact.

The 11th house in predictive work is the house where interactions occur between people without deep emotional content. Thus, it is the realm of your colleagues, clubs, groups, and casual friendships. It also encompasses counseling because counseling is a type of exchange where one individual, hopefully the counselor, does not become emotionally involved. Teamwork and effort put into group projects belong in this house. The 11th house also represents adopted children.

Transit Grids

If the 11th house is found:

In the top row of a grid, it is the advice or action of friends that stimulates events to occur in another part of your life. There is increased socializing leading to events coming to a head elsewhere.

In the middle row of the grid, the friends or groups are now the main area of concern, with the possibility of encountering a whole new group of people or going into counseling or therapy, and so on. The adoption of a child, or having to work with other people's children, could also be a major issue.

In the bottom row of a grid, the ruler of the 11th house is receiving or producing a transit; thus the outcome of the events is the formation of a new group. You could go into counseling, therapy, group projects, teamwork matters, and so on.

THE 12TH HOUSE

Key area of life: alone, that which is hidden; illness, intuition, and the psychic.

The 12th house, with its profound meanings in natal astrology, takes on quite a simple face in the world of prediction. It is the house of being alone, the house of illness or of retreat. It can depict a hidden enemy or can talk of things buried in the past, as well as your psychic or intuitive knowledge.

Large institutions, hospitals, prisons, or working for huge multinational companies are all 12th house areas. Becoming lost, confused, misunderstood, drugged, or developing a vivid dream life belong to the realm of this house.

Transit Grids

If the 12th house is found:

In the top row of a grid, it implies that because hidden things have become visible, or you've had the need to be alone, isolated, or secretive, events occur in other areas of your life.

In the middle row of a grid, the aloneness, illness, or secretiveness becomes your main area of concern. There may be issues to do with large companies, or social security systems, etc.

In the bottom row of a grid, the ruler of the 12th house is receiving or producing a transit. This is a difficult rulership, for when activated, the depths of the 12th house can be stirred up, bringing to the forefront issues that the client may have no or little control over. To be without power. Thus the events that are occurring can lead you to being alone, isolated, ill, or involved with others in such a situation. It can also imply that you may develop your intuitive abilities as a result of the events.

• • •

The definitions given here may seem simplistic, but events are simplistic. Quite often an astrologer questing for the events in a person's life dives deeper and deeper into the mythological, humanistic world and then wonders why the predictive work is falling short of the mark. The astrology of prediction is simple, conscious astrology. The effects of the events that it talks about can be read very deeply, but first it is necessary to get the prediction correct before applying any profound meanings.

Chapter Two

Working with Transits

Transits are probably the most used and discussed form of modern dynamic predictive astrology and, in principle, they are very simple.

Principles of Transits

A chart is receiving a transit when a planet, in the course of its orbit, reaches a point in the zodiac that was previously occupied, or geometrically connected to, a point at the time of birth. This point could be the position of a planet, or a point in the zodiac that was emphasized by the location of the event, e.g., ascendant, MC, or house cusps.

The theory is based on the premise that you, through your life, symbolically represent the planetary positions at your birth. These planetary positions that were abandoned by the Cosmos after the birth are remembered by the individual who acts like a living vessel for these long-since abandoned positions. When a transiting planet reaches one of these "remembered positions," then the vessel—the person who contains their memory—will respond or resonate.

This response is like the strings of a harp, which are plucked one at a time so they may be tuned. A transiting planet will pluck at a particularly remembered position, sounding a discord until the individual string is corrected in the sound it emits. In the world of predictive astrology, events symbolized by transits—or indeed any other technique—are seen not as random occurrences pulling the instrument out of tune but rather the carefully understood plucking of a musician gently bringing the harp into harmony. To be in tune is to be whole, aware, at one's full potential, even possibly enlightened.

You and your chart are therefore like an instrument, striving with an invisible urge to be whole. The predictive astrologer must always be aware that every event is designed to tune the strings.

This string tuning manifests in the everyday physical life as events. These events are designed to modify or adjust the different components of your being by increasing your awareness. This may be a long and rocky road and may contain even the odd broken string. The Hindus believe that this road is so long that the journey could take many lifetimes. In the West, we recognize the road—we are just not too sure of its length.

THE STRUCTURE OF A TRANSIT

Transits, which are one variety of string pluckings, can be broken down into three components:

1) **The planet that is transiting:** the actual planet that, while moving in its orbit, forms a geometric relationship to a natal position.

2) **The aspect being formed:** the nature of the geometry between the transiting planet and the natal position.

3) **The point in the natal chart receiving the transit:** the natal point.

The meaning and importance of the transiting aspect have been discussed in the Alphabet section along with the meanings of the planets and points in predictive work. However, the first point mentioned, the planet that is transiting, will raise an interesting question with which the predictive astrologer will have to deal.

Every planet represents a set of characteristics—archetypal meanings—that have been bestowed on the planet by thousands of generations of humans. However, every planet in a horoscope has its "pure" meanings modified, or filtered, by a zodiac sign, a house position, and aspects to other planets. That is to say, as astrologers, we do not expect to find a "pure" Saturn in a chart but rather a modified Saturn; for example, it may be in Scorpio, in the 10th house, being squared by Pluto . . .

Thus, Saturn in its pure, or universal, principle implies structure and form but each human being will experience this structure in a different way in their lives. Therefore, the question that naturally arises when a chart is receiving a Saturn transit is:

Is the influence of the Saturn transit the person's own version of Saturn, affected by house, sign, and aspects, or is it the universal Saturn that carries no flavor of the individual chart?

If it is the universal Saturn, the whole concept of string plucking for the tuning of the individual falls down, and personal growth through working on and becoming aware of various ups and downs in yourself becomes meaningless. For a single individual cannot change the universal meaning of a symbol.

If the answer to this question, however, is the personalized Saturn, then this must be taken into account when trying to predict the outcome of the transit. So the extra information of house, sign, and rulership that the natal Saturn carries with it must come into consideration. Let's use the analogy of a radio to clarify this concept. There are many different radio waves in the air, but the receiver that you have in your home will only pick up certain ones. Different types of receivers are designed to pick up different signals. The television receiver picks up one sort, the radio receives another. Without these receivers you would not be aware that the signals were there. Furthermore, you don't expect your black-and-white TV to produce color images, even though they are being transmitted in color from the station. The signals are being modified by your receiver.

A Saturn transit is also a signal coming into your world. You will be able to perceive this particular type of signal only through your special design "radio," which you were given at birth. This radio is for picking up signals about authority, and so on. In the same manner as a radio, the incoming signals from Saturn will be modified by your particular receiver, and the transiting Saturn will appear to carry with it the characteristic of the natal Saturn.

So, a transiting planet is modified by the natal chart it is transiting. On the other hand, we could say that the natal chart through which a planet was transiting can perceive the transiting planet only through its own modified version of that planet.

THE HOUSES—THE SPACE IN WHICH THINGS HAPPEN

At different times in your life, events will occur that are the results of a previous situation. These previous situations came from a totally different area of your life. In addition, these events will be dealt with and will then cause repercussions in yet another area of life. It is the nature of any event that it will start in a particular place, or area, in your life, be dealt with in a second area, and have consequences in a third.

Cause = Action = Effect

All events will have a cause, which will lead to some type of action, which will then affect something else. Since the world of transits is concerned with the world of events, all transits will, therefore, have a cause, which will then manifest in a place in the person's life and then have an effect in another place.

There are three phases to any event (transit):

1) **An origin, its cause:** first you have the beginnings of the situation. Because of these events, other events described by the transit are going to occur.

2) **The event itself:** then you have the main theme of the transit.

3) **The consequences of the event:** last you have the outcome, what is affected by the event, and the result of the event.

For example, your friend may borrow your car, leaving you with no transportation, and, as a result, you are late for work. The areas of your life being emphasized, therefore, are friends, transportation, and work. The lack of transportation is the "middle issue," which seems the immediate problem. But the problem starts with the friend borrowing the car, and the consequences result when you are late for work.

Friend = No Car = Late For Work

So events are not abstract. They need a stage on which to perform and they need to manifest in tangible areas of life. If a friend comes up to you and says "I love," you would answer, "You love whom, what, how?" Similarly, if you were looking at transiting Pluto square the Moon, you would know that the person was going to encounter some emotional events. But where would these strong feelings be experienced? Who, what, and how are the natural questions that have to be answered.

When predicting events for a client, the areas of the life with which these events are going to be involved become a major part of the prediction. The houses in a chart are the components of the astrological alphabet that define places, locations, and so on. Therefore, if we involve the houses in our predictive work, we will be able to define the areas of concern for the client, as well as the areas affected by the event's consequences.

So in our above example of:

Friend = No Car = Late For Work

The houses involved would be:

$$11 = 3 = 6 \text{ (or maybe 10)}$$

So in getting back to the three main points of a transit, which were:

1) The nature of the transiting planet.

2) The nature of the transiting aspect.

3) The nature of the natal point.

These points can be expanded to incorporate the natal houses involved:

1) Transiting planet: its natal house, the natal house it rules, plus the house through which it is transiting.

2) Aspect

3) Point receiving the transits: which natal house does it rule?

By taking all of these expanded points into account, the predicted event will not now be some abstract thing floating in the person's life like, "I love," but will have the where, how, and whom attached to it.

SIMPLE GRID

Figure 3 is a simplified chart showing the natal Pluto, natal Moon, and the position of the transiting Pluto. In this figure, transiting Pluto is forming a square to the natal Moon. Transiting Pluto square natal Moon can be delineated using the information in the alphabet section.

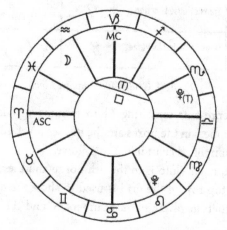

Figure 3. Transiting Pluto square Moon.

In this example you can form the working phrase—Pluto (T) square Moon. Then take the individual components of the phrase and break them down as follows:

Pluto: intense, dramatic, emotional, feminine, transforming, and so on.

Square: The square's key principle is that of events, which are nobody's fault, but which are forcing an action to be taken that has not been taken before.

Moon: emotions, feminine, sensitive, mother, etc.

In putting these ingredients together, we can now formulate a sentence that reflects the concepts of Pluto square Moon.

An event occurs that is very emotional, intense, and transforming that cannot be blamed on anyone and causes the person to act in a new manner. Fine, but we are now faced with the question, "Where in the life is this event going to occur—home, family, lover, children, job, or friends; where?" So let's add the "where" and put in the natal houses as demonstrated in figure 4.

	Transit	Natal Planet
Planet	♇	♇ ☽
Natal House Location	5	11
Transit House Location	7	
House(s) Ruled by Planet	8	4 (IC)

Figure 4. Grid of Pluto square Moon.

This grid represents transiting Pluto forming a square to the natal Moon. The numbers in the boxes are the houses involved in the transit as shown by the simplified chart in figure 3 above.

In the chart, natal Pluto is in the 5th house and the natal Moon is in the 11th. The top row of the grid is used to show the natal house positions of the planets involved, so the numbers "5" and "11" are placed there respectively.

The middle row is used to show the natal house through which the transiting planet is currently moving. In this case transiting Pluto is moving through the 7th house of the natal chart, hence the number "7" is placed on Pluto's side of the grid. The Moon is receiving the transit and is thus a stationary point, so the middle row under the Moon is left empty.

The bottom row shows the houses in the natal chart that are ruled by the two planets. Pluto rules Scorpio, and Scorpio is on the cusp of the 8th house. Thus, the number 8 is placed in the bottom row under Pluto. The Moon rules Cancer, and Cancer is on the 4th house cusp—the IC—so the number "4" or "IC" is placed on the bottom row underneath the Moon. So the grid represents the following information:

1) For the planet that is transiting: its natal house position; its transiting house position; its natal house rulership.

2) The aspect involved in the transit.

3) For the planet receiving the transit: its natal house position; its natal house rulership.

In other words, all the house information involved in the transit as well as the planets and the aspect are shown in the grid.

• • •

In using the concept that all events have three phases consisting of cause, action, and effect, we can apply this to the grid as follows:

Cause: the top row (natal positions of planets involved in the transit) can generally be seen as the area in life where the transit starts to happen.

Action: the middle row (house through which the transiting planet is moving) is the arena where the main event occurs.

Effect: the bottom row (the houses ruled in the natal chart by the planets involved in the transit) shows the areas of life that are affected by the consequences of the transit; that is, the outcome.

These boundaries of beginning, middle, and consequences as defined by the rows are a rule of thumb, and flexibility should be allowed when working with them. At times, it is possible for events to seem to affect all areas indicated all at once.

USING GRIDS

According to the grid, the cause is described by the 5th and 11th houses (the top row). The 5th house is children, creativity, lovers, and recreation, and the 11th house is friends, groups, and unemotional involvements. Putting this together, we have the beginnings of a delineation.

> *A stressful situation starts to develop involving a friend, or group of people, who is in some way connected with your lover, children, or creativity. This results in events occurring that are very emotional and transforming and that force you into new action.*

The main arena of action is the 7th house (the middle row). The 7th house is committed relationships as in marriages, business partnerships, law courts, or open enemies. In adding this to the above description, the delineation begins to be fleshed out.

> *These events are going to occur in the area of the person's marriage—legal or otherwise—or business partnership.*

The consequences of these events are described by the bottom row (the 8th house and the IC). The 8th house is change, transformation, beginnings and endings, and so on. The IC is home, family, mother. Thus, the consequences of these events are:

> *Changes may occur where you are living or in your attitude to home and family or mother.*

Putting it all together, we have:

> *A stressful, emotional situation starts to develop through nobody's fault involving a friend or group of people. This friend, or group, is connected in some way to your more personal life concerned with lovers, children, and creativity. The results of these actions upset your marriage or business partnership to the extent that you have to take action and either move, make some adjustments to your home, or change your attitude to your mother/role as mother.*

So with this transit, there are five areas or houses that are involved and by noticing their involvement, the astrologer gains a great deal of information concerning the nature of the transit.

This is as far as the eagle will fly. To fine-tune this, you would need to either use your intuition—lark—and/or ask your client about his or her given situation. The above delineation would be correct for the following types of scenarios:

The client is going to fall in love with someone she meets through a group of friends, her marriage partner finds out, and, as a result, the marriage breaks up with the client changing her living circumstances.

or:

A woman, while in a love affair, becomes pregnant; the relationship consolidates, and the two people start living together, but not without emotional dramas.

or:

The client's mother gets ill and thus has to be moved into the client's home, which dramatically affects her social life, upsetting the children and causing a change in her marriage as it adjusts to the new family structure. All this is done while the person is worried about the mother's health.

or:

One of the children's friends coaxes them into a lawbreaking situation. They get caught and the child ends up in a juvenile court. As a result of this, the client and her partner change the family rules about how the children socialize.

The number of different ways that people can rearrange a given set of data is almost endless. To pick the exact option that the person will use is definitely lark territory.

Talking to the client about possible meanings can also be helpful. For example, the client's mother may already be ill, in which case the transit will probably manifest as the mother moving into the family home. Or, if the client is having an affair and her partner does not know about it, then the transit is implying that all will be discovered and her marriage may well break up. Let us say that what you picked as the most likely option proves to be incorrect and what actually happens for the client is:

The client's mother dies. In the will, the client is left a partnership in an art gallery. This inheritance forces the client to get involved with artistic people.

Where did you go wrong? If you look at the actual event, all the meanings of the houses are there: mother (IC), business partnership (7), death (8 and Pluto to Moon), art and creativity (5), groups of people through the gallery and mixing with the new group (11), and forcing action that cannot effectively be blamed on anyone else (the square).

All the components are correct, so the eagle is fine. The error, therefore, is in the intuition. When the lark flounders, no amount of rearranging of astrological techniques will help. Only faith—the old Irish word for a seer—and practice can improve its song. On the other hand, the resulting events may not be manifesting in the correct areas of the person's life—the houses—as for example the following event:

The client starts to have difficulties at work due to some health problem that has suddenly arisen. She is forced to resign due to these problems and is very distressed about what to do with her life. However, in a short time she takes up a course of study in childcare or drama.

The areas of the person's life being highlighted by the transit are:

Work: 6th or 10th house;

Health: 6th or 12th house;

Tertiary education: 9th house;

Children or drama: 5th house.

So something is wrong with the houses. The Eagle is on shaky ground. For health, work, and study issues are not contained in the houses that are being emphasized. Therefore, if further work is to be done on the chart, the following points need to be examined:

1) The accuracy of the birth time;

2) The house system being used;

3) The rulerships being used;

4) The astrological predictive technique you are using may not work for that client.

All of these points will be considered later.

Feedback on predictive work that has been carefully and meaningfully worked out should be applied in a constructive way.

Failure is an unexpected outcome and in predictive work should only occur in the area of the lark. If it occurs in the eagle's domain, then it is a golden opportunity to examine your techniques and fine-tune them or possibly even throw them out.

DUAL RULERSHIPS GRIDS

There are of course some planets that rule more than one sign. Indeed in the old rulership system only the Luminaries ruled a single sign with the planets all ruling two signs. Mars ruled Aries as well as Scorpio, Jupiter ruled Sagittarius and Pisces, while Saturn owned the rulerships of Capricorn and Aquarius. Now in the modern rulership, the only allotted dual rulerships are to the two inferior (orbit inside that of earth's) planets— Mercury and Venus.

Using the chart in figure 5, the person has transiting Saturn forming an opposition to natal Mercury.

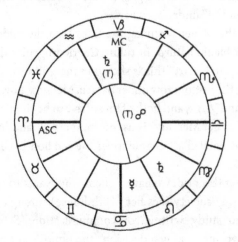

Figure 5. Transiting Saturn opposition Mercury.

The resulting grid is figure 6. Saturn, while forming the transit to Mercury, is passing through the 10th house of the natal chart, represented in the grid by the number "10" being placed in the middle row under Saturn.

	Transit	Natal Planet
Planet	♄	☍ ☿
Natal House Location	5	4
Transit House Location	10	
House(s) Ruled by Planet	10	3, 6

Figure 6. Grid of Saturn opposition Mercury.

Saturn is natally in the 5th house while Mercury resides in the 4th house. Thus the top row of the grid (figure 6) contains the numbers "5" under Saturn and "4" under Mercury.

Mercury is the planet receiving the transit, so the middle row under Mercury is left blank. Saturn, in ruling Capricorn, rules the 10th house in the example natal chart. This is shown in the grid by the number "10" being placed in the bottom row under Saturn. Mercury, however, rules two signs, Gemini and Virgo, and both of these have to be shown in the bottom row of the grid under Mercury. Thus the numbers "3" and "6" placed there show that in the natal chart Gemini rules the 3rd house while Virgo rules the 6th house.

In delineating this grid, we have a client who wants to change her job or change the way society sees her (10th house) through some form of commitment to study, writing, or communication (Saturn-Mercury). This change involves making a decision (the opposition) between home and family (4th house) and personal creativity (5th house). Pursuing the career is difficult due to family needs. The outcome is that the new career is undertaken (10th house in bottom line of grid) by rearranging the household routine (6th house) by getting a neighbor, brother, or sister (3rd house) to help out.

The meanings of the houses used here are very simple, the meanings of the planets are very simple, and the meaning of the aspect is very simple. If these things were not kept to the bare facts, then the astrologer would be overwhelmed by information and lose any chance of a meaningful, correct delineation of the transit. The KISS principle is very important. Small bricks make a big house. Take each piece of information and slowly add it into the delineation as shown in the example with Pluto square Moon.

INTERCEPTED SIGNS IN GRIDS

Charts can, at times, contain signs that are intercepted. That is, the sign is totally contained within a natal house and because of that does not occupy the cusp. Technically, intercepted signs do not rule a house. See figure 7.

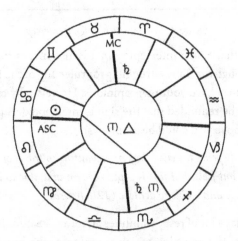

Figure 7. Transiting Saturn trine Sun.

Transiting Saturn, while traveling through the 4th house, forms a trine to the natal Sun in the 12th house. Figure 8 (p. 54) is the grid for figure 7.

Since Saturn is natally in the 9th house and the Sun is natally in the 12th house, the numbers "9" and "12" are placed on the top line of the grid. Saturn is currently transiting through the 4th house of the natal chart (the number "4" placed in the middle row) and rules Capricorn, which is on the cusp of both the 6th and 7th houses ("6" and "7" placed in the bottom row). The Sun rules Leo, and this sign is intercepted in the 1st house. The number "1" is still placed on the bottom row under the Sun, but a circle is placed around the number, indicating that Leo is intercepted.

	Transit	Natal Planet
Planet	♄	△ ☉
Natal House Location	9	12
Transit House Location	4	
House(s) Ruled by Planet	6, 7	①

Figure 8. Grid in which a sign is intercepted.

I believe that a sign intercepted in a house makes that sign stronger, almost as though the Sun is struggling for rulership of the 1st and thus tries harder. You may have your own opinions. However, by circling the number, you will be reminded that the sign is intercepted. A possible delineation of the above grid could be as follows:

> For many years the client has been wanting to travel or study (9th house) but feels that this is a pipe dream and, due to life circumstances, is impossible to achieve (12th house).

She also has a lot of responsibilities at home—Saturn in 4th is involved in the transit. This restraint, which comes from the home or family (4th house), suddenly disappears (trine).

The client is able to gain greater independence (1st house) due to this change in responsibilities (Saturn-Sun) and decides to travel or study. While enjoying a newfound independence, the client forms a relationship (7th house) that totally changes the daily routine (6th house).

When put together as a whole, the information on a grid is quite large, and it may seem as if the astrologer is truly a prophet. But each piece of information is simply like a small brick that, if placed together with others one at a time, will, slowly at first, yield a complete structure.

THE ANGLES IN GRIDS

The other type of transit found in a chart is a planet transiting the Cross of Matter—the ascendant, descendant, and the MC, IC axes.

If a planet is forming a trine to the ascendant, then it will also be forming a sextile to the descendant. In other words, it will be forming a harmonious aspect to the relating axis of the chart. In this example, we would express this as the transiting planet forming the trine to the ascendant and ignore the sextile to the descendant. Similarly, if there is a transit forming a semisquare to the ascendant, it will, at the same time, form a sesquiquadrate to the descendant, and, in the delineation, we would regard the transit as forming a stressful relationship to the relating axis and analyze the semisquare to the ascendant.

The descendant and the IC are points in the chart just like the ascendant and the MC, and all four of these points have meaning in their own right. The sign on the IC talks about your concept of home and the sign on the descendant, your relationship needs. When any of the four points receives a transiting conjunction, then that energy is applied *directly to that point*. If the IC is transited, then the home is taking the focus. If the transit is to the descendant, then it is the relationship that takes the focus.

Thus, for conjunctions, if we have transiting Uranus conjunct the descendant, we would expect events to manifest in the relationship. The common practice of astrologers to delineate this transit as Uranus opposite the ascendant completely denies the existence of the descendant and the existence of any relationships in the clients' lives. Delineation of transits in this manner could lead to some very incorrect assumptions.

The same logic applies to the IC. Transits over this point form conjunctions with the IC, not oppositions to the MC—the events will be focused in the area of home and family, *not* in the career path.

In figure 9 on page 56, we have the same chart as in figure 7, but at a future time when transiting Uranus is forming a conjunction with the descendant.

In figure 10 on page 56, which is the grid for figure 9, Uranus is natally in the second house, so the number "2" is placed in the top row under Uranus.

The descendant is not a planet with a house position, so the top row underneath it is left empty. Transiting Uranus is conjunct the descendant, so in the middle row under Uranus the angle—in this case the descendant—is entered. Uranus rules Aquarius in the new rulership system, and in this chart, Aquarius is intercepted in the 7th house, hence the Number "7" is entered in the bottom row under Uranus. It is circled to show the interception.

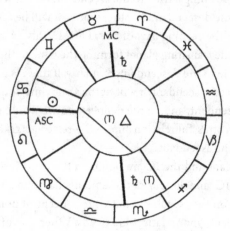

Figure 9. Transiting Uranus conjunct descendant.

	Transit	Natal Planet
Planet	♅	☌ DC
Natal House Location	2	
Transit House Location	DC	
House(s) Ruled by Planet	⑦	5, 9

Figure 10. Grid of Uranus conjunct descendant.

The Capricorn descendant is ruled by Saturn, and natal Saturn is in the 9th house. This information is represented on the grid by Saturn and the number "9" being placed on the bottom row underneath the descendant. Just as a planet has a house that it rules, an angle has a ruling planet. Any angle in a chart will inherently contain the flavor of the natal house of its ruler. In this example, whenever the descendant receives a transit, the 9th house is also involved.

With this transit, the astrologer would expect some sudden and surprising (Uranus) event to occur in the area of marriage and/or business partnerships (descendant). These surprise events would involve the client's self-esteem, value systems, sense of priorities, or personal possessions (2nd house), relationship matters (7th house), and travel or study in a structured way (9th house, Saturn).

So in this example, the client could feel a lack of satisfaction, or feel unappreciated in her relationship (2nd house), and, as a result, leave the relationship to travel or take a course of study; or, another option might be that the client could suddenly fall in love with someone who is an academic or a traveler, engendering feelings of security. The sudden events in the relationship are described by Uranus conjunct the descendant; the studying, traveling, and security issues come from the houses involved.

MULTIPLE TRANSITS GRIDS

There are times when a transiting planet will be making two aspects to natal points at the same time or be aspecting a stellium in the natal chart. Using figure 9 again, suppose transiting Uranus, while conjunct the descendant, could also be forming a square to the natal Moon. Thus a grid could be constructed (see figure 11).

	Transit	Natal Planet	Transit	Natal Planet
Planet	♅	☌ DC	♅	□ ☽
Natal House Location	2		2	10
Transit House Location	DC		DC	
House(s) Ruled by Planet	7	5,9	7	12, 1

Figure 11. Multiple transits grid.

The additional transit is simply added to the original grid. The square that Uranus forms to the Moon stresses the 10th, 12th, and 1st houses, adding an emotional flavor to the transit. This reaction is out of character for the client (Uranus square Moon), and it involves the area of career or social status. The bottom line of the grid is the area that generally shows the outcome of the transits—in this case the 1st, 7th, 9th, and 12th houses plus Saturn. So there could be a permanent change in the relationship due to study or travel, with the possibility of isolation through health matters or study, and so on.

The principle of the grids is to simplify the information that needs to be processed for the correct understanding of a transit. One piece of information that the grid leaves out is the natal aspecting of the planets involved. In doing this, the patterns with which we are working—the grid—become very simple. In my experience, the greater clarity of information is worth the reduction of base data. There may be some astrologers, however, who want to add this information into the system, and they can do so without losing clarity.

A Case Study of Transits

In 1412, a female child was born to a French ploughman and his wife. They were people of the land, and the child, along with her three brothers, was raised to follow a similar lifestyle. The young girl did not receive any formal learning and was educated by her mother in the Christian faith, in reading, and in writing. She was known by her neighbors in Domremy—a village in the French part of the Duchy of Bar—as a hardworking, simple, and very pious child. Her expected future was to marry a man from her village and to raise a family in the same lifestyle as she was raised.

At age thirteen, she began to hear voices in her head telling her to go to France and "raise the siege of Orleans." The child's name was Jeanne d'Arc (known more widely as Joan of Arc), and the France that she knew was at war with the English. The English had invaded France and held nearly all of the northern part of the country, which included the city of Reims, the traditional place of investiture of French kings. Thus, the Dauphin—the heir to the French throne—had remained unconsecrated for over five years and his right to the throne was being seriously questioned by the French people.

Jeanne's voices were urging her to rectify the situation. The fact that she was a simple peasant girl with no knowledge of warfare did not deter her, and in May of 1428, summoning her courage, she traveled to Vaucouleurs, the nearest stronghold still loyal to the Dauphin. There she asked the captain of the guard to take her to see the heir to the throne. The captain did not take the 16-year-old farm girl seriously and sent her back to her village.

There are times when fate steps into a life, lifts it from its expected path, and sets it on a collision course with history. Jeanne, driven on by her voices and visions, was not going to ignore this mission from God. In January of 1429, Jeanne's chart, Chart 1, was receiving three major transits—transiting Jupiter conjunct the natal Node; transiting Saturn conjunct natal Mercury; and transiting Uranus opposite the natal Moon.

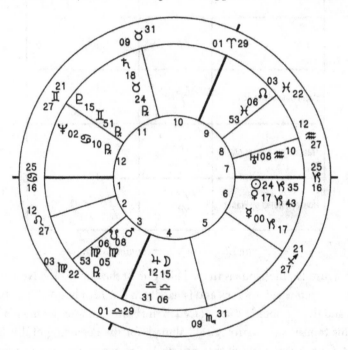

Chart 1. Joan of Arc, born January 15, 1412, N.S., (January 6, 1412 O.S.), 4:30 P.M. LMT, Domremy-la-Pucelle, France, 48N27, 5E41. Data from Profiles of Women. Placidus houses.

Fate did indeed step in and on some deep level Jeanne's "life force" complied and allowed itself to be taken over by energies larger than her own consciousness. The voices could have been from God, or maybe Jeanne became possessed by the collective unconscious of the French people's desire for a king. It is not for us to judge. The important point is that many charts may receive these types of transits, but the actual outcome will be affected by the manner in which the person responds. Jeanne's "life force" surrendered to what it perceived as the larger, more powerful energy.

So, in the fateful January of 1429, Jeanne once again traveled to Vaucouleurs. Jupiter was forming a conjunction to her North Node as the grid (figure 12) shows us:

	Transit	Natal Planet
Planet	♃	☌ ☊
Natal House Location	4	
Transit House Location	9	
House(s) Ruled by Planet	6	♆ 12

Figure 12. Grid of Jupiter conjunct Node.

In figure 12, the Node is treated like one of the angles. The Node is in Pisces. Neptune rules Pisces and is natally in the 12th house. Thus, Neptune and the number "12" are placed in the bottom row under the Node.

This transit is the astrological hallmark for the beginning of this holy quest, for this is the transit that, as astrologers, we might expect to see in Jeanne's chart—a peasant girl, plucked from her farm life by voices from God, commences a divine journey, which was her quest, destiny, or fate. For the North Node represents, among many things, the quest that we seek with our lives.

In examining the grid, there are the 4th and 9th houses in the first two rows. The action comes from the 4th—the mother, the family upbringing, the family beliefs—and the 9th—long journeys, religion, study, and so on. It was Jeanne's mother who taught her her beliefs. It is these religious beliefs (9th house) that propel Jeanne out of her home (4th house) to undertake a long journey (9th house).

The middle row is the 9th house, the place where the events occur. Jeanne takes a long journey for religious purposes.

The bottom row of the grid shows the outcome of the quest from Jeanne's perspective. She totally changes her lifestyle (6th house) and follows to the letter the guidance of "her voices" by having faith in their origins (Neptune and the 12th house). The ultimate end result is, of course, that Jeanne lost her life to the collective need (12th house) and was eventually made a "martyr" by the collective—shades of Neptune and the 12th house.

So, this first transit is the signal for the commencement of the quest and, as transiting Saturn conjoined Jeanne's natal Mercury, the captain at Vaucouleurs finally believed that God spoke through her. The Saturn transit that gave seriousness to Jeanne's words can be represented by figure 13. Clearly the believability of her words is represented by transiting Saturn conjunct the natal Mercury. But figure 13 gives additional information.

	Transit	Natal Planet
Planet	♄	☌ ☿
Natal House Location	11	6
Transit House Location	6	
House(s) Ruled by Planet	7	12, 3

Figure 13. Grid of Saturn conjunct Mercury.

Jeanne sets out to convince a group of people (11th house) that she is on a mission from God as His servant and was instructed to serve the Dauphin (6th house). The manifestation of the transit is in the 6th house, so Jeanne totally changes her daily domestic routine in order to achieve this service to the Crown of France, dictated by her service to the kingdom of Heaven. The captain, in believing her words, allots six men-at-arms to escort her through enemy territory and disguises Jeanne by dressing her in men's clothing—a style of dress unheard of for 15th-century women and a style that Jeanne adopts for the rest of her life.

The bottom row of the grid shows the consequences of the captain believing her words. Jeanne goes on a journey (3rd house). The sole purpose of the journey is to tell the Dauphin of the message that God has given her (3rd house, 12th house is a fair attempt by the chart to describe "messages from God") and to fulfill the mission that "her voices" from God have told her to undertake (7th house: a vocation or mission).

At the same time as this Saturn transit, transiting Uranus was also forming an opposition to Jeanne's natal Moon—exact on February 25, 1429. In this period, Jeanne threw off the expectations of society about the future of a young farm girl. She dressed in men's clothing and left her family home to travel to the French court and there, with the aid of the Dauphin, who finally believed her after she was questioned for three weeks by ecclesiastical authorities, established a military household. The grid for the Uranus transit is shown in figure 14.

	Transit	Natal Planet	
Planet	♅	♂ ☽	
Natal House Location	7	4	
Transit House Location	10		
House(s) Ruled by Planet	8	ASC	

Figure 14. Grid of Uranus opposition Moon.

The Uranus-Moon interaction implies that this is a time in her life where she questions, and changes, her attitudes about her role as a woman. The grid shows that Jeanne is making a decision (opposition) about home (4th house) and her role in life (10th house), caused by her belief in a mission from God. It is God's fault that she is having to make these changes (the aspect is an opposition). If He stopped demanding that she take these actions, then she could settle back into a nice, quiet life. The opposition is pressure, and Jeanne experienced God pressuring her.

This 7th house activity in the top row of the grid shows that it is the commitment to a divine cause that propels her into the changes in her social status (10th house). Strangely enough, this 7th house activity was also evident in Florence Nightingale's chart when she took up her mission of reforming the hospitals. It seems that divine missions are like a "marriage" to the "will of God."

The results of this decision are shown in the bottom line of the grid. Jeanne's old image dies, she changes (8th house) her physical appearance (ascendant) as well as her identity and transforms from Jeanne d'Arc the peasant girl to the "Maid-of-Orleans" (name change), the female, divinely led, warrior and savior of France.

By May of the same year—1429—transiting Jupiter started to form a station conjunct Jeanne's MC. The stationary period lasted from May through September and by May 9, 1429, Jeanne, leading and commanding the French army, had defeated the English at Orleans and cleared the way for the Dauphin to be crowned.

The Dauphin was not crowned immediately, for it was thought that it would be better to clear the English out of other cities first. Jeanne led the French troops to overwhelming victories, to the point where she was thought to be invincible. However, even though her war record was good, she had to fight just as vigorously a verbal and written battle against the advisers of the Dauphin to convince him to hasten to Reims for his coronation. Eventually her arguments won through and, after some minor resistance from some cities along the way, the Dauphin was crowned on July 20, 1429, at the very time that transiting Jupiter was stationary about to turn retrograde at 3°♎ 36'. The Jupiter transit is shown in figure 15 on page 64.

	Transit	Natal Planet
Planet	♃	☌ MC
Natal House Location	4	
Transit House Location	MC	
House(s) Ruled by Planet	6	♂ 3

Figure 15. Grid of Jupiter conjunct the MC.

Jupiter's aspect to the MC is the successful realization of Jeanne's ambitions to get the Dauphin crowned. Her fame and her position with the Dauphin were in their prime, with Jeanne's personal banner being placed next to the Dauphin's at this coronation. The first row of the grid shows the 4th house. The background to this personal fame is her belief system since childhood. Also this implies that the personal fame has grown from Jeanne's establishment as a member of the royal court (new family). The middle row of the MC shows the focus on her social status.

The outcome of the transit is symbolized by the bottom row of the grid. First, for winning her point of view, but then, on a larger level, being captured, tried, and burned for her heretic words. This is an unpleasant meaning to the 6th house, Mars, and the 3rd house.

Jeanne was captured by the English in early May of 1430, as transiting Jupiter squared her natal Sun. In the following January, she was handed over to the Church for trial as a heretic. This period of her trial and eventual execution on May 30, 1431, is symbolized by the transits of Saturn forming conjunctions to her Venus and then her Sun, while transiting Uranus was squaring the natal Sun.

On January 10, 1431, transiting Saturn was exactly conjunct Jeanne's natal Venus. Only seven days earlier she had been handed over for the price of 10,000 francs to the Catholic Church. Being sold for a sum of money to be imprisoned is one way of expressing transiting Saturn conjunct the Venus. The grid of the transit is figure 16.

	Transit	Natal Planet
Planet	♄	♂ ♀
Natal House Location	11	6
Transit House Location	6	
House(s) Ruled by Planet	7	4, 11

Figure 16. Grid of Saturn conjunct Venus.

This transit shows the depths of Jeanne's loneliness and isolation (Saturn conjunct Venus). She feels deserted by her followers and is now in the hands of the Church she sought to serve, only to find herself on trial (7th house). Her services for the group (6th house and 11th house) are challenged by the very foundation stones of her beliefs (4th house). The combined transits of Saturn and Uranus to the Sun can be shown in a multiple grid (see figure 17 on page 66).

Jeanne d'Arc was imprisoned and tried by the Church (Saturn, 11th house, and 7th house) for what she believed was her duty (6th house). Her credibility was challenged, for she was tried not for her efforts on behalf of the French army, but rather on the issue of whether she was a saint or a witch (social status, 10th house). Her freedom was removed and she was forced to defend her concept of who she was (Uranus square Sun). The outcome was that she would not compromise her values (2nd house) by denying her voices from God and, as a result, she was found guilty of heresy by the court (7th house) and was executed as a heretic (8th house).

The 8th house on the bottom row of a grid always shows irreversible transformations or changes.

	Transit	Natal Planet	Transit	Natal Planet
Planet	♄	☌☉	♅	□☉
Natal House Location	11	6	7	6
Transit House Location	6		10	
House(s) Ruled by Planet	7	2	8	2

Figure 17. Grid of transiting Saturn conjunct Sun while transiting Uranus squares the Sun.

On May 27, 1431, transiting Saturn made its first exact conjunction to Jeanne's Sun; on the 29th of May—the day she was found guilty—transiting Jupiter was forming an exact conjunction to her ascendant/MC midpoint; and on May 30, 1431, she was executed.

Jeanne seems to have been a victim of Jupiter with its transit to her Node and its station on her MC showing her rise and fall. Saturn conjoined her Mercury, causing her words to take on authority—thus believability—then conjoined her Sun, showing not her death, but rather the effect that her life would have on the physical world—lasting.

The average client may not have this type of future but, by using the grids, the astrologer will be able to keep on the correct path—even though it may lead to some very strange places!

Grading Transits

Transits can come thick and fast to a natal chart and some method of sorting these transits is required. For example, if a client were having transiting Pluto conjunct the natal ascendant and, within the same time frame, transiting Venus was forming a trine to the natal Moon, most astrologers would be very surprised if the difficulties of the Pluto transit were totally replaced by the effect of the transiting Venus.

Thus, when compiling the list of transits that are affecting a chart in a given period of time, a choice must be made as to which transits are more serious than others. One or two transits will take the lead and be the dominant experience the client feels in that particular time.

If you were writing a story, you would start with a character, and during the course of the story events would occur that would change the main character. There would be, however, not only a main theme that was affecting the character, but also secondary or minor themes that have to fit into the major story line. Think of any play, novel, or film and you will see main themes and secondary story lines. This does not occur just in the world of fiction, for fiction is based on real life. At any given time, people will have main themes running in their lives, as well as secondary issues.

To look at this concept astrologically: if a chart is receiving transiting Jupiter trine natal Sun and at the same time transiting Neptune is forming an opposition to the natal Moon, the astrologer would tend to expect a greater expression of the Neptune transit in the client's life rather than that of the Jupiter. In other words, both transits are happening, but one—the Neptune transit—is being considered the main theme. The main story line. The other transit of Jupiter is being placed as a secondary story line, subject to the first story.

Neptune would take the lead, so to speak. But the expansiveness that the Jupiter transit indicates will be felt only as a by-product of the events of the Neptune transit.

So the person could suddenly expand his or her world by becoming intuitive, visionary, or a healer. It is the healer that is the important event; the expansion is a by-product. If Jupiter were the leading planet—the chief transit so to speak—then, while suddenly deciding to climb the Himalayas (the Jupiter transit and the main event) the client would undergo a mystical experience, or develop food allergies—all hallmarks of the effects of Neptune.

An important decision has to be made. Will the Neptune transit be "Jupiterized" or will the Jupiter transit be "Neptunized"? The answer is based on the combination of the same three points that describe a transit.

1) The nature of the planet doing the transiting;

2) The nature of the planet or point receiving the transit;

3) The aspect being formed between the two.

The first point, the nature of the planet transiting, can be reduced to an issue of frequency.

The Rule of Frequency:

> The frequency of occurrence of a transit is
> inversely proportional to its effect.

Simply put, the slower a planet is moving in its orbit around the Sun, the greater effect it has, symbolically, when forming a transit to a natal chart.

For instance, the transiting Moon, with its orbit through the chart every 27 days, has a much smaller effect as it forms aspects to natal planets and points than the transits of Pluto, which takes 248 years to move entirely around a chart. Accordingly then, the outer, slower-moving planets are going to carry greater weight in predictive work than the faster planets— Mars, Venus, Mercury, the Sun, and the Moon.

The next point to be considered is the nature of the planet receiving the transit.

The Rule of Movement:

> The natal speed of a planet or point is directly proportional
> to its reaction to receiving a transit.

Simply put, the faster, more personal planets seem to produce a greater effect in the physical world when receiving a transit than the slower, more collective planets. That is to say, transits to the personal planets—Sun, Moon, Venus, and Mercury—and to the Cross of Matter, which moves through 361 degrees a day, have a greater effect than transits to the planets of Mars outward. If your Moon, for example, is being transited by an outer planet, this will have a greater conscious effect than if your natal Neptune is receiving the transit.

These rules are guides. There is one notable exception to the above rule and that is the transits of Saturn. This planet seems to have its own private set of rules. Whether it is transiting the natal Pluto, the natal Mars, or the natal Moon, its effect is still very substantial.

The third point is the matter of aspecting. The aspects have varying degrees of strength in their effects in predictive astrology. They could be tabulated in the order of reducing effect.

The Rule of Aspecting:

The smaller the harmonic of the aspect, the greater its effect in transit.

The harmonic of an aspect is the number we must divide 360° by to obtain the aspect:

1st harmonic = 360/1 = 360° (or 0°) = conjunction

2nd harmonic = 360/2 = 180° = opposition

3rd harmonic = 360/3 = 120° = trine

4th harmonic = 360/4 = 90° = square

8th harmonic = 360/8 = 45° = semisquare

and so on, dividing 360 by bigger and bigger numbers. This rule gives us a guide to grading the transiting aspect; e.g., the conjunction has a greater effect in predictive astrology than the square.

1) Conjunction and Opposition: equal

2) Square and Trine: equal

3) Sesquiquadrate, Semisquare, and Sextile: equal

4) Quincunx

All three of the previous points have to be considered together when deciding which transit is going to be the major transit, which transit is going to be the main theme, and which transits are going to be subservient to this main theme. There will be shades of gray, but if the decision is done consciously, then feedback can be usefully employed.

By way of illustrating these concepts, suppose a client is experiencing the following transits at the same time:

a) Pluto square natal Moon

b) Uranus conjunct natal Venus

c) Jupiter opposite natal Uranus

d) Saturn sextile natal ascendant

e) Neptune sesquiquadrate natal Mars

In applying the first rule—the Rule of Frequency—Jupiter is the least important transit. Pluto, Saturn, and Neptune all move slower in their orbits than does Jupiter.

In applying the Rule of Motion, we see that Uranus is a slow-moving natal point. Thus, transit "c" would have the lowest rating of importance in terms of its effect on your client's life. On a score of 1 to 5, we could rate this a 1. The next planet, in terms of speed, is transiting Saturn. Is it aspecting a fast-moving point in the chart? Yes, the ascendant is a very fast-moving point. However, it is doing it by an aspect that is low on the list. Therefore, by comparison to the other aspects we could most likely rate this as a 2.

That leaves the astrologer with "a," "b," and "e." All of the three transits are of outer planets. However, the Neptune transit is relating to Mars whereas the other two are relating to the Moon and Venus. Furthermore, the Neptune is involved in a transiting sesquiquadrate whereas the Pluto and Uranus transits are conjunctions and squares. Thus "e," the Neptune transit, is rated as 3 on our scale.

The remaining two transits are really neck and neck. Pluto wins on the frequency rule, but Uranus wins on the aspecting one; thus they can be rated equally.

In working on this client's chart, the emphasis would be placed on the Pluto-square-Moon and Uranus-conjunct-Venus transits. The houses being emphasized by the grids of these two transits will be the main areas of importance during that period of time.

By this method, the astrologer has graded the transit in a logical manner. If your feedback implies that you have reached incorrect conclusions on the grading of a set of transits, then at least you will be fully aware of how you made your decisions and can thus make the appropriate correction to this part of your eagle.

I have seen astrologers obsessed with the importance of a transiting Uranus semisquare Mars, while totally ignoring a transiting Pluto square Moon, with incorrect outcomes being predicted. By following these rules, the astrologer can minimize such errors.

Knowing how to sort your transits, and being aware of how you are sorting them, is singly the most important process in working with transits.

Retrograde Motion of Transits

Part of the dynamics of a planet forming a transit to a natal point is that it can—depending on the transiting planet—become exact once, three times, or even possibly five times before it moves on through the zodiac.

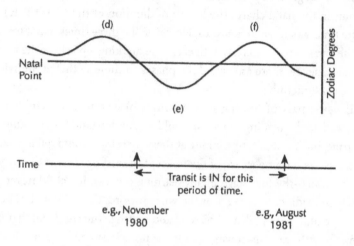

Figure 18. The orb of a transit.

The transit is technically in orb from the time of its first exact touch, to the time of its last exact touch to a particular degree and minute of a natal planet or point as shown in figure 18. Events that start at the commencement of a transit will take the entire length of the transit before those events become completed.

In this figure the transiting planet is shown as the curved line. Its retrograde movement back and forth through an area of the zodiac is visually represented by the curved line moving up and down. Down the page represents the direct movement made by the planet through the zodiac and up the page represents the retrograde movement. In the example, the transiting planet is shown for November of one year to August of the following year. The straight line represents a natal position in the zodiac. Every time the curved line crosses the straight line, the transit is exact. For those astrologers used to working with transit graphs, this figure should look quite familiar. The transit is in orb from November of 1980 to August of the following year, when the transiting planet crosses the line of the natal position for the last time.

The number of times that the transit interacts with the natal point is relevant as it represents the number of times and/or the length of time that fate deems it necessary for the student to learn, or experience, the particular lesson that is crucial to personal development.

The average transit of an outer planet consists of three touches to a point in the natal chart. The length of duration of the transit is for the entire time, as shown in figure 18. However, the three times that it touches can be considered climaxes, with each one marking a phase of the transit. By coincidence, there are also three phases to the way that an individual will learn something.

The first pass of the transit symbolizes observation. As children we observed adults reading to us. We could not understand the markings on the page, but the adult, by looking at these markings, could tell a wonderful story. We became aware of the concept of reading. This is the stage of observation—the first stage of any learning process. If a child never sees someone reading, or never sees the written word, the child will not even conceive of the possibility of reading and writing. The child will therefore grow up with no consciousness of these processes and become an adult without literacy skills.

One hundred years ago, people did not conceive of the world of silicon chips and computers, so no one tried to build one. We can only invent that which is already in our consciousness. Hence we can see the important role of science-fiction writers, who plant the seeds that the world of science tries to grow.

The first touch of a transit, therefore, is something that is not in our consciousness. It is being observed for the first time so that it can become part of our conscious knowledge. Therefore, the first hit of a transit can be the most jolting—like seeing a flying saucer on your front lawn. Sometimes, however, a person will remain detached from the event; "The flying saucer is on my neighbor's front lawn and, therefore, has nothing to do with me." Pluto transits can sometimes be handled like the next-door neighbor's flying-saucer syndrome probably because the person is unwilling to acknowledge the large emotional content generated by this planet's transit.

By noticing this phenomenon in our environment, the flying saucer— or more realistically, our parents reading—we *decide* that we will learn how to read. Recognition, or acceptance, is the second phase of learning.

The second pass of the transit enables us to recognize that possibility that we are also capable of achieving this wondrous feat of reading. Owning the issue, accepting our part in it, not knowing yet what to do with it or how to handle it but accepting that it is there and that it is going to become part of our life, is also the second phase or touch of the transit. The flying saucer is not going to go away so we had better start incorporating it into the garden landscape. This can be a very difficult phase of the transit.

By practicing we, therefore, move into the third stage of learning and that is one of assimilation. We can read. We read so well that we use it unconsciously every day by glancing at street signs, newspapers, and so on. Reading becomes second nature to us. This is the third hit of a transit—acceptance and assimilation—the energy that was once so alien, so foreign, so disturbing, seems to fade into the background with the other daily clutter of memories, resources, and experiences. Thus, in summary, the first touch is a projection or observation. The second touch is recognition or acceptance. The third touch is assimilation.

The first time a particular transit happens, events occur that are outside personal experiences; the second touch is when the person does something that will enable him or her to incorporate the events into his or her world; and the third touch is that of assimilation, the time when the current issues of the transit are no longer an issue but have melted into the background, having been successfully incorporated into the person's life.

If a transit is a long transit with five touches involved, then it is possible that the second stage of "learning how to read" takes longer. This situation implies that there will be difficulties adjusting to the new situations brought by the transit.

When a transit is short—as is the case with some Saturn and Jupiter transits that may have only one hit lasting no more than a week in time—it is an indication that the individual has already assimilated the information at an earlier time. The actual transit issues—that have to be worked out—should be very mild with very few consequences, if any.

Orbs for Transits

Orbs are a very personal part of an astrologer's tool kit. A group of astrologers who may all use the same house system and even the same types of aspects will always, with very few exceptions, vary from one to the other on the question of orbs.

The most standard orb used in predictive work is 1°. That is to say that when a planet is within 1° of an aspect to the natal chart, then the transit should be working. However, I think that this 1° orb is simply a neat figure pulled out of the hat long ago to make for easy reading. Every thinking astrologer will, and indeed should, modify this orb in some way. The following are the modifications I have made, based on my experiences over the years:

Point 1. Orb: 12 minutes of arc.

Point 2. Movement: (a) If a transiting planet approaches a natal point, comes within 13 minutes of arc from the natal point, but turns retrograde before becoming exact, then the person does not start to experience the transit at that time. The transit must come within 12 minutes of arc before its effects can be felt. (b) Once a transiting planet leaves a point for the last time, even though it still may be within 12 minutes of arc, the transit is finished.

Point 3. Exceptions: (a) During transits of Saturn, when Saturn changes direction and commences its movement towards the natal point—and in that forward movement will achieve exactness to the natal point—then that is the commencement of the transit. If the transit is already in orb, then these times of changing direction are also times of climaxes. In other words, when Saturn turns direct and is going to move forward over a point some degrees away, the transit is in orb from the day it turned direct.

In figure 18, the points "d," "e," and "f" would be considered additional sensitive times if this had been Saturn transit. (b) The transits of the planet Uranus are precise and events usually happen on the days of exactness.

These statements should not be taken as gospel but used simply as a starting point. When you find an exception, make a note of it. If it occurs often enough with different clients, then you can start applying it in your predictive work. Good predictive astrologers are not born—they are made from the stuff of sensible logic and feedback.

Feedback on Failure

There will be times in every astrologer's life when the predictive work falls far short of the actual facts. These should not be times of distress or times best forgotten, for they can be the most valuable times of all. Mistakes are feedback into the system. If the mistake falls into the territory of the eagle, then it is a golden opportunity to modify your techniques.

There are three classic ways that the eagle can flounder using the system of grids. Any failure should first be checked against these four points:

1) Using an incorrect birth time.

2) Using the wrong house system.

3) Using incorrect rulerships.

4) The technique you are using doesn't work.

If any of the first three points are involved in your predictive work, then your results will be less than satisfactory. If none of the three points is involved, then you may have to face the fact that option four is a valid statement. If you find that transits are just not working for the client, then go to the section "Older Systems."

INCORRECT BIRTH TIME

This is probably one of largest causes of errors in astrological work. Any change to the birth time can, of course, change the signs on the house cusps as well as the timing of transits to the angles. Thus the first step in predictive work is to ascertain the accuracy of the birth chart. This can be done in two ways: first, check the chart before attempting any predictive work; second, back-check to make sure that the predictive work indicates the correct area of life by implying the correct house cusp.

Since prevention is always better than cure, a technique that can be applied—if the individual knows her birth time within 60 minutes or so— is based on using the transits of the slower-moving planets over the Cross of Matter (ASC-DC and MC-IC axis).

Chart 2, on page 76, is the chart of Thomas Edison. The birth time, according to the source material, is in question, so the chart falls into a classification of dirty data. For the sake of the exercise, let us assume that the birth time is correct to within sixty minutes or so and, by using transits, tune the chart.

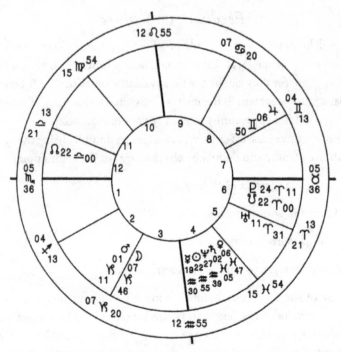

Chart 2. Thomas Edison, born February 11, 1847, 11:35 P.M. LMT, Milan, Ohio, 41N18, 82W37. Data from Circle Book of Charts. *Placidus houses.*

According to the chart, Edison, at different times of his life, would have experienced the following transiting conjunctions to his angles:

Uranus conjunct descendant

Pluto conjunct descendant

Uranus conjunct MC.

We see from the ephemeris that transiting Uranus was at 5° Taurus in May and December 1852, and then again the following February-March of 1853. Edison was five-going-on-six years old at the time. The grid for this transit is figure 19. From this grid, one would expect young Edison to have experienced many changes in his relationship to his parents and the world, with the changes also appearing in his home.

In 1854 Edison's family moved to Port Huron, and Edison was sent to school for the first time. He was expelled by school officials from the school within three months because they thought he was mentally retarded.

	Transit	Natal Planet
Planet	♅	♂ DC
Natal House Location	5	
Transit House Location	DC	
House(s) Ruled by Planet	♏	♀ ♃

Figure 19. Grid of Uranus conjunct descendant.

This was his only formal education, for his mother then undertook to educate him at home. This is a lovely explanation of figure 19. However, these events occurred when transiting Uranus was emphasizing—for the first time in Edison's life—11° to 16° of Taurus and not 5° of Taurus.

If this was Edison's correct descendant, then by consulting a table of houses a new MC could be found. This new MC is 21° to 27° Leo.

Let us check another Uranus transit: According to the angles in Chart 2, Edison would have had transiting Uranus forming a conjunction to his MC in July and September 1874, with its final touch in January 1875. Edison would have been twenty-seven years old. The grid for this transit is figure 20 on page 78.

In examining figure 20, one would anticipate sudden changes in career, job, life direction, or how the world views him (Uranus conjunct the MC). The grid also implies that these changes were due to some creative drive (5th house) resulting in a change of residence (IC) and, possibly, even working from home (Sun and 4th house).

	Transit	Natal Planet
Planet	♅	☌ MC
Natal House Location	5	
Transit House Location	MC	
House(s) Ruled by Planet	IC	☉ 4

Figure 20. Grid of Uranus conjunct the MC.

From 1869 to 1876, Edison worked for the Western Union Telegraph Company. In 1876, when Uranus had long passed the supposed MC and was traveling through the degrees of 15° to 24° Leo, he quit his job. Edison's explanation was that he did not want to be a mere "bloated Eastern manufacturer."* He moved his family to Menlo Park, New Jersey, where he commenced full-time inventive work. He set up the first "scientific village" and the members of his staff were persuaded to settle with their families in the village. Once again, this is a very clear explanation of the grid, particularly with his "family" of staff all living together in a scientific commune. These events happened when Uranus was in the degrees of the proposed MC in 1854. That transit (Uranus conjunct the descendant) indicated an MC of between 21° and 27° Leo. This latest transit (Uranus conjunct the MC) implies an MC of 15° to 24° Leo. We can assume that Edison's MC is possibly between 21° and 24° Leo as these are the common degrees to both transits. This would place Edison's possible ascendant between 11° and 14° Scorpio.

In 1868, transiting Pluto was passing through 14° to 17° Taurus—the possible position of Edison's new descendant. Figure 21 is the grid for this possible transit.

---

* *Encyclopedia Britannica*, p. 1050.

	Transit	Natal Planet
Planet	♇	☌ DC
Natal House Location	6	
Transit House Location	DC	
House(s) Ruled by Planet	ASC	♀ ♃

Figure 21. Grid of Pluto conjunct descendant.

During this period, Edison obtained his first stable job as a night operator for Western Union. He slept little during the day, as he became obsessed with manipulating electrical currents in a new way. This is the obsession of Pluto, and the 6th house is emphasizing the new job, as well as the disturbance to his daily routine—night work. Soon after his 21st birthday, in 1868, he encountered one of Faraday's journals on "Experimental Researches in Electricity."* The young Edison was totally consumed and he proceeded to approach his work using the scientific method. In Edison's own words, this period was the turning point of his life. By September of that year, he had left his job to become a freelance inventor working where he was living. This is the point in his life where Edison met his true love—electric current. The result of this encounter was that he took action to become an inventor and worked from his home (Venus and 4th house).

With the timing of this transit fitting the passage of events in Edison's life, we can hypothesize that Edison's descendant was 14° Taurus instead of the earlier hypothesized 5° Taurus. This would give Edison an MC of 24° Leo, indicating that Edison was born not at 11:35 P.M. LMT, but rather 44 minutes later.

---

* Encyclopedia Britannica, p. 1049.

This simple rectification, based on the events in Edison's life, has not only indicated a later birth time but also caused a major shift.

So taking our new birth time of 12:19 A.M.—44 minutes later than the 11:35 P.M. with which we started—either Edison was born at 12:19 A.M. on February 11, 1847, rather than the 11:35 P.M. of the evening—this would keep his birthday of the 11th correct and give him a birth time "around midnight" on February 11th. Or, maybe he was born on the 12th of February in the early hours of the morning at 12:19 A.M.

This type of problem is not unknown to most astrologers, particularly when dealing with births going back a few years. If you encounter this problem—i.e., knowing the time but not the day—then check transits to the two different Moons in the two possible birth charts, and the correct chart can be found. For example, in 1871 transiting Saturn was forming a conjunction to one of Edison's possible natal Moons and it was in that period that he got married. (Saturn in his natal 4th and the Moon in the new chart in the 2nd.)

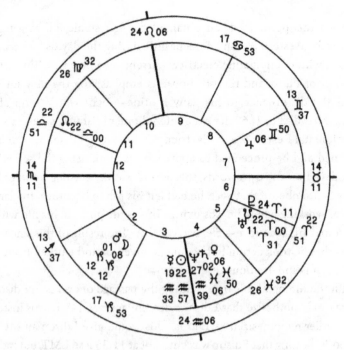

Chart 3. Rectified chart for Thomas Edison. Rectified to February 12, 1847, 12:19 A.M. LMT, Milan, Ohio, 41N18, 82W37. Data from Brady rectification. Placidus houses.

This tends to favor the chart for February 12th at 12:19 A.M., although more astrological testing would need to be done. For the sake of the exercise, Edison's chart is assumed to be the one shown in Chart 3 (p. 80).

The main point is to show that a chart must be checked before predictive work is done. By working with the original chart for Edison, the timing and nature of many of the events predicted would have been in considerable error.

The new chart for Edison shows the Sun and Mercury now in the 3rd house of the chart, not too surprising given his legendary curiosity. This will change the grid (figure 20), because instead of the Sun and the 4th house being emphasized in the bottom row, the Sun and the 3rd house will now be indicated.

The effects of Uranus conjunct the MC, manifested at the time he was setting up a scientific community. All of the members of his staff were persuaded to live in the village whose main objective was for research purposes. Given the fact that we do not lose the IC, the 3rd house inclusion into this picture is more than acceptable.

Thus, prevention becomes better than cure and the astrologer can start to do productive work with the chart with some sense of confidence. The above procedure may seem tedious but it is rather like writing down the method of tying a shoelace: on paper—very complicated; in practice— very simple.

VERIFYING PREDICTIVE WORK

One of the other methods of checking the accuracy of a natal chart is to make sure that the house cusps being used and the respective areas of the life that are being emphasized are correct for the events that have occurred.

If a transit should be emphasizing the 5th house, 9th house, and 2nd house, that is to say:

5th house—Creativity, children, recreation, and lovers;

9th house—Study, culture shock and travel, sport, religion;

2nd house—Personal value systems, self-esteem, personal possessions;

but instead the events that occur to the client are in the area of:

6th house—Work, diet, health, and daily routine;

10th house—Career, social standing, life direction;

3rd house—Siblings, paperwork, local neighborhood;

then it is fairly easy to see that all the houses are being stepped forward by one: 5th to 6th, 9th to 10th, and 2nd to 3rd, indicating that the person was born at a time later than the chart would imply.

There are also times when a house cusp is right on the edge of a sign, either at 29° or at 0°. I believed that a client I had been seeing had an IC at 0° Pisces. Over a period of years, I noted that every time she had any form of Uranus transit, she would either change residences or move her office away from home, and so on. By shaving less than a minute off the birth time, the IC was no longer 0° Pisces but rather 29° 59′ Aquarius. Thus, the observed tendency of any Uranus transits to emphasize the 4th house made a lot more sense. She now has an Aquarian IC.

HOUSE SYSTEMS

The house system that you use will affect the results of your predictive work. Different house systems will, at times, place different signs on different house cusps.

There is no right or wrong house system, and the use of Placidus, Koch, Equal, Campanus, Topocentric, or any of the host available is very much up to the individual astrologer. But the fact remains that different house systems will give different grids for the same transit to the same chart, but only one of those grids will explain the events in a clear fashion. That is to say, one particular house system will work best for a particular chart while that very same house system may fail dismally with another chart. So the first point is to be flexible with the house system that you use. Decide which one you are going to use as a standard but be prepared to be flexible.

The implication is that some people are Placidus people, while some are Koch people, and so on. You may respond to Koch houses personally and you may move in a circle of friends and clients who also respond to Koch. The number of Placidus people that you encounter in your practice may be very small, so you may consider the Koch house system the only one worth worrying about.

However, you may encounter occasions when predictive work for a client seems to "limp a little." You should then ask yourself, "Does a change of house system give a better explanation of the past events?"

Choosing a House System

The same chart should be drawn up using the different house systems that are going to be tested. Some of these charts will have very few differences but others may have planets not only in different houses but also with different signs on the house cusps. This is the case with Jeanne d'Arc's chart when it is drawn up using first Placidus and then Koch houses, as can be seen in Charts 4 and 5 on pages 83 and 84.

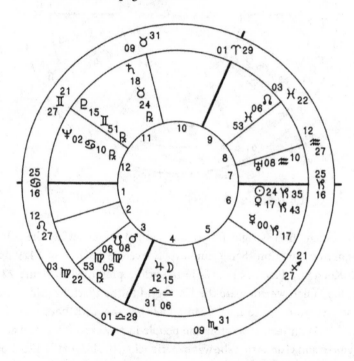

Chart 4. Natal chart for Joan of Arc (q.v.). Placidus houses.

When calculating the chart in Koch instead of Placidus, there are several differences. Saturn moves from the 11th house to the 10th house, Mercury moves from the 6th house to the 5th house, the Node moves from the 9th house to the 8th house, Cancer now rules the 12th house as well as the ascendant, Gemini is intercepted in the 11th house, Capricorn rules the 6th house as well as the descendant, and Sagittarius is intercepted in the 5th house.

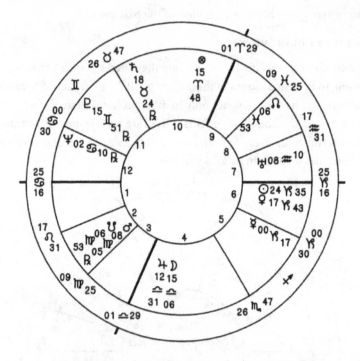

Chart 5. Natal chart for Joan of Arc (q.v.). Koch houses.

So which chart is right for Jeanne d'Arc? We can review the Saturn-Mercury conjunction that Jeanne experienced in January of 1429 using both Koch and Placidus houses in the grid represented by figure 22 on page 85. When we compare the Koch grid to the Placidus grid, the 5th house and 10th house have been added but the 12th house has been excluded. With Jeanne wanting the people in power to listen and act on the voices and visions that she was experiencing, the loss of the 12th house in the grid, particularly with link to the 3rd through the change of house system, is a disappointment. For, in the Placidus chart, Mercury rules the 12th and the 3rd houses, a nice explanation of Jeanne's "voices." However, in the Koch chart, Mercury rules the 11th and 3rd houses. In addition, Jeanne went to the Dauphin because she was told that it was her duty. The removal of the 6th house from the top row, the row that implies the motivation, and the middle row, the indicator of the main area where the person will experience the transit, sadly weakens the potency of the Koch grid. The inclusion of the 10th house in place of the 11th house is quite acceptable, for either house would imply Jeanne's psychic messages being made public. However, the sacrifice of both the 6th and the 12th house influence seems a little too much in exchange. Other transits should be checked in a similar fashion but this tends to imply that Jeanne d'Arc was a Placidus person.

	Transit	Natal Planet	Transit	Natal Planet
Planet	5	☌ ☿	5	☌ ☿
Natal House Location	10	5	11	6
Transit House Location	5		6	
House(s) Ruled by Planet	6, 7	3, 11	7	12, 3

Figure 22. Koch grid compared to Placidus grid.

In checking your house system, take note of what is lost or what is gained. There will always be shades of gray, and if you can't decide using one transit, try another transit until you get a clear result.

Another approach to this problem of what house system to use is to examine transits to a particular planet. Select a planet that will change houses when the house system is changed. For example, examine the history of transits to Jeanne's Mercury and if, in the list of events, a constant theme of daily routine, domestic life, service to others, diet, health, and so on was observed, then the planet is in the 6th house. However, if, every time Mercury receives a transit, events occur that involve Jeanne's attitude toward children, creativity, and so on, then the astrologer could confidently use a house system that would place the planet in the 5th house. In other words, let the client's past tell you which house system to use, rather than just relying on blind faith in one system. Good predictive results come from empirical work, not armchair astrology.

RULERSHIPS

In Western astrology, there are two types of planetary rulership systems: The old rulership system was used before the discovery of the outer planets and was based on a system of dual rulerships apart from the Luminaries, as shown in figure 23a. The new rulership system includes the three outer planets, Uranus, Neptune, and Pluto, as shown in figure 23b.

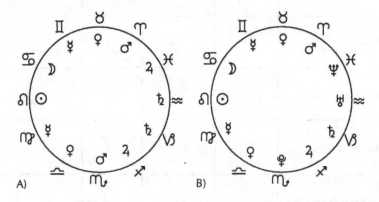

Figure 23. A) Old rulerships; B) New rulerships.

There are times when you may wish to change rulership systems. For example, in the old rulership system, Mars rules Scorpio and may still have some influence in that sign. Would it be correct then in working with ancient charts such as Jeanne d'Arc's to use only planets from Saturn inwards, therefore the old rulership system?

Clearly, as any change in rulerships will dramatically change the grids and therefore the delineation of the transit, by using the grids and examining a few transits while applying different rulership systems, a decision can be made based on logic rather than on the intuitive lark.

So, at this stage, there are quite a few decisions that the thinking, logical, predictive astrologer will need to make. If these decisions are made consciously, then feedback can be meaningfully applied. The following list summarizes the necessary decisions required by any astrologer undertaking predictive work:

◊ A definition of fate and its effect on a person's life;

◊ The nature of the transiting planet—individual or collective;

◊ The house system that is going to be used as a standard;

◊ A method of "grading" the transits at any particular time;

◊ Orbs used and if there are any exceptions;

◊ Rulerships—which set to use.

Chapter Three

Secondary Progressions

The next tool that we have to add to the equipment of the predictive astrologer is that of secondary progressions. There are many types of progressions in this world of computerized astrology, but the most popular are secondary progressions based on the day-for-a-year formula. That is to say, the movement of the planets over the course of a day will represent the movement of the progressed planets over the course of a year. For example, the 30th day after birth will refer to the 30th year of life. (See Appendix 1 for the method of calculating secondary progressions.)

When approaching the world of secondary progressions—henceforth called progressions—one of the first considerations is to look at how progressions differ from transits and the additional information they yield.

All transits and progressions will start to express their energy, or effect, at the deep levels of the unconscious. The first indications of this may occur in the dream world as ideas and energy bubble up to levels of consciousness. However, it is here that transits and progressions go separate ways. The transit, being a totally new piece of energy, is considered so alien by the conscious mind that it is rapidly projected onto the outside world so it can be viewed safely by the conscious mind. From this safe position of observer, the conscious mind can then desensitize to the energy and eventually assimilate the alien transit into itself.

The progression, however, is not alien. It has been recorded at the time of infancy and meticulously collected piece by piece by the individual in the first 90-odd days of life. This familiarity enables it to be assimilated into consciousness without the necessity of first being projected onto the outer world for a period of desensitization. Once assimilated, the person may then generate an outer event due to these new realizations or desires. Thus the progression will seem to manifest first as a *feeling* or need and then as an *action*.

The sphere of the transit is also different from that of the progression. Transits are universal. That is to say, a transiting planet, at any given time, will have a zodiacal position, and that position will be the same for every-body. If a planet is changing its zodiac sign, the entire globe will experience the energy of that planet changing sign. Also, if a planet turns retrograde or direct, it does so on a universal level. Thus, the zodiacal information about a transiting planet's sign, direction of movement, and aspect to other tran-siting planets is not of great importance to a given individual unless the planet is actually aspecting the individual chart.

On the other hand, progressions are *highly personalized*. The position of a progressed planet is unique for any given individual. Its zodiac sign, the direction it is moving, and its aspects to other progressed planets are unique for any given individual, whether they are aspecting the natal chart or not.

One person's progressed Mars changing signs or at a particular degree of the zodiac could, and most likely will, be quite different from the posi-tion of another person's progressed Mars. Progressions thereby specialize in making personal the universal. They take a small slab of the universal—let us say the first three months of a person's life—all the information that the solar system can generate in that three-month period—and give it to the individual to personalize at the rate of one day of universal time equal to one year of personal time. This is astrology's way of subjectifying the objective, of reflecting the outer world on an inner level. "As above, so below" is a statement we all know, but progressions add a time ratio to that ancient statement. They imply that this ratio of one day of "above" is equal to one year of "below."

Progressions are the Cosmos in slow motion. Imagine athletes in slow motion rushing toward the finish line, now turned into elegant dancers, delicately pushing forward in a slow graceful ripple of muscle, closer and closer to the goal only a short distance away, but they seem to take forever. Masses of information pour out to the viewer, information that is normally invisible—hidden by the speed of normal time. This otherwise lost infor-mation is now sharply obvious as time is slowed down.

Thus, progressions offer us a unique opportunity to dip our hand in the river of time and totally process it—to understand the secrets of its meanings and implications. One day of the solar system, with its shifts and changes slowed down, will be played over the span of a year, so that every little movement can be observed and understood. Understood, not in the fast-acting world of the transit with all its external worldly manifestation, but in the world of the personal—the inner life, the inner universe, the "as above, so below"—part of a human being. This is the homeland of progressions.

Progressions are, in a sense, the way the cosmos manifests through us, as compared with a transit, which manifests on us.

Unique Features of Progressions

The unique personalizing of progressions leads to four important features of this style of predictive astrology.

First, it implies that meaning can be taken from the actual zodiacal position of a planet. For example, does a 27° Leo have a meaning in its own right? If it does, then a progressed planet reaching that point will express that meaning through the individual—at that moment only that individual will have a progressed planet at that degree—unlike a transit where the whole world will have a transiting planet at 27° Leo, thereby losing individualization. Even if the Tropical zodiac is dismissed, we could still look at progressions passing over the Fixed Stars as a meaningful statement.

Secondly, a logical extension of this point is that a progressed planet will change its zodiac sign. When this occurs, it is unique for a given individual. Therefore, as progressed planets move through the zodiac, their placement in the zodiac—as well as their sign changes—become relevant.

Next, if an aspect pattern occurs in the world of transits, then it occurs globally. A grand trine forming between three transiting planets is there for everybody. It may or may not aspect a person's natal chart, but it is there for all people. However, an aspect pattern occurring by progression does not relate to everyone. Indeed, it relates only to a small group of people who were all born within a few months of each other.

Last, a transiting planet can turn retrograde or direct—though we may blame the Cosmos for late mail deliveries when Mercury turns retrograde—but the energy of this retrograde planet is global. It cannot be taken personally unless directly affecting the natal chart in some way. However, by progressions, these changes in direction of the planets become personalized. An individual may well be experiencing a retrograde Mercury, while globally there may be a direct one.

So, one of the major points of progressions is that they exist purely in reference to their own phenomena—that is, independent of the natal chart. If your progressed Mars was forming an aspect to your progressed Venus, then this has meaning for you even if the progressed planets are not forming any recognized aspect back to your natal chart. However, if transiting Mars was forming an aspect to transiting Venus, this will only have meaning if one of these planets is also forming an aspect to your natal chart.

In summary, a progressed planet has meaning for an individual as it:

◊   changes zodiac sign,

◊   changes direction of movement,

◊   forms relationships to other progressed planets, or

◊   emphasizes a degree of the zodiac.

Of course, they can also interact with the natal chart in the same way as a transiting planet—forming aspects to the natal chart and moving through the houses.

This leads to two types of progressions:

(a) Progressions yielding information via the four points mentioned in the previous section—that is, non-chart–related. This means progressions relating to other progressions or other zodiacal information. It could be progressed Mercury changing sign, or becoming retrograde, etc., but not actually forming an aspect back to the natal chart.

(b) Progressions that relate back to the natal chart in the same way as a transit. This means progressions that form aspects to natal points and move through natal houses; i.e., progressed Mercury changing house or aspecting natal Sun, and so forth.

When people exhibit intense desires arising from deep inside, from the center of being, from God, or from intuition, then they are manifesting a progression of the non-chart-related type. As a hallmark of this type of progression, people will display an unshakable faith or determination without compromise.

When people express feelings or desires but are willing to let the world change them, then they are manifesting a chart-related progression. The hallmark of this type of progression is having a desire to proceed in a certain direction but also being prepared to compromise along the way.

Progressions are, therefore, a richer source of information than transits. They tap into the realm of the inner, personal world, showing both day-to-day motivations as well as unshakable life statements or desires.

A good example of this personalization of the Cosmos can be seen if Jeanne d'Arc's life is reconsidered using nothing more than the Cosmos's activities (progressions) for the 19 days after her birth.

Non-Chart-Related Progressions

The following ephemeris page (figure 24) is the portion of time given to Jeanne d'Arc in her short life. She was born on January 6, 1412, and died on May 30, 1431, at age 19. The period in the ephemeris that represents her life in progressions is from January 6 to January 25, 1412. There are four obvious astronomical phenomena occurring during this time period:

0:00 at			Tropical Geocentric Longitudes for January 1412									
d	S.T.	Sun	Moon	Merc.	Venus	Mars	Jup.	Sat.	Uran.	Nep.	Pluto	Node
1	7:13:04	18♑48 00	5♏10	24♐59	10♓36	8♍19R	12♎15	18♏29R	7♒51	2♈18R	15♊36R	7♈11R
2	7:17:01	19 49 05	17 07	25 47	11 51	8 18	12 18	18 28	7 55	2 16	15 55	7 08
3	7:20:58	20 50 09	29 10	26 38	13 07	8 17	12 21	18 27	7 58	2 15	15 54	7 05
4	7:24:54	21 51 13	11♏21	27 34	14 22	8 15	12 24	18 26	8 01	2 13	15 53	7 01
5	7:28:51	22 52 16	23 44	28 33	15 37	8 12	12 27	18 26	8 05	2 12	15 52	6 58
6	7:32:47	23 53 19	6♎23	29 34	16 53	8 08	12 30	18 25	8 08	2 10	15 51	6 55
7	7:36:44	24 54 21	19 21	0♓39	18 08	8 03	12 32	18 24	8 12	2 09	15 51	6 52
8	7:40:40	25 55 23	2♏42	1 45	19 23	7 58	12 34	18 24	8 15	2 07	15 50	6 49
9	7:44:37	26 56 24	16 29	2 54	20 39	7 52	12 36	18 24	8 18	2 05	15 49	6 46
10	7:48:33	27 57 25	0♐43	4 05	21 54	7 45	12 38	18 23	8 22	2 04	15 48	6 42
11	7:52:30	28 58 25	15 21	5 18	23 09	7 37	12 40	18 23	8 25	2 02	15 47	6 39
12	7:56:27	29 59 24	0♑20	6 33	24 25	7 29	12 41	18 23D	8 29	2 01	15 46	6 36
13	8:00:23	1♒00 21	15 30	7 49	25 40	7 20	12 42	18 24	8 32	2 00	15 46	6 33
14	8:04:20	2 01 20	0♒42	9 06	26 55	7 10	12 43	18 24	8 36	1 58	15 45	6 30
15	8:08:16	3 02 16	15 47	10 25	28 11	6 59	12 44	18 24	8 39	1 57	15 44	6 27
16	8:12:13	4 03 12	0♓34	11 45	29 26	6 47	12 45	18 25	8 43	1 55	15 43	6 23
17	8:16:09	5 04 06	14 57	13 07	0♈41	6 34	12 46	18 25	8 46	1 54	15 43	6 20
18	8:20:06	6 04 58	28 53	14 29	1 57	6 21	12 46	18 26	8 50	1 53	15 42	6 17
19	8:24:02	7 05 50	12♈22	15 53	3 12	6 07	12 46	18 27	8 53	1 51	15 41	6 14
20	8:27:59	8 06 39	25 24	17 17	4 27	5 53	12 46R	18 28	8 57	1 50	15 40	6 11
21	8:31:56	9 07 27	8♉04	18 43	5 43	5 37	12 46	18 29	9 00	1 49	15 40	6 07
22	8:35:52	10 08 14	20 26	20 09	6 58	5 21	12 45	18 30	9 04	1 47	15 39	6 04
23	8:39:49	11 08 59	2♊34	21 37	8 13	5 04	12 45	18 31	9 07	1 46	15 39	6 01
24	8:43:45	12 09 42	14 32	23 05	9 28	4 47	12 44	18 33	9 11	1 45	15 38	5 58
25	8:47:42	13 10 24	26 24	24 35	10 43	4 29	12 43	18 34	9 14	1 44	15 37	5 55
26	8:51:38	14 11 05	8♋14	26 05	11 59	4 11	12 42	18 36	9 18	1 43	15 37	5 52
27	8:55:35	15 11 43	20 06	27 36	13 14	3 51	12 40	18 37	9 21	1 41	15 36	5 48
28	8:59:31	16 12 20	2♌00	29 08	14 29	3 31	12 39	18 39	9 25	1 40	15 36	5 45
29	9:03:28	17 12 56	14 00	0♒41	15 44	3 10	12 37	18 41	9 28	1 39	15 35	5 42
30	9:07:25	18 13 30	26 07	2 15	16 59	2 49	12 35	18 43	9 31	1 38	15 35	5 39
31	9:11:21	19 14 03	8♍22	3 49	18 14	2 28	12 33	18 45	9 35	1 37	15 34	5 36

Ephemeris Copyright (C) 1986, Astrolabe Software

Figure 24. Ephemeris for January 1412.

1) On January 12th, Saturn turned direct.

This date is the progressed date for when Jeanne was six years old. There do not appear to be any records covering that period of her life.

2) On January 19th, Jupiter stationed turning retrograde.

This date corresponded to when Jeanne was thirteen to fourteen years old. At this time she started to hear voices in her head telling her of her mission. A slow-moving planet will take a whole year to change direction, so one can't place an exact date in Jeanne's life for this astrological event. However, it does symbolize a Jupiterian event manifesting from the very depths—or heights—of Jeanne's unconscious. From her perspective, God spoke to her, giving her a message. She felt this message so strongly that it propelled her into taking action that not only totally changed her life but also led to her death. The retrograde movement is a movement towards the inner reflection and introverted quality of that planet's energy. Hearing the voice of God fits this symbolism.

3) On January 23rd/24th, Venus conjoined Uranus.

This exact conjunction between these two progressed planets corresponded in Jeanne's life to February 14, 1429. In January of that year she went, for the second time, to the army at Vaucouleurs and insisted that her voices be heard.

She left Vaucouleurs (having convinced the Captain of the Guard of her genuineness) about the 13th of February, 1429, dressed in men's clothes and accompanied by six men-at-arms.*

With this Venus-Uranus progression, Jeanne had the strength to confront the Captain a second time, after an earlier attempt to convince him had failed. She had summoned the determination and desire to encounter a whole new group of people—the French Court. Throughout the rest of her short life she willfully continued to dress in men's clothes, even after being ordered by the Church to stop dressing in that fashion. One speculates that—had she lived long enough—the progression would have passed and Jeanne could have returned to the expected and accepted behavior patterns of a 15th century maiden.

4) On January 24th, Mars conjoined the South Node.

This conjunction relates to the time when Jeanne was eighteen years old. The exact conjunction between Jeanne's progressed Mars and her progressed South Node (mean) corresponded to May 7, 1429.

---

* *Encyclopedia Britannica,* p. 377.

On the evening of May 4th (1429), when she was resting, Jeanne suddenly sprang up, apparently inspired, and announced that she must go and attack the English.*

This was her first entry into battle and produced a victory for the French and the liberation of Orleans by the "Maid of Orleans." Jeanne was driven to this point—driven by a deep force from within.

In these examples of non-chart-related progressions, we have Jeanne hearing voices in her head. This was a totally subjective, internal experience or, as Jeanne insisted, a very real and personalized message from God—or the Cosmos. Either way, it was a phenomenon that Jeanne experienced inside herself. The determination to wear men's clothing—regardless of conflict or consequence—and the sudden inspiration to fight, when she was meant to be resting, are the results of a deep internal subjective process, which is the domain of the non-chart-related progression.

These are only brief examples of the power of the Cosmos on your subjective world. There is intense determination to move in a given direction generated by a deep feeling that—despite all advice—you *know* you are right.

Chart-Related Progressions

There are only three major chart-related progressions, excluding the progressed Moon, during the period of Jeanne's recorded life. These are:

1) Progressed Mercury sesquiquadrate natal Mars on May 3, 1429.

The first chart-related progression occurs during the same period that her progressed Mars conjoined her progressed Node in the earlier example. Is it any wonder that she leapt out of bed on that fateful morning of May 4th, 1429! Due to Jeanne's great victory on that day:

[She] left Orleans on May 9th, 1429, and met the Dauphin at Tours. She urged him to make haste to Reims for his coronation. Though he hesitated because some of his counselors were advising him to undertake the conquest of Normandy . . .**

---

* *Encyclopedia Britannica*, p. 378.
** *Encyclopedia Britannica*, p. 378.

All the ingredients of a Mercury sesquiquadrate Mars are present—haste, hesitation, counselors, and so on. However, the whole process seems external. But history records only external events, and this whole period of Jeanne's history is full of haste and unfinished battles because she keeps rushing back to the Dauphin urging him to hurry up. She feels the need for haste—through the frustration of the sesquiquadrate—and this is reflected in her behavior. Once again from the unbiased source of the *Britannica:*

> Instead of pressing home their advantage by a bold attack upon Paris,
> Joan and the French commanders turned back to rejoin the Dauphin
> . . . she argued all the time to overcome his hesitancy and the advice of
> hostile counselors.*

Here is a chart-related progression functioning on quite a different level of behavior from the non-chart–related progressions seen earlier. It would seem, by effect alone, to be manifesting just like a transit. Gone is the flavor of fate, sense of right, and determination that cannot be stopped. As an unknown farm girl, she convinced the Dauphin to give her an army and go to war with the English. Now, under chart-related progressions, as a successful general whose opinions have proved to be correct, Jeanne is unable to convince him to ride into a conquered city and to be crowned the King of France.

2) Progressed Sun trine natal Jupiter, September 10, 1429.

With this progression, one would expect a sudden and quick end—the trine—to the frustrations of the Mercury-Mars. This was indeed the case. By this stage the Dauphin had been crowned and Jeanne had won some important victories. By late August, a four months' truce was in force in most of France. Jeanne then turned her eyes to still-unconquered Paris.

Jeanne strode into battle, feeling that her very presence was all that was required for the citizens of Paris to surrender to the King. Indeed, this very same tactic had worked only days earlier with other enemy strongholds. The attack failed and by the 22nd of that month the army had disbanded. The fighting was finished. A rapid ending—the trine at work.

Once again, this program seems external, but it is Jeanne's personal sense of being unstoppable—Jupiter trine Sun—that makes her decide to

---

* *Encyclopedia Britannica,* p. 378.

attack Paris. But she does not have the burning conviction of a non-chart-related progression, and she allows the attack to be called off after only one day. If this had been a non-chart-related progression, she would have had an inner conviction and would therefore have persisted, projecting her determination onto the troops and pushing through for a victory.

3) Progressed Mercury conjunct natal Sun, May 4, 1430.

After the army was disbanded, Jeanne kept herself in contact with events around the country by letters and messages. By mid-April, concerned at the number of letters asking for help, Jeanne was, once again, riding out to do battle with only a small group of men-at-arms to aid a town under threat from enemy forces. By May 14th, she had been captured.

These last events don't give much insight into the actual progression except to show Jeanne's intense restlessness and that it is a letter that acts as the final stimulus for her to embark upon a short journey.

There is a subtle but clear difference between the non-chart-related progressions and chart-related progressions. The first is characterized by actions that grow from a deep conviction. It is a conviction so strong that it fuels a fire of determination or stubbornness to achieve a certain aim that nothing can tear asunder. The latter characterizes attitudes and methods of approach by which an individual tries to achieve an objective without truly having any deep commitment or determination.

Orbs for Progressions

Orbs vary from one individual to another, but a good gauge is to use an orb of 1°. The most useful attitude to progressions is not so much to note when they are in orb and when they are out of orb, but rather to consider them on a sliding scale—growing in intensity and then fading off.

WAXING AND WANING ASPECTS

A progression moves into orb—usually 1°—over a period of time, with the individual experiencing a growing groundswell of slowly building attitudes or emotions. When the attitudes, desires, and emotions are at their strongest, the progression becomes exact, and as the progression moves on, such feelings start to subside.

There are two phases to a progression's movement, the waxing or growing phase as it is coming into orb, and the waning or reducing phases as it passes out of orb. This movement is shown in figure 25. This figure also shows a progression forming an exact aspect to a natal point over a period of time. The bottom line is the period of time when the progression is within an orb of 1° of the natal point or planet. The vertical line is intensity or closeness of orb. The closer the orb, the greater the intensity, so a way to talk about the intensity of a progression is to refer to its orb. Thus, a progression with an orb of 10 minutes of arc would be considered of greater intensity than if it had an orb of 20 minutes of arc.

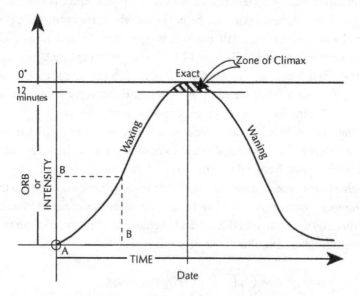

Figure 25. Waxing and waning phase of a progression.

Therefore, the progression starts to come into an orb of 1° at point "A." As time passes, the progression becomes closer to exactness and, therefore, more intense. At some stage in this waxing phase, you will start to become consciously aware of the energy and express physical action in the manner suggested by the progression. If you are very sensitive, you may start to act on the energy at point "A" in time. Or possibly, you may not sense the internal changes until point "B" is reached. This will vary from person to person and from progression to progression. Eventually the progression becomes mathematically exact. However, it seems that as soon as a progression is within 12 minutes of arc to either side of the exact point, then a zone of climax is reached. Within this zone, the energy of the progression transforms and is just as strong but expresses itself in a different manner.

As the progression enters the waning phase and moves away from exactness, the feelings, attitudes, and focus that the progression represented slowly fade into the background of the person's mind—the situation having changed forever. A good example of this is a pregnancy. When a woman becomes pregnant, the family is pleased and, as time passes, the issue of the pregnancy and the unborn child becomes larger and larger in the family's mind. This is the waxing stage of the progression.

Eventually the family enters a waiting stage, while the mother-to-be awaits the birth of her child. The only thing on the family's mind is the unborn child. The child is born (this could be equivalent to the exact period of the progression) and the energy is transformed. No longer is the issue the unborn child; it has changed to become an issue of a newborn child.

The level of intensity is just as strong and, indeed, it is still the child who is the center of attention. But the expectancy has gone, the climax has occurred. For a while the mother and child are the center of attention. The mother comes home with the child and slowly, over a period of time—the waning phase—the family's mind shifts to a new interest. The family has been permanently changed by the addition of the new member.

EXAMPLE USING JOAN OF ARC

A similar example of this waxing/waning nature of a progression can be observed by examining the major progression that was happening to Joan of Arc's chart at the time of her rapid rise in history.

Figure 26 (page 100) is of the progressed Sun trine her natal Jupiter. On September 14, 1428, the progressed Sun moved into an orb of 1° from exactness to Joan's natal Jupiter. We have already seen Joan's sensitivity to Jupiter, for it was the transiting Jupiter conjoining her North Node that heralded the beginning of her quest. The progression was a trine—speed, no barriers, no delays. By January of 1429, Joan's desire to be taken to the Dauphin had become intense enough to cascade into physical action (point "A" in figure 26).

The progression was still waxing, so the conscious desire to pursue a particular path was growing. By May of 1429, Joan had won decisive battles. The French had control of Reims, and Joan was urging the Dauphin to be crowned: point "B" in figure 26. When this waxing progression was within 10 minutes of arc to being exact, the Dauphin was crowned: point "C" on the graph, the area of the progression's "zone of climax," the area of 12 minutes either side of exactness where the progression transforms the expression of its energy. Joan's quest, the center of her thoughts—the obsession she had had for over a year—was to get the Dauphin crowned. The baby had been born.

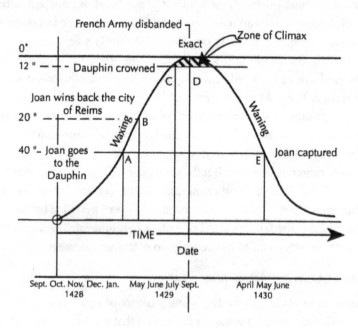

Figure 26. Progressed Sun trine Jupiter.

The progression continued in this climax zone and, on September 10, 1429, the progression formed its mathematical exactness. From this point, the progression was still traveling through the climax area and on the 22nd of September, only 12 days after the point of exactness, the French army was disbanded: point "D."

The progression was now sliding into its waning phase. Joan had achieved her goals. Her energy was still high but she was now concerned with the mop-up operations to protect the newly crowned king. Although she kept traveling through France, the urgency had gone.

In May of 1430, Joan was captured by the English: point "E." The most remarkable thing about this progression is that the level of its intensity was the same when Joan started her quest (point "A" in waxing phase) as when she was captured (point "E," waning phase)—40 minutes of arc.

Thus 40 minutes waxing was the commencement of the undertaking and 40 minutes waning was the completion of that undertaking. For Joan, her orb—level of sensitivity to chart-related progression—is 40 minutes of arc. For other charts it could be more or sometimes less.

SUMMARY

There are two major types of progressions:

◊ Non-chart-related types of progression are very subjective. You will not be persuaded away from your obsession.

◊ Chart-related types of progressions are still subjective and felt as the desire for movement or action. However, you are willing to listen to other opinions or you lack the confidence and determination to follow through with an action.

The orb for a progression should be about 1°:

◊ The *waxing phase,* or the approach of an aspect, is the stage of growth building toward a goal.

◊ The *exact phase*—12′ arc either side of exactness—is the period in which the goal will be achieved, lost, or altered.

◊ The *waning phase,* or separating aspect, is the time to deal with the consequences of the goal.

Interpreting Progressed Planets

The planets most commonly used in progressions are the faster-moving Moon, Sun, Mercury, Venus, and Mars. The outer planets are relevant, but in terms of a day of movement in the ephemeris being equal to a year of life, these outer planets may move only a few degrees from their natal placements during the course of an entire life. Thus in terms of chart-related progressions, the outer planets tend to emphasize the natal aspects of the time of birth. However, if one of those natal aspects becomes exact by progression, then that progression becomes extremely important—more on that later.

THE PROGRESSED MOON

The fastest-moving progressed planet is the Moon, moving at a rate of approximately 12° per year. There are two features of the progressed Moon that are non-chart–related: one is the change of zodiac sign, which occurs approximately every 2½ years; and the other is the angular relationship to the progressed Sun—the Progressed Lunar phase.

The Moon, like any other progressed planet, transits through the houses and makes aspects to the natal chart. Her rapid movement, compared with other progressed planets, means that she will interact with the natal chart more than any other progressed planet. Thus the progressed Moon becomes a major tool of astrologers.

So what does the progressed Moon mean? I believe it means nothing in its own right. If you are shocked by this statement, think back to the world of transits. Not many astrologers work with the transits of the Moon to the natal chart because they are so frequent, with the Moon aspecting everything in the chart—in every possible way—every 27 days. If we were seriously affected by such prolific transits, we would experience major life changes every few days.

The ancients saw this rapid movement and called the Moon the "Translator of Light," a carrier of energy from one planet to another. This does not belittle the Moon but rather elevates her. For the Moon gives a pulse to the chart—a heart producing a blood beat. Thus, the meaning of the Moon was that of a carrier of energy.

The astrologer can easily extend this concept of the Moon being a carrier of energy to the progressed Moon, suggesting that she has no meaning of her own but rather acts to highlight other planetary energies.

This implies that the progressed Moon yields predictive information but does not flavor it with natal lunar meanings—feminine, mothering, nurturing, and so on. That is, she acts as a torch shining on an object in the dark so that attention is focused onto the object rather than onto the source of the light. The object can be a zodiac sign, a natal house, or a planet.

In examining these objects more carefully, we can start with the zodiac signs. The progressed Moon, in moving through a sign, is performing a non-chart-related type of action. Therefore, the information is going to be on the deep internal level of a human being, and the energy will be expressed almost unconsciously as a fundamental approach to the world. The progressed Moon in a zodiac sign illuminates the type of energy you are currently seeking—the type of experiences toward which you will unconsciously gravitate. These needs seem to come from the deepest troughs of our being; thus, we do not question them nor do we challenge them. They are considered of-the-self.

PROGRESSED MOON THROUGH SIGNS

There are two basic types of zodiac signs: Yang—Fire and Air—and Yin—Earth and Water. When the Moon is traveling through a Yang sign, you desire to direct your energy outward into the world. When the progressed Moon is traveling through a Yin sign, you are more withdrawn.

Aries: Yang/Fire/Cardinal

Independence and clarity of action. The desire here is to experience freedom of action without heeding the consequences. To do what you desire. If you act within parameters of the current situation for most of your life, you will start to act more independently. When the progressed Moon travels through this sign, you want to face confrontations and challenges, for unconsciously you desire to measure yourself against others to compete with them and thus will become involved in competitive, aggressive, or angry situations.

Taurus: Yin/Earth/Fixed

From the fiery competitiveness of Aries, the Moon enters Taurus, where the battle weary lose the desire to compete and turn to the quieter world of security. This is the stage of consolidation. You feel less impatient and angry and start to withdraw, pulling away from the competitive world. The issue here is on slowness of approach, less haste, consolidation, and larger projects that take longer time but yield greater benefit. Patience and persistence are the keywords. The main desire is to improve your position—emotionally, materially, spiritually, or all three—and you do this not by conquering new ground, but rather by tending the ground that is beneath your feet. Look to your resources, for among them you will find what you need.

Gemini: Yang/Air/Mutable

From the fertile soil of Taurus, on the farmlands of the personal self, the crop of curiosity is grown. Suddenly you require more information and, in seeking this information, you stride down from the hills into the cities of the external world. Input is the keyword here and you have an inner motivation to seek it above all else. You feel the need to increase the base of your knowledge, to encounter ideas in a productive, non-threatening way. Books, courses, languages, conversations, and people will now start pouring into your life.

Cancer: Yin/Water/Cardinal

Your desire once again turns inward. Courses are finished or carried into personal study. If the Gemini Moon has taken you away from home, this Moon will call you back. Your focus becomes home and family life. Your prime need during this progressed Moon is to recognize and establish the safeness of your nurturing source. The intellect and the feeding of it are no longer key issues. The desire is to nurture and grow—yourself and others—in a safe environment. We call our safe environment home, and you instinctively turn your steps in that direction.

Leo: Yang/Fire/Fixed

From the safety of the hearth—the family fire—you are given a center of security and a base from which you feel strong enough to explore your creativity. Your skills have been developed in the protective warmth of the family environment where they may not have been criticized or challenged. You now instinctively present your talents to the world, naively confident of your ability. The chief desire is to display your talents and to test them in the marketplace. It is a time of expression and action, with a touch of naive over-exuberance. It is the desire to be seen.

Virgo: Yin/Earth/Mutable

From the marketplace of creativity and talent come success, failure, or both. Whatever the outcome, as the progressed Moon moves into Virgo, the issues of practicality become a major focus. The lens moves from the macro of the Leonian marketplace to the micro of the individual. This involves finesse of detail—polishing and perfecting the creativity into a craft. You desire not the perfection of one piece, but the perfection of all pieces. This shows a mastery of the creative area—the craft. The instinctive need is for quality of life—its routines and practical needs.

Libra: Yang/Air/Cardinal

From the introverted precision and craft of Virgo, you start to relax your vigil in your constant striving for practicality. You start to feel that balance and flow are greater assets then precision. You desire the smoothness of life rather than its correct procedure. You re-emerge from the cocoon of self-oriented ideas and encounter others with whom this smoothness can be generated. Sociality, relating, communicating—these are the instinctive desires of a Libra Moon.

Scorpio: Yin/Water/Fixed

The social needs of balance crumble as you instinctively seek to express strong emotional needs. You hunger for intensity. The potential for this intensity to throw a situation out of balance is no longer a concern for you. Human relationships are now worthy of energy only if they contain strong emotions. Women can quite often give birth to a child while the progressed Moon is in Scorpio, as the Scorpio Moon engenders very strong earthy bonds with another—permanent bonds.

Sagittarius: Yang/Fire/Mutable

The shackles of intense, one-to-one relating start to ease as you see the expansiveness of the unexplored world. You now have a burning desire to increase your worldview, to do things that have never been done before, to go to places that have never been seen before, and to think things that have never been thought before. Such desires cause you to push for greater independence. The key issue is to encounter that which is new. You no longer desire intensity, as it reduces your ability to have an overview.

Capricorn: Yin/Earth/Cardinal

Your concept of the world has grown fast, but the expansive inspiration belonging to Sagittarius now fades as the focus shifts to control of the environment. You may feel that your world has become oversized, and therefore threatening, as a result of the Sagittarian phase. Your energy turns inward again and you seek to put your house in order. No new input is required since the new internal furniture—supplied courtesy of Sagittarius—is marshalled into some semblance of order. Fear also belongs here, the fear of chaos out of which can come failure.

Aquarius: Yang/Air/Fixed

From the dominating, controlling desires of Capricorn come the realization of group energy. The desire here is to achieve something for or with the group. You start to socialize and find yourself being drawn into the group and identifying with it. This is the time when the needs of the many outweigh the needs of the one. You feel strongly in control of your own world, and you reach out to help the group's world. You no longer desire personal control of situations for purely personal gain or stability. Instead, the focus is on group recognition of rights within a situation. This can become a personal crusade where your emotional needs are satisfied within the group's structure.

Pisces: Yin/Water/Mutable

The non-emotional, non-personal energy of Aquarius leads you into a drought of deeply personal inner relationships and away from your own feelings. As the Moon enters Pisces, this drought is broken. The unconscious desire is to reconnect with the deeper self, the god/goddess within, or the higher self. You cascade into a waterfall of your own unconscious and turn away from groups. Dreams flood into your life and your inner world becomes a fantasyland that is irresistible. The desire here is to become reclusive so that your inner world can be explored. The self can be lost in this sort of terrain and your boundaries become unclear. But recognize that this cycle, in turn, leads to Aries—the ultimate overreaction to the boundlessness of Pisces.

• • •

These meanings should be regarded as a guide rather than as laws chiseled in stone. In the example of Joan of Arc, her progressed Moon was traveling through the sign of Gemini when she left her farm life behind and entered into the world of war and politics. While her progressed Moon was in Gemini, she also wrote numerous letters urging that her ideas be followed. Her progressed Moon entered Cancer in August of 1430. By May of 1430 she had been captured by the English and imprisoned. If she had turned her steps toward home in that year, she might have avoided being captured, for with the Moon traveling through Cancer, the Cosmos wanted her settled—not moving around the countryside—confined one way or another.

Look back at your own life through the lens of the sign of your progressed Moon. You will notice, as it changes signs, that those changes will show up in your life as attitude changes and changes in lifestyle.

SECONDARY PROGRESSED LUNAR PHASES

The second type of non-chart-related progression in which the Moon is involved is lunar phasing.

During the course of a month, the Moon passes through phases due to its angular relationship to the Sun. (See figure 27.)

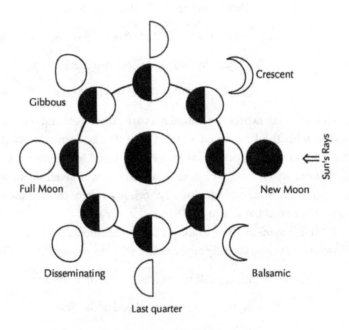

Figure 27. Lunar phases.

The net of progressions captures not only a small period of time for personalization, but also the lunar phases that occur within the first few months after a person's birth.

As shown in figure 27, there are eight phases of the Moon in any one cycle, e.g., New Moon to New Moon, and each one of these phases, when captured by secondary progressions, represents a gear change in the inner realms of the individual. We cannot allocate specific facts or dates from the life to the lunar phases and, like all "non-chart-related progressions," the information is subliminal in nature and the individual may become aware of it only in retrospect.

Traditionally the lunar phases are measured as follows:

New Moon = 0° to 45° ahead of the Sun

Crescent = 45° to 90° ahead of the Sun

1st Quarter = 90° to 135° ahead of the Sun

Gibbous = 135° to 180° ahead of the Sun

Full = 180° to 135° behind the Sun

Disseminating = 135° to 90° behind the Sun

3rd Quarter = 90° to 45° behind the Sun

Balsamic = 45° to 0° behind the Sun

However, in practice the boundaries are not so neat and precise. When dealing with the Progressed Lunar Phase that is currently occurring in any given chart, it appears that as the progressed Moon moves to within approximately 12° of one of these phase changes, as given above, then the next phase starts to come in. This 12° orb is a rule of thumb; the orb will vary from one individual to another.

With this in mind, then, a new set of measurements can be given for the conscious *effects* we actually experience of the Progressed Lunar Phases:

New Moon = 12° behind to 33° ahead of the Sun

Crescent = 33° to 88° ahead of the Sun

1st Quarter = 88° to 123° ahead of the Sun

Gibbous = 123° to 178° ahead of the Sun

Full = 178° ahead to 147° behind the Sun

Disseminating = 147° to 102° behind the Sun

3rd Quarter = 102° to 57° behind the Sun

Balsamic = 57° to 12° behind the Sun

These may look tedious but they are actually more realistic in the world of predictive astrology. They are easy to remember if you realize that, as the progressed Moon approaches a phase change, that phase change starts to be felt inside the person up to a year before the traditional geometry—the first list given—actually acknowledges the change.

LUNAR PHASES

"To everything there is a season . . ." All life has its own timing. You can do anything at any given time, but things work out better if they are done in their own timing.

New Moon

This is the beginning of a cycle, the commencement or emergence of the flavor of the next 29 years. People of average life expectancy will experience two to three progressed New Moons, and these progressed New Moons will usually be in consecutive houses and signs.

The house and sign in which a New Moon occurs are important as a pointer and will indicate the background theme for that 29-year period. This is the phase where you will begin a new development in your life. There is an urge for new activities, new desires. Some of these new desires may not manifest externally for a few years. However, when they eventually emerge, they can be described by the house and sign in which the New Moon has occurred.

This is a beginning. The way of life will change from this point onward.

Joan of Arc experienced a New Moon in the sign of Aquarius in her 7th house in June of 1419. She was only seven years old at the time, and it was the energy of this New Moon that would sketch the big picture of her life for the next 29 years, in her case for the rest of her life.

The 7th house is openness: open enemies and court cases; unions or partnerships; divine or human. Aquarius is the desire to work with the group, sublimating the self to the group needs. Under this New Moon, Joan took up a divine vocation to lead a group into overthrowing its oppressor.

So a New Moon is a very important pointer for the predictive astrologer as it shows the unconscious desires, needs, and expectations that will unfold under the orchestration of transits and progressions over the following 29 years. An astrologer paints a picture for a client, and the location of the secondary progressed New Moon gives the astrologer the size of the canvas and the colors the client can use.

New Moons are seeds. Seeds that will grow into a plant. If you are working as a predictive astrologer on "what is going to happen to the plant," then it is important that you have some type of idea of the nature of the plant.

All other lunar phases stem from this phase, each one building on the previous one by taking that initial statement of energy (house and sign of the New Moon) and evolving it through its stages of development: something is born, grows, culminates, declines, and dies, making space for another type of energy to be born. This is the cycle of life, the cycle of the Moon, the cycle that is present in every known living thing in the universe—as we know it.

Crescent Moon

This whole time span, from New Moon right up to just before the First Quarter, is a time of new beginnings, new ideas starting to bubble up to the surface of the person's mind. Growing from the seeds of the New Moon, the individual reaches a time when he/she tentatively starts to manifest the drives or desires symbolized by the New Moon some three years earlier.

The Crescent Moon Phase implies the end of this planting season as the deeds and actions of the previous few years start to take root, for better or for worse. Any new concepts or lifestyles brought into the life now will not take hold, for the ground has been planted and there is no more room. The Crescent Moon Phase is thus like a marker giving the timing or cut-off point for the incorporation of new things the person wants to develop with the next cycle.

This is the time of the *emergence* of the seed, the sprouts pushing up through the ground. Before the Crescent Moon Phase, the seed was planted but invisible. Only the farmer knows what has been planted in the field of life. The Crescent Moon Phase is the time when everyone can see the type of plant.

You start publicly to display the new direction that your life is taking. The new idea, the new hobby, the new interest quietly pursued before, now starts to emerge and make a bigger statement in your life.

First Quarter Moon

Occurring seven years after the New Moon, we have the waxing square: a time of action. The action springs from the essence of the New Moon. You feel a deep need to physically materialize the desires implanted seven years earlier. It's an ego-building time, with personal achievement taking the lead role.

If a client is in this lunar phase, all her predictive work will be flavored with this essence of action—the energy of the square: manifesting, pushing forward, obvious to the world. The seeds of the New Moon are now visible to the world and during this time the plant is growing rapidly, achieving most of its strength and height before it is needed to support fruit.

Joan was fourteen years old when she started her First Quarter lunar phase. It was then that she started to hear her voices. This was the time when others became aware that Joan was hearing voices.

The First Quarter Moon is the physical manifestation of the energy of the New Moon.

Gibbous Moon

Working with the energy. Understanding it. Becoming aware of its uses. Incorporating it into one's life. By this stage the energy has been obvious for about three years. You will feel confident with it and will start to experience a desire to express your knowledge. This is the time to have faith that you are strong enough, wise enough, and stable enough to express your own ideas and opinions, even in the face of adverse conditions. It is a time of *expression*.

This is the stage at which the plant is setting its fruit. The rewards are not yet ripe but are visible on the vine. The years of hard work are starting to pay off, and the fruits of your labors—weeds or crops—are in sight. When in this phase, you will either be content, working hard, confident of the outcome; or panicky, knowing that the road you are traveling is leading to an unproductive outcome—a crop of weeds.

Joan of Arc was experiencing a Gibbous Moon from August of 1430 till her death. If we allow the 12° orb, discussed earlier, then most of Joan's life work was produced under a Gibbous Moon Phase. Action and confidence in her outcomes were definitely her hallmarks.

Full Moon

The time to reap the rewards. This is not a time for new projects or ideas but rather a harvesting of that which is already there. This is the time to collect, the time to receive, to pick the fruit, for now it is in its prime. This is the climax to the cycle where the energy is at its peak. Collect the fruits of your labor. They are ripe.

The Full Moon Phase states that the seeds have grown and you experience the fulfillment or outcome of the new beginnings made 14 years earlier. These rewards may be positive or negative, depending on the crop that was planted back at the New Moon Phase.

The important point to make about this lunar phase is that regardless of the energy or the area into which you have been putting your energy, the process has now culminated, reached its peak, is in its prime. The confronting part of this harvesting lunar phase is in *recognizing* that this is harvest time. For some, this can be easy, with the harvest being bountiful; others may be discontented with the harvest and wait for it to get better. "I'll just stick this job out for a few more years and then I'll get the promotion that I want" is the sort of statement that can occur around a Full Moon. However, the Full Moon doesn't get any better than this. There is no more promotion. This is the peak of the cycle.

Disseminating Moon

The harvest is over. That which has not been reaped now has to be left behind. Whether this is a good or bad thing, you are now at a stage of realizing that the lovely swelling energy of the Full Moon has stopped. People quite often change jobs in this phase, for all that can be achieved has been achieved from the present pathway. It is now time to examine the crop and re-evaluate, to think about the current position, to extract the most from what has recently been harvested.

This phase represents the first *waning* phase of the Moon and, thus, is the commencement of a more internal, reflective, and productive period that will last, in varying degrees, for 14 years.

Thus the reason many people change jobs is because they sense that the time has passed when that job or goal could continue to offer a challenge. You are aware of periods when life is growing, bubbling, surging forward, and in the same way you are aware of the times when that growth stops.

Now is the time to use the skills or advantages gained in the growth period by manifesting these in the community.

Third Quarter Moon

This phase is the *waning square* and has all the energy of the First Quarter but directed towards reorientation: the rearrangement of old skills. If the First Quarter was symbolized by a young warrior using a sword for the first time, then this phase is the warrior putting a new handle on the sword or realizing that the sword needs sharpening in some way.

You start to review your life situation. New ideas may start to come but they are concerned with old issues. Clients in this phase will happily take action and seek action, but it is action that restructures old skills, rather than that which brings in new skills.

This is also a very productive phase. It is a square, and the action implied by the square is coming from the wisdom learned in the earlier phases of the cycle. If the waxing part of the cycle can be likened to growing grapes, then the waning phase and particularly the third quarter can be likened to the making of the wine.

Balsamic Moon

This is the last phase of the cycle. For most of us, this closing lunar phase will occur in the same house and sign as that of the New Moon, which started the beginning of the cycle. Calmness and security are the hallmarks of this phase as the individual releases the old cycle. Friends change, old papers stored for years are tossed out, the very foundation stones of your life start to develop cracks, resulting in the need for many things to change in your world.

This is the clearing of the old ground to make sure that there is room in your life for the new cycle to come in. You are future-oriented, rather than preoccupied with the here and now or the past. It is a time of *release*. If something wants to leave your life, let it go, for its space will be filled with the seeds of the New Moon.

This can be the hardest lunar phase of all, as we are conditioned to keep our lives full. This phase is all about clearing a space. As this space opens up, you may panic, fearing that there is something wrong. We are taught to believe that it is unnatural to pull away from so many things, to eliminate so much from our lives for no apparent reason—a seeming whim. If the clearing is resisted, then the Cosmos will take charge and you will experience an uncontrolled exodus of people and things from your life.

HOW LUNAR PHASES WORK

The effects of the secondary progressed lunar phases can be summarized in figure 28.

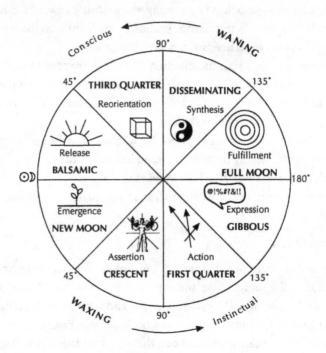

Figure 28. Graphic summary of Lunar phases.

A good illustration of the implicit, unconscious drives that secondary progressed lunar phases will produce is shown if we examine Galileo Galilei's life and chart (Chart 6, page 115).*

Galileo was an Italian mathematician, astronomer, and physicist. He was the first person to use the telescope to study the sky. He also amassed evidence to prove that the Earth revolves around the Sun. He pioneered work in the field of gravity and motion and is revered today as the father of modern mechanics and experimental physics. His views represented such

---

* The Old Style or Julian calendar gives Galileo's birthday as February 15. The New Style or Gregorian calendar that is now in use gains one day per century. This gives a birth date of February 24 for Galileo.

a radical departure from the accepted thought of the day that he was tried and found guilty of heresy by the Inquisition in Rome and was put under house arrest for the last eight years of his life.

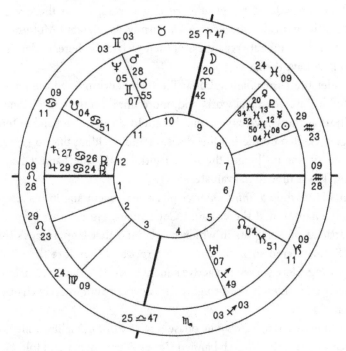

Chart 6. Galileo Galilei, born February 15, 1564, 3:18 P.M. LMT, Pisa, Italy, 43N43, 10E23. Data from The Round Art. Placidus houses.

The first *New Moon* that Galileo experienced was in May of 1590. It occurred at 2° 10′ Aries and, therefore, fell in his 9th house.

This Aries New Moon in the 9th house wonderfully describes a man who is remembered for pioneering work and ideas (Aries) and who had published in the academic world (9th house). Indeed, in 1589 Galileo published his first treatise on the center of gravity in solid objects. Here we see the 12° orb coming into effect.

The *crescent* lunar phase occurred in July of 1593, so the period from 1592 to 1595 was his Crescent Lunar Phase. This is the phase, remember, that is concerned with emergence, being seen. In 1592 Galileo took up the post of Mathematics Lecturer at the University of Pisa, a post offered to him as a result of his earlier treatise. He stayed in this position for 18 years and during this period produced the bulk of his most outstanding work.

Galileo experienced a *Full Moon* in May of 1605. The years 1604 and 1605 are considered his greatest of that period, for in those years he proved, theoretically, the Law of Uniformly Accelerated Motion—bodies fall at the same rate regardless of their weight. So here, under the Full Moon, we have the harvest.

Under the *Disseminating* Lunar Phase, he encountered the telescope, started his astronomical work, and, more importantly, left his long-held position at the University so that he could do more research. One can imagine Galileo pondering this decision and deciding that to stay at the University was no longer the most fruitful path. The harvest had happened. It was time to re-evaluate.

In 1613, while a *Third Quarter* phase was occurring in his chart, he openly championed the cause of Copernicus. He did this by publishing articles on sunspots in which he claimed that Copernicus's theory of a Sun-centered solar system was correct and therefore that Ptolemy was wrong. Here we see the active square period working again, but you notice that Galileo is not bringing in a new concept, merely championing an old one.

In June of 1616, a *Balsamic* phase was at work in Galileo's life and in March of 1616, the Church banned Copernicus's theory and told Galileo he must stop any investigation or work in this area. The Balsamic Lunar Phase is one of letting go or releasing, and here we see Galileo almost cut off from his life's work. As a result of this warning, he went into retirement and published nothing for seven years.

The next *New Moon* occurred at 0° 55′ Taurus in his 10th house in the year 1619. History does not oblige us with events at this stage of his life but one can imagine the genius of Galileo working but not letting the world, or more importantly, the Church, see any results.

The New Moon in Taurus implies a phase of consolidation, of steadfastness. Its occurrence in the 10th house of his chart presages that his next 29 years will be in the public eye or he will gain public recognition. Indeed, this is Galileo's last New Moon Phase and in this cycle he wrote the great book that guaranteed his place, in retrospect, as the Father of Modern Mechanics and Experimental Physics. He did not add new thoughts or theories in this time but consolidated his life's work (Taurus).

The next *Crescent* phase was in January of 1623, and in the true form of emergence, Galileo stuck his head out of his hole and published an essay on comets in which he made his famous quote "the Book of Nature is ... written in mathematical characters." With this crescent lunar phase, the reclusiveness that began under the Balsamic Phase ended. Galileo traveled to Rome and pleaded that he be allowed to work and write about the "systems of the world." He was given permission to do so as long as his conclusions supported the Church.

The *First Quarter* Moon of 1626 is the period where Galileo wrote and completed his great book—a nice expression of the action-oriented First Quarter.

The *Gibbous* Moon occurred in December of 1630, and this was when the book was published: expression, claiming the energy as one's own, working with it. The book was released and Galileo did not come to the conclusions that the Church had dictated to him. It was here, in this waxing stage of expression, that Galileo stood up to be counted.

The *Full Moon* of December 1634 represented the reaping of the crop sown by the New Moon of 1619. In 1633, Galileo stood trial for heresy. Although he was convicted, due to his age he was not imprisoned but instead placed under house arrest. In this Full Moon period, in forced seclusion, he wrote his second book. This book represented the summation of his life's work and laid the foundation stones for the immortalizing of his life in the world of physics—a fine harvest from the tenth house Taurean New Moon in 1619.

Galileo died while still under house arrest on January 8th, 1642.

Clearly an astrologer could not have predicted all of these events for Galileo by progressed lunar phases alone. But armed with knowledge of these phases, astrologers can ascertain the direction of the client's energy flow and use this knowledge as an adjunct to the predictive arsenal. As counseling astrologers, if we advise a client in the third quarter lunar phase to begin new projects, then the client will founder. Lunar phases that wax and wane are like tides affecting a beach. A surfer catching a wave does so at the appropriate phase, as the wave is growing, swelling, and beginning its push toward the beach, not when it is ending.

Secondary progressed lunar phases give the *big* picture, the ebb and flow of life. The lessons or opportunities that the Progressed Lunar Phases offer us are to push when your world says push—when your energy is surging—for that is the time when you will achieve the most benefit, and to let go when your world says to relinquish.

THE PROGRESSED MOON THROUGH THE HOUSES

The second ebb-and-flow phase of the progressed Moon is a member of the "chart-related progressions." This is the passage through the circle of houses.

Because this is a chart-related progression—i.e., a relationship between the progressed Moon and a natal chart—the expression is more conscious and therefore less dogmatic. There are two ways of working with this movement:

1) to take note of the individual house through which the Moon is moving; and

2) to take note of the Moon's position in relationship to the MC.

The progressed Moon takes 27½ years to complete one circuit of a chart. During that time it spends, on average, 2½ years in each house. However, since in most house systems the size of the individual houses can vary, the Moon will spend more time in some houses than in others. It is an interesting point, for it starts to give meaning to these uneven houses. (The larger the house, the longer the transiting or progressed planets will influence it; therefore, the more you may need to learn about that house.)

At this stage, it is wise to emphasize the importance of choosing the house system with which you feel the most comfortable and using this for both transits and progressions. If a house system is working for transits, then that same house system will be the one you will find valid for progressions.

As the progressed Moon moves through a house, then the area represented by the house becomes your theme. For example, if the Moon is moving through the second house, then the theme is one of increasing security, of consolidating your position in life, or of re-arranging your value systems. You express the energy by consciously setting out to achieve security. If you are projecting your needs, you will attract issues or people to you that will affect your security.

The house through which the progressed Moon is moving describes the desires, needs, emotions, and issues represented by that house. Each house is encountered in sequential order—the one flowing from the previous one. This may seem a simple logical statement, but it also implies a certain flow or rhythm to your life. For example, creativity (the 5th house) is followed by hard work (the 6th house) and is based on the foundation of a sense of place or home (the 4th house), and so on.

The 1st House

This house is encountered after the wilderness of the 12th. You find that you can now take effective action and move into a mode of *"I, myself, doing my own thing and striving for my own independence."* A progressed Moon in this house propels you into an active, visible phase. You are pushing forward—a time for action. It is time for personal effort with visible results. You make your own decisions.

There can also be an emphasis on your physical body, your physical appearance, your name, your signature, and so on.

The 2nd House

From the personal action of the 1st, you then desire to consolidate your resources. This may lead to a period of having to pay back debts due to rash or impatient actions. Alternatively, you may receive benefits from the personal actions of the 1st house, whose rewards can be financial, emotional, or spiritual. However they express themselves, the driving force is the need to consolidate, to secure, to repair, or to build your base of security.

The 3rd House

From the security of the 2nd house Moon, you enter the 3rd house, seeking knowledge or activity and wanting to express ideas. Movement, journeys, new forms of transportation, classes, and issues to do with siblings are highlighted. You will be open to new ideas, willing to explore different methods of doing things. You will be restless and keen to communicate.

The 4th House

When this house is activated by the progressed Moon, issues of home, house, family, and hearth become the important themes. Children may be born, representing a change in the family. You may change residence. There may be issues of mothering, or about mother and your immediate family. This is the house representing hearth, and your energy is firmly ensconced there. Travel, business, new careers, learning, classes, and other issues fade in importance unless they are directly connected to the home and hearth.

The 5th House

Personal creativity usually occurs when one has gained the security of the hearth and home. The progression of the Moon through 5th house is the period when you are able to express these personal creative skills, either through a craft or on a biological level by producing children. Expression is the emphasis and flavor of this house placement and you will use any available transit to push your energy out into a visible form. This is also the house of lovers and recreation, so there can be new relationships formed, new activities or hobbies taken up.

The 6th House

Once you have creatively flourished and/or become a parent in the 5th house, you now feel the hard work and daily grind of health or routine. The entry of the Moon into this house signifies that work and effort are required, either in coping with children when they are toddlers or in polishing the craft. This is the house of perfection, requiring a body of work to be built through steady effort. If you are a creative person, having had your first flush of success, you now work to perfect the creation through routine and hard effort. With a progressed Moon in this house, you are dealing with issues of duty, service, and follow-through. In Babylonian astrology, it is interesting to note that the 6th house was the house of slavery.

The 7th House

This is a time of relationships—both positive and negative—that may culminate in a legal process, e.g., marriage, divorce, or lawsuits. This is a time when you are prepared to incorporate another into your plans, reviewing what you require in a relationship. New relationships could start with the progressed Moon in this house or old ones could re-arrange themselves by breaking up or consolidating. Any transits during this period will be biased toward incorporating another or taking into account how another will view your actions.

The 8th House

From the relationship-oriented attitude of the 7th, you find yourself (gently or not so gently) pushed into the changes symbolized by the 8th. Here life's events become more intense and the focus is on beginnings or endings—life, birth, or completions. This is a time when your life situation changes. This is also another house relating to giving birth—becoming a parent.

Issues of money and power, big business, taxes, wills, and inheritance take focus. You will be aware of the importance of the events around you, seeing the deeper issues in things. You may surround yourself with issues that are more dramatic than normal. The purpose behind this lunar progression is for you to allow change to enter your life.

The 9th House

As the progressed Moon moves into this house, the overview—the big picture—becomes important. You will seek input that will satisfy this need, so matters of travel, overseas issues, and/or study start to take the limelight. Foreign affairs, immigration, philosophy, and publishing all belong to the 9th house. Any way that you can expand your world will be pulled into your life patterns at this time.

The 10th House

Career and social status are highlighted, with job changes or even marriages/divorces occurring in this time slot. You are aware of how society judges you and will make changes to that classification. This could entail gaining a promotion, losing a job, becoming a parent for the first time, getting married, getting divorced, winning a million, or losing a million. There are hundreds of ways that you can change your standing in the community. This is also a time when you can achieve a goal that you may feel is out of reach.

The 11th House

As the Moon moves through the 11th house, groups start to take on a higher profile. You feel impelled to work with, for, or through a group, and the group's opinions take on great importance. You find yourself involved with other people's issues, minority group problems, the activities of clubs, or societies. This is the period in your life when you are open to socializing and social interactions.

The 12th House

The progressed Moon, by moving through the zodiac, will travel above the horizon of the chart by moving through the 7th house, across the MC over to the 12th house. Thus as it enters the 12th house it is "setting"—preparing to sink into the 1st house. Thus the 12th house secondary progressed

Moon is a very interesting phenomenon in astrology. The 12th house is that which is hidden—the collective unconscious—and while the Moon travels through this area, it is a time for retreat. It seems that a person can put energy out into the world for 25 to 26 years, as the Moon moves through the 1st through 11th houses, but as it enters the 12th house, this is the time when the outer focus must be given over to the inner life. You are hidden in this period. If you seek acclaim or recognition at this time, it will not be achieved.

This is the time for the artist to head for the hills and withdraw—for two years or so—to create a whole new body of work. The work will not be recognized until the Moon crosses over the ascendant, because the ascendant is the boundary between that which is hidden and that which can be seen.

If you use this period to explore the inner life or to work quietly with your own creativity, then the rewards can be great when the Moon enters the 1st house. If, however, you spend the time denying your inner world and life, then the harvest of these two or so years will not be bountiful.

The progressed Moon traveling through the 12th house is the best chance you have for clearing the "unconscious air" and sorting out deeper issues and problems that generate in the hidden areas of your mind.

DEVELOPMENT CYCLE OF THE PROGRESSED MOON

The second way the progressed Moon yields information from a chart with regard to houses is its relationship to the MC.

The Moon takes approximately seven years to move through a quarter of the chart. This timing, of course, varies from chart to chart, but as the Moon moves through these quarters, it moves through groups of houses that seem to have common themes. These common theme houses can therefore be clustered together in groups. The whole chart can therefore be divided up into slices containing one, two, three, or more houses, with each slice or section carrying a particular theme. See figure 29 on page 123. This theme of a group of houses will be the background energy surrounding a person in any given time.

Building

The first and second houses can be seen as one unit (see figure 29) sharing a common theme—*Building of the Self*. While the progressed Moon travels through this area, you will be concerned with developing your personal self, in terms of independence and security. All of the transits experienced in this period will be used with an emphasis on self and personal gain—the personal building of a strong base. Your individual growth or maturity is the bias during this period.

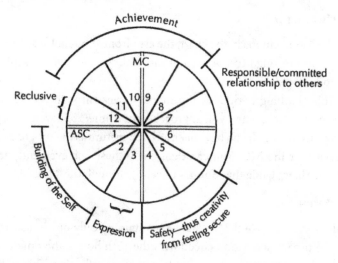

Figure 29. Development cycle of the progressed Moon.

Expression

The 3rd house alone defines the domain of expression and learning.

Safety and Creativity

The next phase encompasses the 4th and 5th houses. You feel safe enough to express creative ideas; therefore, this is the most creative period that the progressed Moon can offer. You resolve any problematic family issues in this period and can begin to free your energy for personal creative expression. This can manifest as children, hobbies, or any of the recognized creative forms—writing, painting, and so on. By being aware of this period, you can use it to very great satisfaction. This is like the New Moon of the progressed lunar phase, for the progressed Moon at the Nadir is starting on its journey of climbing up the chart.

Responsibility to Others

The area contained by the 6th, 7th, and some of the 8th houses is concerned with responsible relationships to others—relationships that require commitment—so the consequences of these relationships will also surface at this time. Additionally, this is a time when you experience the results of your actions—the results of your creative expression. You encounter commitments and can become involved with others. You may have to be practical, responsible, and aware of the consequences of your actions.

Achievement

As the Moon climbs in the chart, the area from about halfway through the 8th house through to the cusp of the 12th we can call the achievement period.

This climbing period, as the moon moves through the 8th and 9th houses, is a time when you approach your prime. Achievements, desires, and goals for which you have been striving mature as the progressed Moon passes over the MC. You can then enjoy these achievements, and even expand them, while the Moon is traveling through the 11th.

Reclusiveness

This is an area (like the 3rd house) containing only one house, the 12th. As the progressed Moon encounters the 12th house, the time comes for sitting back, resting on your laurels, and inner reflecting. This is the time-out discussed in the previous section on the 12th house.

During each set of 27 to 28 years, you experience periods in which you can, respectively, build and mature personal strength, express ideas and learn, establish and strengthen the home, dabble with creativity, take on commitments, experience success, and rest.

A predictive astrologer needs to be aware of the position of the progressed Moon because it flavors the entire predictive work. This cycle is a chart-related progression; thus an individual feels the drive but can be distracted from the progression's correct course and valuable periods can be lost.

For example, you may be experiencing a Jupiter transit conjunct your natal MC. Your astrologer may advise you to go into business. But if the progressed Moon is traveling through the 12th house, the Jupiter transit should be used for traveling alone, or withdrawing from the world to learn or study. Accepting the astrologer's advice, you push against your natural urge to withdraw and try to open the new business. You find, to your financial dismay, that "no one can see you." Thus, the business may fail, and you have wasted a beautiful period of self-discovery and understanding, as well. The astrologer may wonder why, on such a good transit, the business failed.

These cycles are like the landscape through which you are walking—the terrain that you are going to encounter. There is no use in taking along dancing shoes when the terrain is a mountain trek.

• • •

Referring back to the earlier example of Galileo, we can observe these patterns, or slices of the chart, as his progressed Moon traveled through the houses. Galileo had gone to the university to study medicine, but he accidentally overheard a lecture on geometry that so inspired him that he changed his career direction toward the world of mathematics. This occurred in 1581 as his progressed Moon was around the 5th house cusp. Thus, his Moon was in the creative stage.

The next time that Galileo changed his career direction was when he encountered the telescope, which turned his mind to astronomy. This occurred in 1609 when the progressed Moon was again around his 5th house cusp. Clearly, both encounters—with geometry and with the telescope—occurred when he felt safe enough to drive headlong into a totally unknown area where his highly creative mind could be given full rein.

By 1585 Galileo had to withdraw from the university, due to lack of funds, and start working for a living. In September of 1584, the progressed Moon entered his 6th house, the stage of responsible relationships and hard work—having to pay one's way.

By the time the Moon was moving into his 9th house, he was well on the way to using his achievement stage and, in this period, he became renowned throughout Europe as a mathematician. As the progressed Moon formed a conjunction to the MC, he was offered the prestigious position of the Chair in Mathematics at Padua University.

Moving forward in time to 1611, once again the progressed Moon was entering the 6th house—the area of responsibility and consequences. It was in this period that Galileo started to come into conflict with the Church. Now he was being held responsible to another group—the Church. By 1616 Galileo was forbidden to work in fields that could contradict the scriptures. Since most of the modern world—as Galileo was now perceiving it—contradicted the creation myth of the scriptures, this meant that Galileo was effectively forced to stop working. His progressed Moon was traveling through his 8th house.

Nothing is known of his next achievement stage, because—shackled by the Church—there was very little he could do. However, as the progressed Moon entered the 12th house, he was given permission to write his first book. He did this from 1624 to 1626, the period when the progressed Moon was in the house of reclusion, a beautiful way to use such a reflective period.

Galileo's book was published as the progressed Moon traveled through the 3rd house. He was placed under house arrest—forced to stay at home—as his progressed Moon entered the 4th house.

In another example, if we look briefly back at Joan of Arc's chart, her entire career occurred as the Moon passed through her achievement stage and, with a timing that is eerie, as soon as her progressed Moon went into the 12th house—the house of reclusion—she was imprisoned.

PROGRESSED MOON ASPECTING THE NATAL CHART

The Moon offers a greater variety of aspects in its progressed form than any other progressed planet. Due to her fast motion, she can aspect most of a chart within a few years.

It is probably because of this large natal aspecting potential and the speed at which the aspects are formed and then finished that the progressed Moon, in forming aspects to other progressed planets, has very little obvious meaning. Perhaps, if a careful study were done linking these fast, internal aspects to dreams, we might see some connection, but, in the conscious world, the effect does not seem to manifest.

However, there are three principal applications of the progressed Moon's aspects to the natal chart.

The first role is that of a highlighter. This is a key issue with the progressed Moon since, as mentioned earlier, she has no meaning in her own right, except to act as a pointer or catalyst.

As the progressed Moon moves through the chart, she carries energy from one planet to another, throwing a spotlight on a particular planet and house. The aspect employed acts as a colored filter giving information as to the nature of the interaction, and the planet encountered by the aspect is the stuff that is activated.

The progressed Moon conjunct natal Mars will indicate that you are going to become either enthused and motivated, or angry and rash in your actions. The progressed Moon trine natal Mars will imply that you are going to suddenly become active, get results, and desire to become further involved or activated—but in a way that does not cause any waves. Progressed Moon opposite natal Mars is indicative of a time period in which you are going to be asked to make a decision to take action in some way. The progressed Moon quincunx natal Mars is letting go of anger, or ending physical activity, or losing personal motivation.

A book could be written containing the different combinations that can be generated. But it is far better for astrologers to understand the basic components of aspects and planets and to put the pieces together by themselves.

So the progressed Moon acts as a spotlight, with the aspect represented by the colored filter. By working with the meanings of the aspects given earlier and the basic meanings of the planets (remembering at all times to keep the meanings simple), the correct delineation can be achieved.

The second major application of the progressed Moon is timing. You may be having a major transit that will last for over twelve months. When will that transit actually manifest as events in your life? This can be a hard question, particularly with a planet like Saturn, to which we are so sensitive, or even Neptune, which can have up to five "hits" on a point before moving onward. If the progressions of the Moon and other fast movers are examined, then there will be periods in the time span of the transit where the progressions are thick on the ground. That period will be when the transit is expressed. This concept will be expanded in the section on Time Maps.

The third application of the progressed Moon—not used frequently but nevertheless interesting—is the progressed Moon becoming Void-of-Course. This occurs when the progressed Moon is not going to form another major aspect until it enters a new sign. This Void-of-Course period can last for just a few months or up to a year or more. This, traditionally, is a period where activities are not as productive and the energy is best spent on personal development no matter the Moon's house position.

We can summarize the importance of the Progressed Moon as follows.

Summary of Progressed Moon

◊ The progressed Moon has no meaning in its own right but rather acts as a highlighter as it aspects natal planets and points.

◊   The progressed lunar phases set your tidal energy—driving outward or moving inward.

◊   The movement of the progressed Moon through the natal houses points to where the energy of the progressed lunar phase is going to be expressed.

◊   All transits should be read in the light shed by the progressed lunar phase and the current natal house position of the progressed Moon.

◊   The progressed Moon aspecting a progressed planet or point seems to have very little conscious manifestation.

◊   The progressed Moon, in aspecting a natal chart, gives information about the timing of the expression of a major slow-moving transit and can show periods of wilderness by becoming Void-of-Course.

In conclusion, the progressed Moon is probably the most important tool that the predictive astrologer has for coloring in the picture of your life.

PROGRESSED SUN

The progressed Sun represents the unfoldment of your Sun's story. Like a seed, every natal Sun contains the story of a person's life, and the Sun's sign refers to life's theme. Definitions for the natal Sun, in its particular zodiac sign, are not a bunch of dry, dusty keywords, but rather a living story. As the progressed Sun travels through its birth sign, it will make aspects to other members of the chart and will then continue into other zodiac signs. Each time the progressed Sun involves itself in these activities, it is making statements about your life's path—the story of your life—the unfoldment of your personal story.

Sign Change

The progressed Sun moves, on average, about 1° per year. The Sun at birth will be in a particular sign, which is known as the Sun sign. This Sun sign will have a whole set of meanings, but inherent in these meanings is the unfoldment of the Sun as it, through progression, passes into another zodiac sign.

For example, all Pisceans, after a maximum of 30 years of life, experience their progressed Sun moving into Aries. After another thirty years, the progressed Sun will move into Taurus. Therefore, to be a Pisces is to experience the unfoldment of the energy of Aries and Taurus, and perhaps Gemini. This varies from Pisces to Pisces, for if you are born with your Sun at 20° of Pisces, then by the age of ten, the progressed Sun has entered Aries. That young Piscean will therefore develop the self-orientation and self-centeredness of Aries much earlier than another Pisces whose natal Sun is at 2° of Pisces. The earlier Pisces will not experience the Arian energy until he or she is twenty-eight years old.

Every Sun sign, therefore, matures with the qualities of the following signs. Unfolding gradually over the period of the life, this maturing mirrors the major movements of the progressed Sun.

The self-oriented, self-motivated Aries becomes more settled and calm with the energy of Taurus. The security-conscious, invariable Taurus learns to be curious and enjoy change. The changeable, curious Gemini settles down into the home and hearth, while the nest-building, creative Cancer gains the confidence to display talents and skills. The exhibitionist, Leo, learns to bring patience and precision to innate talents, while the craft and precision of Virgo recognizes that harmony and balance, rather than correctness, may be a greater prize at times. The harmony-at-all-costs Libra realizes that a little intensity is not a bad thing, while the intense, one-to-one Scorpio learns to relax and step back to view the big picture. The big-picture-oriented, independent Sagittarius learns lessons about responsibility and "being there," while the responsible, establishment-loving Capricorn slowly allows the group energy and group needs to become an issue worth considering. The team-oriented Aquarian learns to become emotional and discovers a spiritual inner world, while the sensitive, impressionable Pisces without boundaries gains the self-orientation of Aries.

The sign change is therefore very important, as it marks phases of maturing, or unfoldment. Thus, this particular progression is a huge background swell in the astrologer's predictive work.

Although the progressed Sun will change its zodiac sign on an exact date for a given individual, the expression of its energy is blurred over a period of time. For some years before the change, you will start to experience deep desires vaguely flickering to the surface of your mind. As the Sun actually enters the new sign, no obvious effects may be visible, but within a few years, you will have made great changes in the way that you lead your life and the issues that are considered important.

Joan of Arc's progressed Sun moved from Capricorn into Aquarius by the time she was six years old. Thus, for thirty years, from the age of six, she would have had the capacity to understand the group's needs. At the same time, with her natal Capricorn Sun, she had the skills necessary to be a leader. It is inherent in the expression of Capricorn that the sign produces leaders. However, they lead more effectively once their progressed Sun enters Aquarius.

Looking at two more examples: Neil Armstrong, the first man on the Moon, was born on August 5th, 1930, with his Sun at 12° Leo. By the time he was eighteen years old the Sun had entered Virgo, so the flavor of adding precision and craft to his skills colored his years from 18 to 48. At the age of 17, he became a Navy Air Cadet. Although he had obtained his pilot's license at the age of 16, he wanted to improve his skills and build his career—a nice Virgo-progressed Sun expression.

It was while this progressed Sun traveled through Virgo that he walked on the Moon. After this event, Neil then worked as a professor of aerospace engineering at the University of Cincinnati. As the Sun moved out of Virgo, in 1979, he gave up his teaching position and gained employment with a firm supplying oil-drilling equipment to the Middle East. He no longer wanted the Virgo expression of precision and correctness in his life, so he moved out of the academic world and into commerce.

Martin Luther King Jr. was the leader of the American civil rights movement until he was assassinated in 1968. He was born on January 15, 1929, with a 25° Capricorn Sun. King experienced his progressed Sun entering Aquarius by the age of five. This, curiously enough, was the same pattern as for Joan of Arc. From the age of 5 to 35, King's progressed Sun was traveling through Aquarius and entered Pisces in 1964.

Martin Luther King Jr., as the leader of the civil rights movement, is a classic example of a Capricorn Sun moving into Aquarius. As his Sun entered Pisces, a huge peace movement of over 200,000 people had formed, and to this group he made the famous emotional speech where he announced, "I have a dream. . . ." in which he emphasized his faith that all men someday will be brothers. This powerful speech moved the nation and the world, resulting in the passage of the Civil Rights Act of 1964. In this same year, King was awarded the Nobel Peace Prize. The Sun's movement into Pisces occurred when his life's ambition was fulfilled by the outpouring of emotional and spiritual energy. Sadly, with his assassination a few years later, he became a literal expression of another Pisces trait—that of being a martyr for the group.

Leaders are more inclined to become martyrs because inherent in the sign of Capricorn is the eventual movement into Pisces. Martyrs to a cause who are not leaders belong to the Aquarians, for that sign also moves into Pisces. If old leaders are not martyred, then they may also be turned into gods or put on a pedestal—another expression of Pisces. Pisceans don't escape this pattern either. If a guru is going to fall from grace, it will be in matters of ego and money, for Pisces matures into Aries and then Taurus.

These examples highlight the importance of the movement of the progressed Sun through the signs. This progression does not give the daily, or even monthly, prediction, but shows the momentum of your life. It shows the general timing of your unfoldment, the big themes and the deep, driving desires that are a part of your personal natural development. You are almost unaware of these urges until their time has come.

Changing House

Of equal importance in this large picture is the progressed Sun's travel through the houses. As the Sun moves through the houses, the area of life symbolized by the house becomes emphasized and, as in sign changes, shows the phases of unfoldment. House changes signal the times when new interests and attitudes come into your life.

The major difficulty with house changes is that small errors in the birth time can lead an astrologer into an error of several years with regard to timing. In addition to this problem, the house system used will also dramatically alter the time of the house change. This does not mean that we have to disregard the whole system, but it does mean that it should be handled with care.

The house system that is working for the transits should be the house system that you use for progressions. As long as you keep in mind the variation in timing that can be caused by shifts in the birth time, then you can still use this astrological phenomenon as a pointer to periods of change in your client's life. For example, the 9th house academic Sun will, in the fullness of time, progress into the 10th house—success and social acceptance. Thus study and academic achievement are considered the way you progress in the world.

In comparison, creative artists with their Suns in the 5th house are not considered to be on a "sure-fire" career path, for the image of the artist is of someone living on the borderline of poverty—a slave to art. The 5th house Sun—creativity—progresses into the 6th house—hard work and commitment. Not all artists will fit into this category, but these are the popular images. The homemaker wants to have a family—4th house leading to 5th house of children. The spiritual guru's ego may become enlarged, leading to a downfall—the 12th moving to the 1st house.

These images have become popular because they are standard patterns that can occur. There are standard ways certain character traits seem to develop, but not all people fall into these patterns. Enough do, however, to support these common beliefs. The passage of the Sun through the houses and, indeed, the passage of any progressed planet through the houses, as well as any transit through the houses, will result in these common patterns. These patterns are inherent in the basic meaning of the houses and, more importantly, the sequence in which they unfold.

So, at this level, the progressed Sun yields valuable information regarding the phases of life and life interests.

PROGRESSED SUN ASPECTING THE CHART

The progressed Sun, unlike the progressed Moon, does contribute Solar symbolism to all of its progressions as it moves slowly through the chart. When the progressed Sun makes an aspect, the sense of self is being altered. For the symbolism of the Sun is the sense of self and the sense of being—the concept of who you are and what you feel you can achieve. The Sun can form aspects to the natal planets or points and can also yield meaning when it forms aspects to other progressed planets.

For example, the progressed Sun forming a conjunction to natal Uranus can turn a conservative person into an individual who does not care what the Establishment thinks—one no longer afraid to rebel. Be aware that this person can be dissuaded from rebelling because this is a chart-related progression. However, if we have *progressed* Sun conjunct *progressed* Uranus, then we have the same conservative person becoming the rebel—but now it is unshakable. The basic meaning of Sun-Uranus manifests with a stronger or weaker determination, depending on whether it is the natal Uranus or progressed Uranus being aspected.

The next point to be aware of is that, in the case of the outer planets, movement by progression is only a few degrees over a lifetime. Therefore, the progressed planet will always be very close to its natal position, and thus the effect of any progression to these points will be felt at both the unshakable as well as the changeable levels.

Whether it is to a natal planet or a progressed planet, the progressed Sun in forming aspects will give you a new definition of yourself.

Joan of Arc's progressed Sun trine natal Jupiter implied that she felt invincible, full of god (Jupiter). If your progressed Sun aspects Saturn, you are feeling responsible, able to take control, or else intimidated or weighed down by commitments—caged in.

Vincent Van Gogh was born March 30, 1853. In December of 1880, Vincent's progressed Sun had conjoined his natal Uranus. This was the time when he was pushed out of missionary work and was in the depths of despair. In this state, he started to draw and discovered his true vocation. His self-confidence is reported to have been fully restored, for he was re-defining himself as an artist—rejoicing in his newfound talents and a new personal definition.

His progressed Sun conjoined his natal Saturn in June of 1890. History tells us that he committed suicide a few weeks later, thinking that he was a failure.

Summary of Progressed Sun

◊ The progressed Sun changing sign is an indication of a significant unfoldment in your life story.

◊ The progressed Sun moving through the natal house shows the times when new life interests or expressions are coming into your life, and is very connected to the sign change unfoldment.

◊ The progressed Sun contributes solar symbolism to the planets it aspects.

◊ The timing of the aspects of your progressed Sun shows the times when you are re-defining your sense of self.

PROGRESSED MERCURY, VENUS, AND MARS

All three of these planets can also change sign as well as house, with similar effect to that of the Sun. Not with the same encompassing, wholistic life effects as the Sun, but rather with implicit individual meanings that relate to that planet.

Mercury changing house or sign will show changes of intellectual pursuits or communication skills. Venus going through this process shows changes in relating patterns and value systems and what pleases the person, while Mars, which could spend a lifetime in a house or sign, will point to a change in what motivates the person.

We will use Leonardo da Vinci's chart (see chart 7 below) as an example to best illustrate this. He was born three hours after sunset on April 14, 1452, near Vinci, according to his grandfather's diary.* Because of the possible inaccuracy of his birth time, only the movement of progressions changing signs will be examined here.

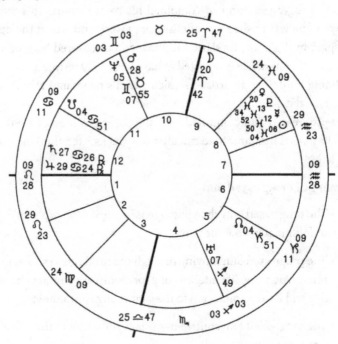

Chart 7. Leonardo da Vinci, born April 14, 1452, o.s. 3 hours after sunset (10:00 P.M. LMT), Vinci, Tuscany, Italy, 42N25, 11E52. Data from Circle Book of Charts. Placidus houses.

---

* S. Erlewine, *Circle of Book of Charts.*

During the course of Leonardo da Vinci's 67-year life, Mercury progressed from its natal position at 9° Aries to 12° Leo. He was twenty years old when it entered Taurus in February 1472. In that year, he finished his apprenticeship and was admitted to the Guild of St. Luke as a painter. For the next five years he continued working with his teacher, after which he accepted commissions and started his studies in anatomy. This period was one of building his skills. It was the most stable period of his career.

Progressed Mercury entered Gemini in September 1488 and remained there until August 1502. The years of 1490 to 1495 are considered his "stage of writing." From within him arose a growing need to record all of his perceptions and experiences. The need to think on paper, the development of the illustrated technical work, unheard of before this time, his constant doodling of inventions next to the rent that he owed to the landlord—all of these were manifestations of this non-chart-related progression.

In 1502, Leonardo started his work in cartography and town-planning, developing the aerial view and revising the whole system of maps of cities. This was the time of progressed Mercury in Cancer, from August 1502 to December 1518. He worked on the concept of connecting Florence to the sea by a canal, so there would be greater security in trade, as well as protection against attack. Security of cities, town-planning, etc., are all very nice expressions of a progressed Mercury traveling through Cancer.

Leonardo's progressed Mercury moved into Leo in December of 1518 just a few months before his death. One wonders, had he lived longer, about the art he would have produced under this Leonian Mercury.

Over the period of his life, Leonardo's progressed Venus moved from 24° Taurus to 16° Leo. The period of progressed Venus in Cancer was August 1481 to September 1506. In 1481, Leonardo was twenty-nine years old and, in true Saturn return style, he had finished working for his teacher and decided to freelance. All was going well, for he received two fairly substantial commissions from his native city of Florence. The young artist was on his way to a very good career. He had begun the first commissioned piece titled "The Adoration of the Magi" but, for reasons that leave the historians confused, he suddenly abandoned the work uncompleted and moved to Milan. The *Encyclopedia Britannica* states of that period: "That he gave up both projects despite the commitments he had undertaken—not even starting on the second named—seems to indicate deeper reasons for his leaving Florence."*

Clearly, given the Venus emphasis at this time, there may well have been some relationship issues playing out in this part of Leonardo's life. He stayed in Milan for 17 years and eventually left there in 1499.

Progressed Venus was in Leo from September 1506 until his death. The year of 1506 found Leonardo, now fifty-four years old, working in Florence on a monumental mural titled "Battle of Anghiari" when, once again, he left Florence and returned to Milan. "Unsuccessful technical experiments with paints seem to have impelled Leonardo to stop working on the mural. One cannot otherwise explain his abandonment of this great work."**

Here once again is his move to Milan. Here once again is the confusion of the historians. History does not give us any more information. The subtle meanings of the Venus in Cancer changing to the Venus in Leo are not obvious. However, the effects of these personal upheavals, good or bad, have left their marks on his history.

Leonardo's natal Mars was at 15° Aquarius and moved to 29° Pisces during the course of his life.

Progressed Mars entered Pisces in November 1472 when Leonardo was only twenty years old. The only reference made for that period is that in 1472 he was accepted into the painters guild in Florence. This means that he had finished his apprenticeship and could now, if he wanted to, start working for himself.

As we know from history Leonardo was strongly motivated by ideas (natal Mars in an air sign). In addition, his progressed Mars was in Pisces for all of his adult life, while it traveled through his 3rd house. So with Leonardo's Mars energy being Aquarius/Pisces and 3rd house, it is no wonder that his genius produced ideas for bicycles, helicopters, fluid mechanics, wave motion, and ballistics, not to mention submarines, revolving stages, and aerial perception—most of these inventions being 500 years before their time.

As a note of interest, from the same period of history when Michaelangelo's Mars moved from Aries to Taurus, he was relieved of his artistic commissions and put in charge of fortifying a city. He became a "general," a very reluctant one at that, who kept disappearing.

---

*   *Encyclopedia Britannica,* p. 960.
** *Encyclopedia Britannica,* p. 962.

PROGRESSED MERCURY ASPECTING THE CHART

Mercury carries with it the theme of paperwork, words, studying, and movement. When involved in a progression, you will desire, or find yourself surrounded by, words. This type of progression can show the commencement of studying or the starting or finishing of a Mercurial job. The aspect involved will give the type of action: square—contest, opposition—decisions, quincunx—abandonment.

When Florence Nightingale returned from the Crimean War, she urged the army to change its ideas about the health of the common soldier. She forced a Royal Commission to be held on the "Health of the Army." At this commission, she presented extensive reports covering the whole field of army medical and hospital administration. Just a few months before this commission, Florence had her progressed Mercury forming an opposition to her natal Neptune. She spent months of working and writing about health and hospitals and was motivated by the idea of winning her case.

PROGRESSED VENUS ASPECTING THE CHART

The progression of Venus affects your relationships, not only the personal, intimate relationships, but also those with colleagues or casual friends. Issues of money can also be involved in this progression, or the way you use your resources can come under question. Once again, the aspect supplies the action, and an excellent example of this planet in progression is seen if Vincent Van Gogh's chart is examined (Chart 8 on page 138).

Just before his progressed Sun conjoined natal Uranus, Vincent experienced progressed Venus conjunct his natal Pluto. At this stage of his life he was working as a missionary with the poor. He became so involved with his work that he gave all of his worldly possessions away to the poor. Due to this rash action, the Church dismissed him for taking Christ's words too literally. He was penniless and in despair. His very faith in the Church and its "god" had been shaken. He was in a crisis of "value systems." In this state of depression, he cut himself off from everybody. It was in this period of isolation that the progressed Sun conjoined his natal Uranus and he discovered his painting.

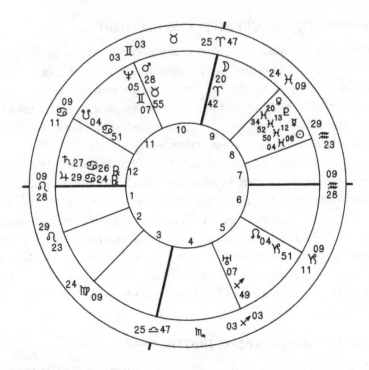

Chart 8. Vincent Van Gogh, born March 30, 1853, 11:00 A.M. LMT, Zundert, Groot-Zundert, Netherlands, 51N28, 4E40. Data from Circle Book of Charts *quoting Gauquelin. Placidus houses.*

PROGRESSED MARS ASPECTING THE CHART

The progression of Mars intensifies a person's motivation, desire, and determination to achieve something. The flavor of progressed Mars brings in energy and action. It is a little like receiving a jolt of energy—either constructively or destructively. At this time you are able to take action.

When Florence Nightingale was finally allowed to study nursing, when she was finally allowed to get into a hospital and actually work with sick people, she was having progressed Mars trine natal Mercury. She was suddenly being allowed to study what she wanted and was able to take the action that she desired.

The outer planets in progression are really relevant only if they make an exact natal aspect, as discussed earlier.

NATAL ASPECTS BECOMING EXACT BY PROGRESSION

The natal aspects in a chart can become exact by secondary progression. The faster-moving progressed planets will become exact in their applying aspects within the childhood of a person's life. Natal Sun forming an applying square to natal Pluto will probably, by progression, make that square exact within 4 to 5 years, depending on the orb of the square. However, what is of greater importance to the predictive astrologer is the other type of aspect, i.e., where the natal Sun is a separating square to the natal Pluto. During the course of the life, the secondary progressed Pluto may move into an exact square with the natal Sun.

When a slow-moving planet makes an exact natal aspect through progression, the meaning of the natal aspect becomes emphasized in the life. It is a time when the person can become conscious of the implications of the natal aspect—a time of realization. For example, you may have your natal Venus square Pluto. You may never have considered yourself as needing strong, intense relationships or needing a little drama in your personal life. If the progressed Pluto moves into an exact square with the natal Venus, then it is in this time period—which will be a period of a few years—that you suddenly realize that these are your characteristics rather than everybody else's. Once this is realized, it seems that the aspect, in this case Pluto square Venus, becomes a major theme in life.

A good example of this is the life of Vincent Van Gogh. He experienced two of his natal aspects becoming exact through the movement of the slower-moving progressed planets. (See Chart 8.) The first was in February of 1883, when a progressed Uranus moved into the exact semisquare to the Natal node.

His first vocation in life was to be a religious missionary and help people. This failed because he was overzealous. His next vocation was to bring consolation to humanity through art. He wanted to help people but experienced immense frustration in this area and, indeed, considered himself to be a total failure. He found it impossible to gain satisfaction from his work—the semisquare. His art was born from conflict because he refused to conform to the established art methods of the time and was always at loggerheads with art schools and the public.

By February 1883, as the Uranus aspect to the Nodal axis had become exact by progression, he became obsessed with being alone and took himself off into very isolated parts of the Netherlands to reconnect to his paintings and nature. He was a recluse for over three months and, upon his return, started to use his painting as social commentary. His most famous paintings in 1885 were "The Potato Eaters" and "The Weavers." Van Gogh's genius was his ability to touch the common nerve, reaching the life of the people. However, his life was tormented by a lack of any satisfaction in his work. Out of over 800 oil paintings and 700 drawings he only sold one in his lifetime—Uranus semisquare Node.

The other natal aspect in his chart that falls into this mode is that of Jupiter conjunct the South Node. This aspect became exact by progression in January of 1890. This aspect natally supports the desire to be a missionary in his early life and his determination to help humankind. When this aspect became exact, Vincent was voluntarily in an asylum at Saint-Remy-de-Provence. Twelve months earlier he had requested that he be "shut up" in the asylum so that he could be under medical supervision. However, he began to feel immensely homesick—South Node—and realized that his art needed life and nature around it—Jupiter—for it to grow. He left the asylum to return home. Immediately his work became broader and more expansive. A whole different style began to emerge. However, the despair of never succeeding overcame him, and he committed suicide in July of that year.

In another example, Florence Nightingale set up her famous school of nursing—which ensured that her life's work would live on after her death—when her progressed Neptune made the natal square to the Node exactly.

Your life may contain only one or two of these types of aspects becoming exact by secondary progression. The predictive astrologer needs to be aware of these, for they can override all else during their period of exactness. All transits and progressions that you may also be experiencing in that period will play second fiddle to these big progressions.

PROGRESSED PLANETS CHANGING DIRECTION

Progressed planets can also change their direction during the course of a lifetime. They can move from direct to retrograde or retrograde to direct. Each time a planet changes direction, it goes through a period of being stationary. A stationary planet in astrology implies a great emphasis on that planet. So a progressed planet can become stationary, thereby directing acute, stressed planetary energy into your life.

Mercury

When Mercury turns retrograde, it does so for 19 to 24 days. So, if you are born with a retrograde Mercury, then sometime between birth and age 24, Mercury will turn direct. The year that this event occurs marks the change in your life with regard to your communication skills.

If progressed Mercury turns retrograde, then it will be so for 19 to 24 years. The turning from direct to retrograde marks a time of greater inner communication. There is greater thinking or planning with less expression, or more carefully measured expression.

Venus

With Venus, the retrograde period occurs for approximately 40 days. Thus, if you have a retrograde Venus at birth you will experience the Venus turning direct by the time you have reached forty years old. The year that Venus changes direction is a year where you experience changes in your relating skills and self-esteem.

If progressed Venus turns retrograde, then it will be in that condition for 40 years. This figure of 40 days and 40 years is very reminiscent of Christ's 40 days in the desert and also the Israelites's 40 years in the wilderness. This retrograde period represents a time of shyness, reclusiveness, or withdrawing in some way.

Mars

When Mars turns retrograde, it is for a period of 58 to 81 days. Therefore, if you are born with a retrograde Mars you may have this planet retrograde for the rest of your life, or it may change direction. If Mars does change direction, then this shows astrologers that you are going to be changing the way you manifest your energy. Someone who appears to be passive may become much more confronting. Or if the situation is reversed—the Mars turning retrograde after birth—this may signify the energy turning inward, with the confronting individual settling down and becoming quieter.

SLOWER-MOVING PLANETS

Jupiter will stay retrograde for about 4 months; Saturn, 4½ months retrograde; Uranus, Neptune, and Pluto, 5 to 6 months retrograde. All of these planets, therefore, may or may not change direction during the course of a person's life. However, if they do change direction, then it can make a lasting impression, where the energy of the planet becomes very strong and almost "possessive."

Joan of Arc with her Jupiter turning retrograde at the age of 14 is a good example of this. Jupiter, if strong, yields an obsessive, unstoppable, totally-consumed-by-an-idea type of individual.

For Leonardo, Neptune turned direct in 1501, and the drive in him, in this last period of his life, was to find the wholeness of his life: a connection between machines, energy, and life—the unified field theory. This was Neptune with its entropic—all energy and things being the same—overtones, manifesting through his great mind.

Henry Kissinger's retrograde Saturn in Libra changed its direction when he was twenty years old. He became a naturalized United States citizen in that year and spent the rest of his life working hard—via the Saturn in Libra energy—to keep the balance—the most predominant feature of his life.

Not all cases will be as clear as the above examples, but it does pay to be aware of these slow movers and their potential to change direction.

PUTTING THE CYCLES TOGETHER

Life is a continuous journey, and these progressed cycles and large events create a picture in which you can be placed. Knowledge of that picture gives astrologers a guide to the daily ups and downs. If no knowledge of the terrain or picture is available, then making sense of the ups and downs or bumps along the way is almost impossible.

If a playwright plots a character hitting another character and then asks you to guess what happens next, you would immediately want to know more detail. A small child accidentally hitting its mother is going to have a grossly different outcome than if the scene is a barroom brawl and the two characters are angry boxers.

Background information is the key to drawing the correct conclusion in every single case of forward planning. If your car is running out of gas, you rely on your knowledge of the length of your journey and how much gas your vehicle consumes to make a judgment on the situation. You take into account additional information concerning the two things—car and trip—and work out a possible outcome.

Doing predictive astrology also requires that astrologers have background information—a map of the countryside through which the client is walking. Without this information, the astrologer is looking at events like the two characters hitting each other in our supposed play and trying to guess the outcome with that information alone. If the astrologer is psychic, then all is well, but for most of us, it is a nearly impossible task. The use of progressions in terms of house, sign, direction, or phase gives the astrologer that map. They give us the nature of the two characters in the script and, most importantly, they create the background into which transits and other progressions will drop.

THE COMPONENTS OF THE LANDSCAPE

The landscape is made up of the following points:

1. The current progressed Lunar Phase;

2. The natal house through which the progressed Moon is traveling;

3. The zodiac sign through which the progressed Moon is traveling;

4. The position of the progressed Sun with regard to house or sign change;

5. Any other progressed planet changing sign or house;

6. Any progressed planet changing its direction of movement;

7. Any natal aspect becoming exact by secondary progression.

The first three points are an ongoing, constantly changing landscape in the person's life. The latter four are only going to occur on rare occasions, but those rare occasions should not be missed as they will be predominant in their expression for several years surrounding the mathematical event.

Let's pretend that the year is 1610 and you are an astrologer in Padua, Italy. The professor of mathematics at Padua University is coming to see you. He is in a dilemma, as he has been offered another position that would enable him to do more research. However, he has been at the University for 18 years and it is a secure job, one he can have for the rest of his life. After all, he is forty-six years old now and should be thinking of his security. He is hoping that you can cast some light on the future to help him make his decision. The professor is Galileo.

The landscape where Galileo is standing is as follows:

(a) His current lunar phase is Disseminating;

(b) His progressed Moon is in the late degrees of Sagittarius;

143

(c) His progressed Moon is in the 5th house and will be there until the end of 1611;

(d) His progressed Sun is at 22° Aries, so he has eight years before it enters Taurus.

The Disseminating Lunar phase means that something just behind Galileo, in his past, has reached its fullest expression. He will now be passing through a stage of synthesizing his achievements and wanting to push on with his life. It is the Disseminating Moon that has opened him to the offer of the other job. This is the pragmatist. What is causing the tension in the story is the issue of security.

His progressed Moon is in the late degrees of Sagittarius about to enter Capricorn, so the need to make a commitment will be upon him very soon. Either way, the decision is very close, and he will have to make a decision to commit to the old job or take the plunge into a new job. Neither of these two points answers the question, but they are providing the reasons why the dilemma has arisen and are giving some sense of timing to the decision being made.

His progressed Moon is in the most creative area of his chart and will be until the end of 1611. This favors research. Whatever decision Galileo reaches about this job, he should start to become involved in research during this period because it could be extremely successful. Any decisions that would bring greater research into his life should be favored. It will be many years before such creativity will again be available for his use.

His Sun still has 8° of Aries to travel before it reaches the security-conscious Taurus. For eight more years, he can sail on with his independence, or personal creativity. For although he is forty-six years old, it will not be until he is 54 that security will become a more important issue.

Galileo's dilemma is not unlike that of the modern client's—when to leave and when to stay in a job, marriage, etc.

Thus, before any transits or progressions to the natal chart are considered, the astrologer can build up quite a detailed picture of the current countryside in which Galileo is standing as he tries to make the decision. He is blind, using only his "gut" feelings. The astrologer, however, holds the map of this time-dimensional world, where the past and the future are seen simultaneously clustering around him.

Although you, the astrologer, can't make decisions for your client, Galileo, it is clear—even before you've done any detailed work such as transits or progressions to his natal chart—that indications are favorable for Galileo to take the new job, allowing him to spend greater time doing research. Of course, history gives us the answers. Galileo did leave his old job. In the summer of 1610, Galileo left his lifelong appointment as professor at Padua to become the "first philosopher and mathematician" to the Grand Duke of Tuscany.

Chapter Four

Time Maps

A strologers work with time. Unlike any other profession, we can travel backward or forward in time. For most people, time is a shapeless void, only visible in retrospect. The journey of life can be like moving forward while looking backward, knowing what is going to happen only after the event has occurred.

However, with predictive work, we as astrologers can turn this future void into a landscape. So instead of thick, pea-soup fogs where only vague shapes loom, we can see stormy mountains or sunlit plains rolling off into the distance. An approaching Pluto transit can be seen as a thunderstorm, while a Uranus transit could be an approaching circus caravan. Enchanted forests with hidden bogs; leafy glades; stony, barren steppes; rich, green valleys; and craggy mountains to climb are all part of the traveler's future landscape.

Each piece of predictive astrology, each unit, each snippet of data is a part of the map that our client, the traveler, is using. Some of the data gives the overall nature of the landscape: city, desert, mountains, etc.; other pieces show the events that the traveler will experience in that particular landscape; while another sort of data will illustrate what the traveler is trying to achieve and how he or she is feeling.

Once all the data has been collected by the different predictive techniques, it is laid out onto a Time Map. If too much information is placed on the map, then it becomes cluttered and unreadable. So transits, in particular, must be sorted and graded so that they don't flood the map.

The type of format for the Time Map must be simple enough, yet contain all the necessary data. For the information contained in the Time Map will not be only transits and their grids, but also secondary progressions and possibly a few of your pet methods.

Setting Up a Time Map

Write the months that you are going to examine across the top of a sheet of paper. This is your time scale—a calendar of months. See figure 30.

Having sorted out the most important transits using the methods discussed in the section on Transits, the first step is to write them onto the sheet of paper under the appropriate months for when they are going to occur. Most transits occur three times, so only bother to do the grids for one of the hits. If all the hits are placed in grids, there will be too much information on the page, and you may not be able to read it.

You will see we have transiting Saturn forming a conjunction to Mercury. The transit first occurs in early March and then returns in mid-July and early October.

Above the transits, or below if you wish, mark in the progressions. By drawing them in as short lines, the length representing the approximate length of time that the progression is effective, you can also see them overlapping and stacking up on each other. In figure 30, the period of mid-January to mid-February is influenced by the progressed Moon forming a square to natal Mars. At the same time, from early February to March, the progressed Moon is forming a semisquare to natal Sun. In August to September, the progressed Moon is forming a trine to natal Pluto.

The slower planetary progressions are entered as long lines at the bottom of the page, with the climax, or exactness, marked with an arrow. In figure 30, the progressed Sun is forming a trine to natal Moon. Using an orb of 1°, the progression starts in April, becomes exact in September, and continues on into the following year, waning.

I usually use color when constructing maps. I do all the hard—or 8th Harmonic progressions—with red lines and the soft—or 12th harmonic progressions—in blue. Use whatever color coding you like, but I strongly recommend that you do use color.

This is a very simple Time Map. You can put more and more information onto it—Solar Arcs, eclipses, more transits, and so on. However, once you put too much on it, then you see nothing.

The second step is examining your Time Map. In figure 30, you can see that there is an area of activity in January and February and that this energy seems to clear or climax in August and September. If you do nothing more than this, you have just turned, for the client, the fog of the future into a light morning mist.

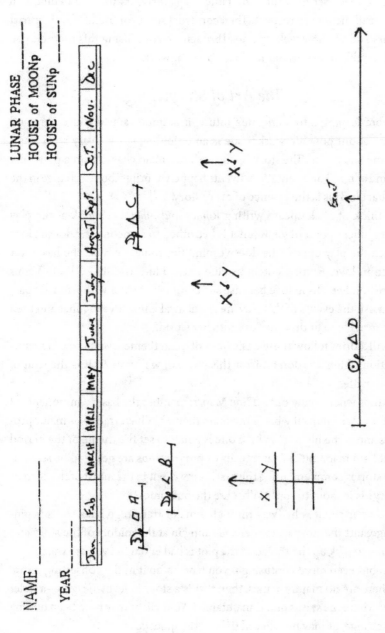

Figure 30. Time Map of transiting Saturn conjunct Mercury.

The following are examples of how to set up Time Maps and how they can be read. Set up your own Time Maps for years that are behind you and read them in retrospect. Then construct some for friends for their past years and see how well you do. Through practice, using this method you will be able to get instant feedback on your work.

The Art of Storytelling

Before leaping into someone's future, it is important to pause here and think about how life works. Life is an unfolding story. Every story has a theme and a plot. The story opens with our main character in a particular frame of mind or orientation. Events happen to bring about a change in the character. This is the essence of every story.

Think of Shakespeare writing *Romeo and Juliet*. Let's look at the play from Juliet's point of view. Juliet is betrothed to someone she doesn't love when the play opens. She doesn't mind this much because she has never been in love. Romeo enters her life like a Pluto transit—a Pluto-Venus transit. Juliet falls in love because she comes in contact with Romeo's passion. All the events of this play are about awakening love in Juliet and then the struggle to fit this new love into her world.

All stories follow these basic lines of main theme, events, and transformations. Humans don't mirror this process; we create it. It is the stuff of human life.

Thus when laying out a Time Map, remember the basic components of a story. Ask yourself what is the main theme? Which transit or major progression is the biggest? Which one is going to set the theme of the period that I am mapping? What transits or progressions are going to be secondary stories complementing the first? Is my client in the midst of the current story? Is it about to start? What are the outcomes?

If your client is halfway through a major transit, go back to its beginning. Start the story from there. Coming in at the middle of the story and trying to pick up the thread of the plot is bad enough if you are watching a film but even more confusing if you have to do it in the consulting room. If there are no major themes, then that is a story in its own right—a quiet year where the status quo is maintained. Your client may have been hoping for change, or may be relieved to have the quiet year.

Case Studies of Time Maps

The following are some examples of Time Maps; however, the best examples are always going to be the Maps you draw up yourself.

MARIE CURIE

Pretend that Madame Curie is coming to see you in August of 1905 for predictive work, so the Time Map you draw up will be from August 1905 to July 1906. You are aware that she won the Nobel Prize a few years earlier under her Full Moon phase. (See Chart 9.)

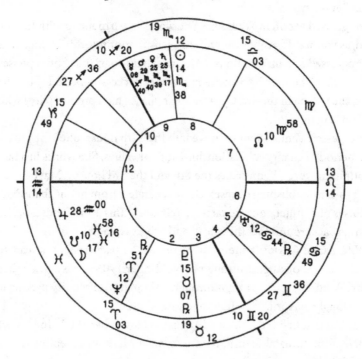

Chart 9. Marie Curie, born November 7, 1867, 1:30 P.M. LMT, Warsaw, Poland, 52N14, 21E00. Data from Profiles of Women, time speculative. Placidus houses.

Background Information

Progressed Moon is in Leo in the 7th house.

Mars is progressing into the 11th house (depends on the accuracy of the birth time).

Progressed Sun is in the 10th house.

Progressed Venus is moving into the 12th house.

Lunar Phase is Disseminating and not moving into 3rd quarter until 1908.

Background Landscape

Lunar Phase: Disseminating. The client is in a stage of stepping back from an achieved goal and starting to look for other areas of life into which to direct her energy.

Progressed Moon in 7th house. She works in partnership with her husband, as you are already aware, and she plans to continue this arrangement.

Progressed Sun in 10th house. Although her progressed Lunar phase is now waning, she may be moving into a very successful period—in a few years, she will be in the 3rd Quarter lunar phase (high productivity) while the Sun is in the 10th.

Progressed Venus about to move into the 12th house. She is approaching a period of change in relationships and/or values. She works in a team situation; however, Venus rules the 8th and the 3rd houses. Maybe she is going to start publishing or researching separately from her husband?

This is our "Juliet," our character in our story. This is our landscape. It is into this background that the transit and progression will fall.

With Marie Curie's Time Map (figure 31 on page 153), you can see that the period of August through to November 1905 is busy. Then there is a break from December right through to March with activity picking up very strongly in April, May, June, and July of 1906.

Look at that first busy patch of August to November 1905. The transits are: Neptune to natal Saturn, Saturn to natal Mars, and Neptune to the natal MC.

What is the theme of this period? The aspects imply frustration (sesquiquadrate) and change, separation, or someone leaving (quincunx). The transiting Saturn square Mars only emphasizes this. So even before we start looking at each transit or progression, we have a sense that there is frustration and/or change in this time slot. The Neptune-Saturn aspect that starts in this period does not complete until July of 1906. This is a transit, remember, so it is marked on the map as three separated hits, September, November, and then finally July 1906.

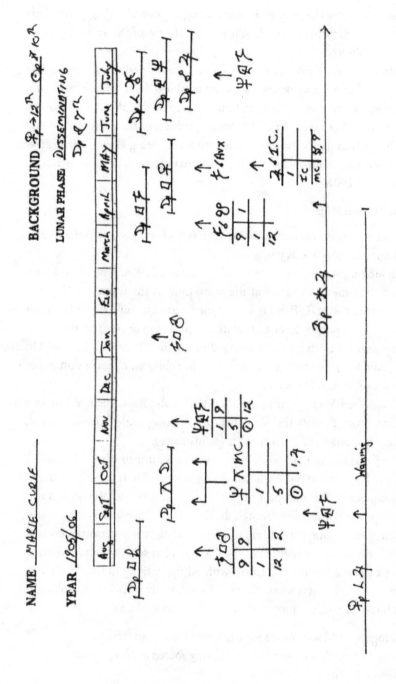

Figure 31. *Time Map for Marie Curie, August 1905–July 1906.*

153

The second patch, in April and May, is mostly composed of Saturn transits, but here the progressions are piling up on each other, particularly after a very Saturnian period. What is the theme of the second period? Responsibility?

However, the astrology indicates a very heavy period in her life. This is a period of hard work and illness or tiredness (Neptune-Saturn), and for every Saturn transit, the 12th house is emphasized through the Saturn rulership of that house. The 12th house position in the grids is as an end result—it is in the bottom row: working alone, being alone, doing secret work, working in hospitals. The Saturn climax seems to be in the period of April–May 1906.

Reading the Map

Start at the beginning and delineate each transit and progression in order, building the storyline as you go.

In looking at the progressions in September of 1905, progressed Moon quincunxes the natal Moon at the same time as the transiting Neptune quincunxes the MC. There is some type of parting here, either from her job, or from a particular line of creative exploration or research that she is doing, since the 5th house is involved in the middle row of the grid. Or, she could be temporarily separated from her children due to a shift in her workplace or current project.

Progressed Venus semisquares Jupiter, so she feels frustrated by this change. Even though she feels that she is being undervalued (Venus), there is nothing she can do about it (semisquare).

By January, the hard work aspect of the Saturn-to-Mars has passed, but the Neptune-to-Saturn is still going strong. The transiting Neptune sesquiquadrate Saturn aspect is coming from the 1st and 9th houses and the Neptune is transiting through the 5th house. This illness or tiredness, which is generating frustration, is being caused by her personal research work; and the consequences of the 1st and 12th seem to imply working alone or being alone. One senses with all the activity in the April–May period of 1906, that is where the transits will really manifest. In looking at that heavy period, the progressions can be examined first.

Progressed Moon square Saturn: being forced (square) to stand on one's own feet (Saturn); being forced to accept greater responsibility.

Progressed Moon square Venus: forced action (square) and feelings concerned with her husband or friends (Venus). A difficult time for socializing that is nobody's fault may also be indicated.

Progressed Mars sextile Jupiter: an opportunity (sextile) that suddenly occurs or is offered to her (sextile in Yang elements) which expands her career or is good for her career (Jupiter rules her 10th house).

Is it possible that Marie Curie is going to be offered a really wonderful job, but that job will mean she would no longer be able to work with her husband? The astrology is quite clear: good job opportunity, forced increase in responsibilities, difficult socializing time. These are the transits for the period.

Jupiter conjunct the IC: a change in the home with consequences in the 9th house and the MC—a new job or new research.

Saturn conjunct South node (and remember, Neptune is still aspecting the natal Saturn): this is difficult. Illness, or family problems (South Node). The result of this illness or problem is the 12th house. Is a member of her family going to get ill, or is *she* going to get ill?

Saturn is also forming a conjunction to her Anti-vertex: a point of letting go, releasing.

But what about the good job offer? You are aware, as her astrologer, that her progressed Venus is also about to enter her 12th house, the exact date depending on chart accuracy, but nevertheless, another indicator of a relationship change.

Your eagle has given you a lot of information. There is a great deal of frustration and hard work in the August, September, October period that may result in Marie getting ill from the workload that she is carrying. This hard work clears by January of 1906 after which things run fairly smoothly until April of 1906.

Starting in April, there are two themes: one of loss and/or illness with a strong indication of being alone; and the other of sudden job opportunities that are very good.

It is at this point that the lark (the astrologer's intuition) needs to come into the picture, hand in hand with talking to the client to see what her plans were for the period.

The period of June and July, after the climax, contains first a lot of frustration concerning a new idea or new colleagues (progressed Moon semisquare Uranus). Next, personal confusion (progressed Moon sesquiquadrate Neptune), which is cleared by a decision that she makes in July (progressed Moon opposite natal Jupiter).

History does not give us all the personal details of Marie Curie's life. However, on April 19, 1906, her husband Pierre was killed in an accident, and a month after that she was given his job as a professor at the Sorbonne. She was the first woman to be appointed to lecture at the Sorbonne.

Loss, grief, standing alone, being alone, a new job, a sudden opportunity occurring for a new job, loneliness, isolation, and pain, all of which she translated into hard work. After her husband's death, she devoted the rest of her life to research.

The landscape tells us of changes. She is moving toward success but also isolation and lonely or hidden periods. Marie Curie was walking toward a forest of magnificent trees, but this forest also contained some lonely hidden places.

Listing both transits and progressions on the same sheet, laying them out so that you can see when they are piling up on each other and making note of the recurring house placements, allows you to pick the correct character of an approaching time period. Astrology can never tell the precise events that are going to occur. However, the nature or energy of the events and the areas of life that are involved are very clear.

NAPOLEON BONAPARTE

Napoleon's birth data is speculative; however, this version of his chart (Chart 10) does give a wonderful and interesting example of working with Time Maps.

Pretend that Napoleon has an appointment to see you in March 1814, for predictive work spanning the next couple of years.

This general/emperor is fighting for the life of his army. The French people are no longer supporting him and the allies of Russia, Prussia, Austria, and Great Britain have joined forces to conquer him.

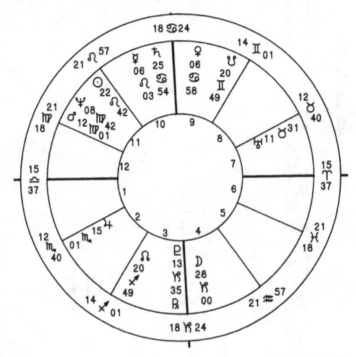

Chart 10. Napoleon Bonaparte (Napoleon I), born August 15, 1769, 10:08 A.M. CET, Ajaccio, Corsica, France, 41N55, 9E44. Placidus houses.

Background Information

The progressed Moon is in the 12th house. It does not cross over the ascendant until the end of 1815. It is a time of inwardness, a time of isolation, a time of personal growth.

The Lunar Phase is Balsamic, with a New Moon occurring in the 12th house in February of 1815. It is a time of endings with a new period of life starting, but one that is reclusive, metaphysical, or without ego.

The progressed Sun is in Libra in the 12th house. Once again a huge theme of withdrawing to find balance or to write, and so on.

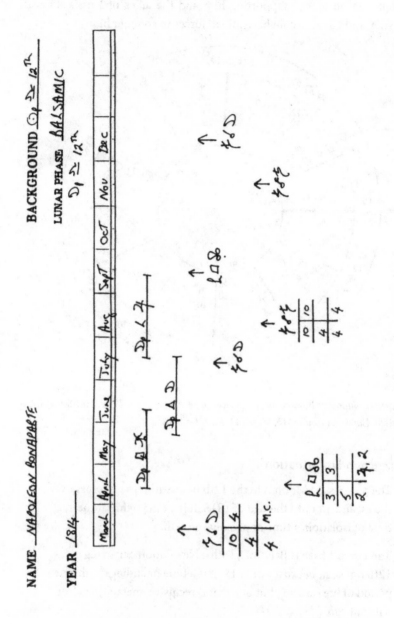

Figure 32. Time Map for Napoleon, March 1814–December 1814.

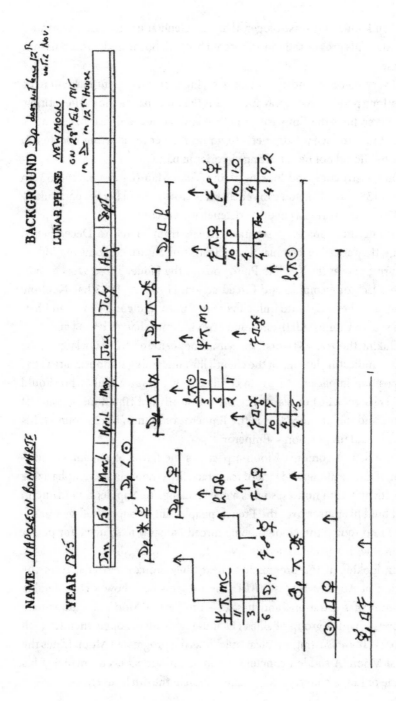

Figure 33. Time Map for Napoleon, January 1815–September 1815.

You know, as the astrologer, that this General unsuccessfully invaded Russia as his progressed Moon entered his 12th house under this Balsamic phase.

Every piece of landscape data is saying that your client has entered a very long period of withdrawing. This is the time that he should be retiring. However, he is the Emperor of France and wishes to defeat his enemies. You, the astrologer, really need to go no further to draw the conclusion that he should not be expecting victories in battle.

In constructing and looking at the Time Map (figures 32 and 33 on pages 158 and 159), you can see that it is crowded and hectic, particularly in 1815, designating a chaotic existence for the client.

While there are three separate transits from March to December in 1814, they are all of a similar flavor. Transiting Saturn conjoins the Moon, Saturn opposes itself, while Pluto squares the Node. These aspects indicate a lack of resources and forced action. However, 1815 has Neptune quincunx the MC, Pluto quincunx Sun, Saturn quincunx Venus, and Saturn square Uranus. All these quincunxes indicate change, letting go.

Taking the year 1814 first, the Saturn opposition Saturn is a large cyclic transit indicating lessons in the client's life concerning responsibilities; the opposition implies that he is in conflict with a group about "who should be in charge." The houses concerned are the 4th and 10th houses, issues of home and job or, since this is the Emperor of France, home country, his people, and his position—Emperor.

The Saturn conjunct Moon aspect has the flavor of loneliness, isolation, standing alone, and lack of resources. This transit is also emphasizing the 4th and 10th houses, so it is a real challenge to Napoleon to maintain and hold his power over the French people. This is supported by transiting Pluto square the Node—being forced (square) to struggle for power (Pluto) with a group of people (Node).

In looking at the progressions next, they are concentrated from the period of April to August 1814. The progressions show a considerable amount of frustrations and hassles—progressed Moon sesquiquadrate Uranus—with a group of allies (Uranus) who are his open enemies (7th house). These frustrations clear quickly as the progressed Moon trines the natal Moon. A sudden conclusion and an emotional event involving his home or home country occur (natal Moon in the 4th house).

This sudden clearing of issues, however, leads him to a period of frustration and a sense of being in a "stuck state"—progressed Moon semisquare Jupiter. By July, he is going to be feeling blocked or checked in his ability to tap his resources (Jupiter in the 2nd house).

Putting It All Together

This is not looking good for your client. There is a great deal of struggle while the progressed Moon is in its Balsamic phase—the end of a cycle—and in the 12th house. He is going to encounter a lot of difficulties in raising support from the French people with his progressed Moon in such a hidden house, as well as transiting Saturn conjunct his natal Moon. Indeed, the allies, in attacking France, have assured the French that they are attacking only Napoleon—not France. It would seem that the 12th house Moon is starting to take on a scapegoat characteristic.

He experiences these draining, difficult times in March, with a lot of intense, strong activity in April, the time that he is struggling to hold power and raise support among the French people. As the General moves into May, there is frustration with his open enemies, leading to events happening very fast in May and June. These events seem to be a change of home or power base. This change leads to feelings of isolation (Saturn conjunct Moon) and a feeling of being blocked in August of 1814. This period of isolation continues through to the end of the year, until the transit of Saturn conjunct Moon completes.

Napoleon actually surrendered to the Allies in April 1814. He was moved to an island called Elba in May 1814, where he was meant to live in exile with a small band of men, while still retaining his title of Emperor.

Looking to 1815, we find him alone on Elba, with only a small band of men. We would expect the Emperor's Time Map to be fairly calm; however, it is evident that he is going to be very active. Let's look at taking these transits one at a time.

◊ Transiting Saturn is forming an opposition to the natal Mercury: a difficult decision, serious thinking, making plans involving his career and social standing (10th house), and his home and people (4th house). The consequences of this transit are in the 4th, 9th, and 12th houses. A home far away? A home by oneself? Seclusion in one's home while studying? This transit occurs in February 1815, and then again in September, and finally in October 1815.

◊ Transiting Saturn is forming a quincunx to his natal Venus. Key phrases for this aspect are separation, letting go of a group of people, reduced socializing, ending a relationship, and giving up responsibilities. The transit is coming from the 10th and 9th houses, his career, study, or travel aspirations. The consequences of the transit are indicated by the 4th and 8th houses plus the ascendant. He (AC) will change (8th house) his home or residence (4th house).

◊ In addition, there is also the transit of Pluto forming a quincunx to his natal Sun, symbolizing an ending, a letting go of one's 3rd, 10th, 6th, and 2nd—career, communications, resources, and health or daily routine. This transit starts in May of 1815 at the same time as a string of quincunxes appear in the progressions.

To summarize 1815: Napoleon needs to let go. If he can do this, then all may be well. There is a huge emphasis on a change of residence and a very strong indication of loss or power—the Pluto-Sun transit.

His moon is still in the 12th house, but a progressed New Moon occurs for him in February of 1815. However, as his astrologer, you advise him not to start new projects until the Moon is in the 1st house (December 1815). In addition, Jupiter will be conjunct his ascendant in the end of 1815. This is a much better time to start the new life shown by the New Moon.

But it would seem that your client does not want to let go of his old life, for all those quincunxes are implying that letting go will take most of the year. His new life is described by the New Moon occurring in Libra in the 12th house. This does not seem to fit into Napoleon's idea of being the supreme ruler of France.

The progressions start to unfold the story. Three big progressions are climaxing in February and March of 1815. The first one is progressed Mercury square Saturn, which indicates a desire to take action in regard to communication concerning his social status (Mercury in the 10th house), and this has an element of restraint or hard work about it (Saturn). The second progression is the progressed Sun square Venus—more action: the personal desire (Sun) to take a journey to claim his rights (Venus in the 9th house). The third is a Mars-Uranus quincunx. Hasty action will bring sudden change.

Linking these progressions with the faster Lunar ones, we have, in February, the progressed Moon sextile Mercury. An opportunity suddenly occurs (Yang sextile) through some form of communication (Mercury) to help his social status (Mercury in the 10th house). This opportunity leads him to feel a need to take action—progressed Moon square Venus—and make a journey (Venus in the 9th). This action, once taken, leads into a period of frustration and being in a "stuck state"—Moon semisquare Sun.

Well, you have your hands full with this client! There is a need to let go but a determination to take action. Action of some form is obviously going to occur in February–March of 1815. He will regret this action by the late March–April period, for he does not have any support.

The second strong period is in May–June, when the Cosmos is really making strong statements about letting go. The progression of Moon quincunx Uranus occurring at the same time as the transiting Pluto is quincunx the Sun is a real indicator that this is now the period in which this big transit will manifest. To suddenly let go (quincunx to Uranus) and to change one's social status (Pluto quincunx 10th house) are very compelling aspects.

The client should be advised to willingly let go of his ambitions. Take some time off. Wait until the Moon and Jupiter move into the 1st house and then, with that clarity, decide what he wants to do with his life, reminding him that his future life path is now a 12th house one.

Of course Napoleon does not take your advice. In March of 1815, he returned to France like a thunderbolt, fighting to regain his former power. By March 20th, he was in Paris with a large army behind him. He was officially recognized and brought back to power. However, he quickly lost support because he found himself caught between whom he should support and whom he dared not support. In this confusion, he set up a reign that was without any real meaning for the French people.

By June he was in the battlefield again, fighting the allies who had amassed on his borders. He fought the battle of Waterloo. He was overpowered. He fled. He once again abdicated and by early July was trying to take a ship to the USA.

Just think how the history of that country would have changed if Napoleon had been able to make his journey! However, he was captured and by October of 1815 was imprisoned on the island of St. Helena, stripped of all his rights, destined to live a solitary 12th house life. This would be a difficult case for any astrologer, mainly due to the immense amount of important predictive data present in the client's chart. A good rule with such cases is not to try to delineate each transit and progression but rather to look at the overall flavor.

The big theme for Napoleon in 1815 was the change of residence and a need to let go of an old cycle. The constant repetition of the 10th and 4th house, the large number of quincunxes, the 12th house Moon, the Balsamic phase with the New Moon occurring in the 12th house, all these point to some kind of release and isolation, either voluntarily or forced.

ELIZABETH—DAUGHTER OF HENRY VIII

The year is 1558 and Mary I of England is ill and childless. Princess Elizabeth, the popular heir to the throne, consults you about the possibilities for the coming year. See Chart 11.

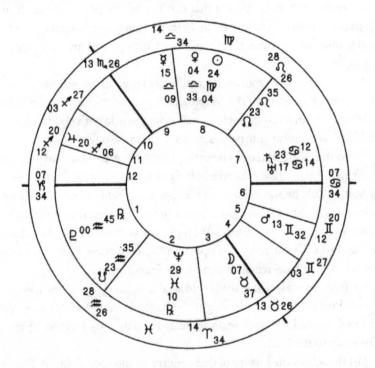

Chart 11. *Queen Elizabeth I, born September 7, 1533 O.S., 3:00 P.M. LMT, Greenwich, England, 51N29, 00W00. Data from* Profiles of Women. *Placidus houses.*

Historical Background

Elizabeth was one of two surviving daughters of Henry VIII. Her older sister Mary I, strongly devoted to Catholicism, married Philip II of Spain to re-enforce the return to Catholicism of the English people. Elizabeth, the heir to the throne, was connected to the Protestant cause and was thus considered a threat to Mary. As a result, Elizabeth's early life was precarious and indeed she suffered a period of imprisonment in the Tower of London at her older sister's hand.

Astrological Background

The Princess is in a Gibbous lunar phase that will become Full in May of 1559.

The progressed Moon is in Aries in the 2nd house. The progressed Sun is 19° Libra in the 9th house. It will not cross over the MC for approximately 24 years. However, progressed Venus will cross the MC in 1564.

The Princess is moving into a time of fulfillment with the Gibbous Lunar phase about to become a Full Moon. In addition, with her progressed planets, Mercury, Sun, and Venus, in the 9th house moving slowly toward the MC, you sense that this woman will achieve power somewhere in her life. The implication is that it will occur within the next few years with her Full Moon phase.

The Time Map

The Time Map (figure 34 on page 166) has been constructed for the period from May 1558 to August 1559.

In looking at the Time Map, the period of November 1558 to January 1559 stands out as a busy period for both transits and progressions. The major flavors of the period are first, the Uranus opposite Moon, and second, the Uranus conjunct the MC.

Considering transiting Uranus opposite Moon, which is the earlier transit of Uranus, you can surmise, as her astrologer, that Elizabeth is awaiting the decision or actions of another (opposition). The first row of the grid is the 7th house, 3rd house. She has already told you that her half sister Mary (3rd house) is ill. She is aware that she is the popular heir to the throne but there are other contenders (7th house, open enemies). In addition, she is the popular heir because of her ability to form an alliance. By being unmarried, if made Queen, England could choose a new alliance

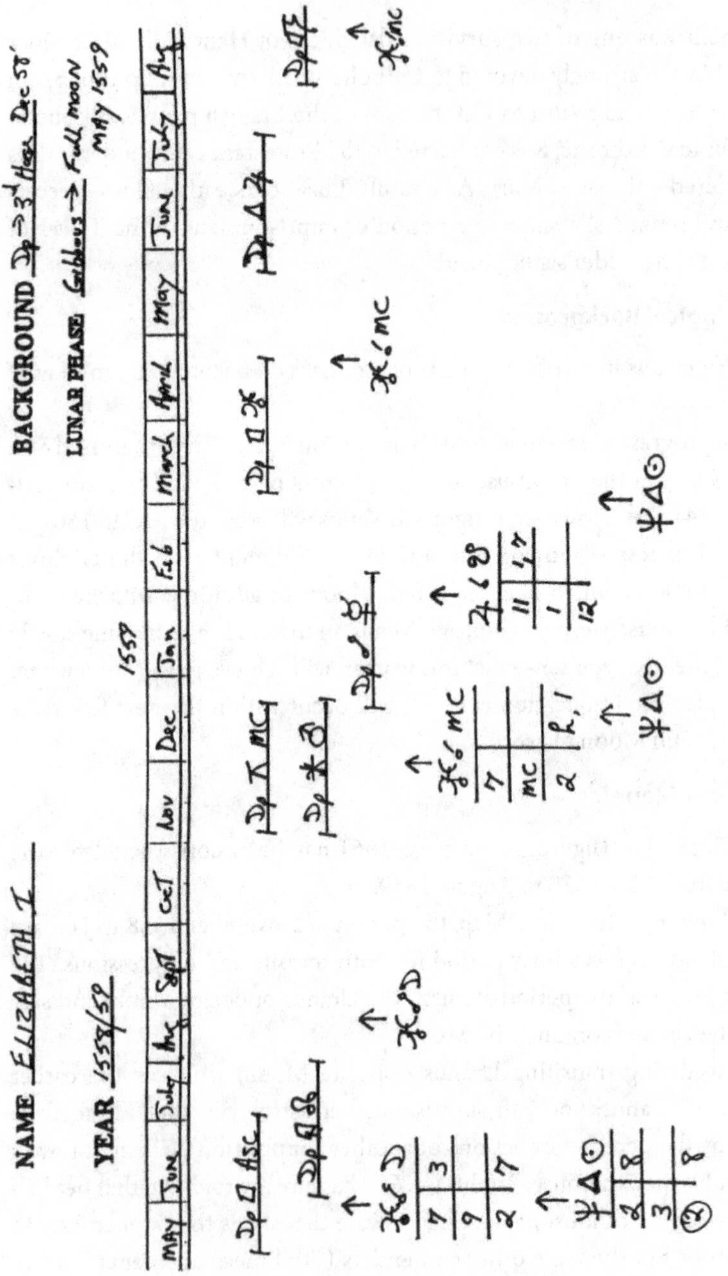

Figure 34. Time Map for Elizabeth I, May 1558–August 1559.

by the selection of a husband from one of the powers of Europe. This is far better than crowning an individual who already had alliances that might be diplomatically embarrassing.

The energy of Uranus-Moon is of sudden events involving a woman, a mother, or emotional reaction to situations suddenly changing. Since this is an opposition that always involves another person, it seems to be referring to Queen Mary. Elizabeth is virtually waiting for her sister's health situation to resolve itself. She recognizes that Mary's Spanish Catholic connections—9th house being in the middle row of the grid—could challenge her claim to the throne.

The outcome of the transit is the 2nd house and 7th house. These houses indicate that the young princess may be going to use her resources by forming or promising to form an alliance or a marriage.

This is a good transit for your client. If the end results were the 8th house or the 12th house, then the chances of coming to the throne would be slim. As it is, the transit is implying that the area of worry is the Spanish and/or Catholics (9th house) but by an alliance, she can win.

The transit of Uranus conjunct the MC shows sudden changes in social standing. The origin of this is the 7th house (her ability to form an alliance) and the outcome is the 2nd house, as well as Pluto in the 1st house. This is a very powerful outcome. Elizabeth will take and hold power, or come into power, or personally hold sway over a large number of people. Thus, the sudden change of social status increases her personal power or strength.

The transit of Neptune trine the Sun supports this last transit, as there is a fast (trine) change in personal charisma (Neptune-Sun) originating from the 8th house, which could be about the death of her sister. The 2nd house in the first row of this grid is indicating that Elizabeth has the resources that she needs—that is, that she becomes the heir to the throne. The 3rd house is logical in this transit as Mary is her half sister. The outcome of the transit is the 2nd and 8th house: increase of resources through an inheritance, death, or sudden change.

This could also be read as a loss of resources, or an ending to resources, but there is nothing else in the predictive work implying this type of event. This is an important point because, by seeing the general flavor of the predictive work, you can start to judge which way certain transits and progression should be read.

The transit of the Neptune trine Sun starts in May of 1558, returns in December, and returns again in February of 1559. Also in January of 1559, transiting Jupiter conjoins the South Node. Gaining her birthright, maybe?

To summarize: the strong Uranus transits are implying that Elizabeth's status is going to change. This, in addition to her lunar phase moving towards Full, indicates a climax or peak in Elizabeth's life. The trine from Neptune to the Sun also implies an easy passage to power, so the threat from the 9th house (Catholics and foreign powers), indicated by the Uranus-Moon transit, is more than likely not going to eventuate.

The progressions give the rest of the picture and, most importantly, give you a sense of the timing involved. In May of 1558, as the Uranus-Moon transit occurs for the second time, Elizabeth is feeling much easier about her ascension to the throne. For the progressed Moon square ascendant indicates that she is effectively taking action. With transiting Neptune starting to trine her natal Sun, things would be starting to move for the young princess. However, by June–July, she is going to become impatient as the progressed Moon sesquiquadrates the Node. This implies delays, waiting, and frustration with groups or associations. However, there is nothing that Elizabeth can do and she must bide her time.

By November, things are starting to move. Uranus to the MC shows a sudden change to her social status at the same time as the progressed Moon quincunxes the MC, which also implies a change of social status. There is also a sextile to the Mars: sudden opportunity occurring. Elizabeth can use this opportunity as there is no restraining influence on the map. On top of this, there are, in the December to January period, two more hits of Neptune trine Sun, as well as transiting Jupiter conjunct the South Node.

In scanning the rest of the Uranus to the MC transit, this is the only time that the progression supports the transit. In September of 1559, on the last hit of Uranus to the MC, there is a progression of Moon square Saturn, implying that she is being forced to take on additional responsibilities or to deal with matters regarding authority. But there is no other activity around this point and although this time period could be a contender for the ascension to the throne, a safer bet would be the earlier one.

Thus, it would be possible to suggest to Elizabeth that she should come into power at the end of the year and that, if her birth time of 3:00 P.M. was absolutely correct, it would be late November or early December, since Uranus transits tend to act very close to their exact dates.

As it was, Elizabeth ascended to the throne on November 17, 1558. As her astrologer, you would most likely have shaved 30 seconds or so from her birth time to bring the Uranus transit a little closer to November 17th.

Thus, as her progressed lunar phase became Full, she became Queen of England. With the progressed Venus conjunct her MC a few years later, it was not surprising that history records that for the first twelve years of her reign she worked very hard to establish herself as a loved Queen. It is also interesting that when her progressed lunar phase was Full for the second time in 1588, her Navy defeated the Spanish Armada and Elizabeth was held, by all of Europe, to be a great Queen.

KING EDWARD VIII OF GREAT BRITAIN

The date is February 1936. There is a new King on the throne, and you are the court astrologer who is trying to ascertain the results of the emotional involvement that the King has with a married American lady. (See Chart 12.)

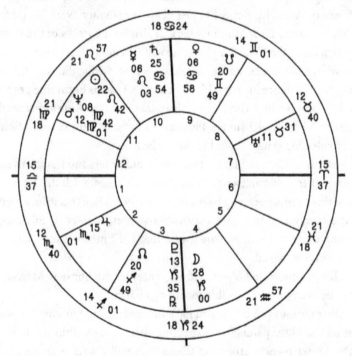

Chart 12. King Edward VIII, born June 23, 1894, 9:55 P.M. GMT, Richmond, Surrey, England, 54N24, 1W44. Data from American Book of Charts (latitude and longitude corrected). Placidus houses.

Background

The Prince of Wales, future King of England, has gone through a very difficult time with relationships, as transiting Pluto was conjunct his descendant from September 1933 to June 1935. During that time, he developed a relationship with a married American lady, Wallis Simpson. Their relationship/friendship seems to have survived the Pluto transit.

Edward is currently in a Crescent Lunar phase. The New Moon occurred in the 7th house during the course of the Pluto transit over the descendant.

All of this energy of the Pluto transit occurred while the chart was in a New Moon phase, the new seeds being planted, and thus the Crescent phase of emergence will probably bring these intense transforming relationship issues to the surface. However, as the astrologer, you are most likely to be anticipating a scandal about the King's relationship, which will then, hopefully, blow over.

To complicate these deep issues, which are just starting to emerge for the Prince of Wales, his father has just died—in January 1936. Tangled up with his 7th house New Moon issues will also be the issues of the British monarchy, for in the Crescent phase, he will ascend to the throne.

But what really concerns the astrologer is that, during the year, Edward is going to experience his natal Pluto quincunx Uranus becoming exact by secondary progression. This is the only quincunx in the King's chart and it is from the 9th to the 4th house. Pluto is ruling the 9th house natally while Uranus' rulership is intercepted in the 1st house.

The nature of Uranus-Pluto is to collapse old orders and traditions suddenly, and then construct a new order from the ashes. With the 1st house flavor of this natal aspect, you have always suspected that this Prince would alter the family tradition in a reasonably sudden way. With this aspect becoming exact in 1936, you are aware that the time for expressing this natal aspect has arrived.

The King's progressed Moon will also enter his 8th house in May, so he will not be averse to the possible incoming change.

Another curious point that you have noticed while preparing the work is that all the outer planets are aspecting themselves within the next 18 months. Outer planets aspecting themselves will always indicate cycles reaching different levels of climax. As an astrologer, you will be aware that great changes are in the wind.

Time Map

This is the Time Map (figure 35 on page 172) for the first year of the King's reign. In glancing at the map, to gain a broad overview, you can see that the progressions are running fairly constant from January right through to December. After December, there are no progressions for some months, so it would seem that the issues of this troublesome relationship will settle down by early 1937.

With regard to the timing of transits, there seems to be a similar story. The transits are difficult from February right through to December, and then as transiting Jupiter opposes his Sun, the transits seem to clear, once again indicating that the current issues will take until December and then will be completed. At times, just giving clients this type of timing information is enough data for them to make their decisions.

The transits are divided into two types: firstly, the cyclic transits of Neptune square Neptune and Pluto semisquare Pluto.*

Both of these transits indicate a time of redefinition. The Neptune transit refers to issues of integrity and the recognition of the creative and/or spiritual path that one desires. The Pluto transit is the reassessing of where to put deep emotional involvements via the lens of the semisquare.

The King will be doing some hard thinking for the first half of the year. He will be making decisions about what is the most important thing for his life. Will he decide to take the American lady as a mistress after a legal marriage to a suitable wife? His great uncle, William IV, had ten children by his mistress. Will he devote himself to the British monarchy? Will he devote himself to Wallis Simpson? These are the types of questions that Edward would be pondering under these big cyclic transits.

There is also the transit of Saturn quincunxing its natal position.

This is of further concern, for this is the release or ending of responsibilities. The houses indicated by the grid are also supporting change and stating that it is the King's own personal actions (1st house in middle row) that will bring about his change in responsibilities. The bottom row of this grid is most ominous: the 12th house and the ascendant. He takes himself into hiding or solitude. He withdraws.

---

* For current generations, Pluto will normally be squaring Pluto as Neptune squares Neptune. However, due to the irregular speed of Pluto, the generation to which the King belonged was experiencing the semisquare.

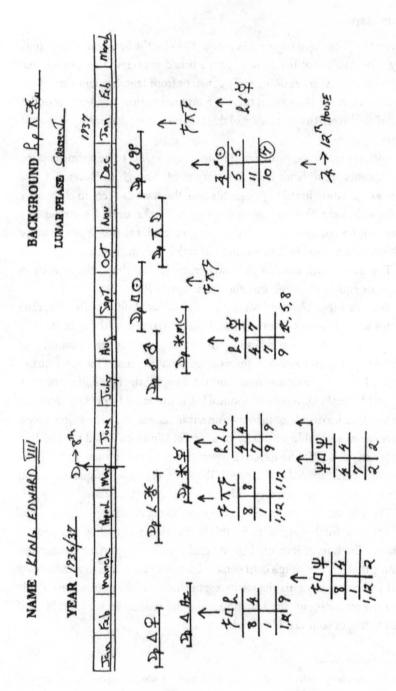

Figure 35. Time Map for Edward VIII, January 1936–March 1937.

Transiting Pluto is going to commence a conjunction with the natal Mercury in August. The Pluto to Mercury transit indicates that the King is going to become obsessed with an idea. Given the background Pluto-Uranus statement already mentioned, this idea could be very revolutionary. The transit starts in August, returns in January of 1937, and finishes later that year.

The top row of the transit grid contains the 4th and 7th houses, so this decision, or idea, is coming as a result of the family's attitude to his marriage partner, choice of marriage partner, or his marriage partner's opinions as to where they should live. Here is the relationship issue of the earlier New Moon phase in the 7th emerging under the Crescent phase. The middle row of the transit grid is the 7th house, so the action is all going to be focused onto the issue of relationships. The outcome or consequences of this transit are described by the bottom row of the grid: the 9th house (overseas, or study), the IC (home, family tradition), 5th house (love, children, creativity), 8th house (change, to make an end, to transform).

Is it possible that the king will take an obstinate attitude to a matter concerning a relationship, and is it this relationship issue that causes the revolution promised by the Pluto-Uranus natal quincunx?

The King has already started his reign in conflict with the Prime Minister over matters of court procedure—his support of the poor and starving during the miners' strike and his all-too-unhealthy interest (as far as the Prime Minister was concerned) in the new ideas of the Nazis, just starting to emerge from Germany. All signs of his Pluto-Uranus quincunx coming to the fore.

In looking at the individual progressions, we can see that by April he will be feeling restricted and blocked, with his freedom reduced. This will lead to frustrations that he can take no action to resolve (progressed Moon semisquare Uranus). It is in this period that the first touch of the Saturn quincunx Saturn occurs. He starts to feel/think that he has to let go of something. By May of 1936, there is an opportunity that he develops (progressed Moon in a Yin sextile to natal Mercury) that is supportive to his relationship with Wallis (Mercury in the 7th house). It is at this time that his Moon enters the 8th house.

In July, the King will be making a decision (progressed Moon opposition natal Mars in the 2nd house). This decision concerns ways of taking action with regard to his resources or changes in his priorities. As he makes, or ponders, these decisions, the Pluto transit to Mercury begins, and he starts to become very intense about an idea or concept. He sees these new ideas as an opportunity that drops into his lap (progressed Moon Yang sextile to his MC). During the month of September, the King will be forced to take action with regard to someone he loves or to some creative endeavor (progressed Moon square natal Sun in the 5th house). At the same time, the Saturn quincunx Saturn transit returns, signaling the change or release from responsibilities.

By late October or early November, the changes are showing in the progressions. He separates from something or someone with whom he is very emotionally close (progressed Moon quincunx natal Moon in the 1st house). This is the important period. The King will either let go of the relationship with Wallis and then become intensely involved with some form of radical transformation to the system of monarchy and its place in society, already indicated by the King's lack of concern for protocol. Or, he will decide in favor of the relationship and thus isolate himself from his family, a course of action indicated by the Saturn quincunx Saturn transit.

The final card is played in December, as the progressed Moon forms a conjunction to the South Node. The inherited family tradition is being emphasized here for better or for worse. The January period sees a winding down of the energy. Jupiter opposes his Sun as it enters his 12th house and the Saturn transit completes.

History provides us with the answers. However, the astrology also shows the information or events very clearly. Wallis Simpson received a divorce in late October of 1936, and within a few weeks the King had informed the Prime Minister that he was prepared to abdicate in order to marry Wallis (progressed Moon quincunx natal Moon). He signed the necessary papers, which put his abdication into effect from December 10, 1936. Could an astrologer have picked these events long before 1936? Since Edward was born, this period of revolution, most likely stemming from relationship issues, had been written in his chart. However, it would take the beginnings of the events to give the astrologer the clues as to the details of the transits and progressions.

And how would an astrologer advise the King? The King, with transiting Pluto conjunct his Mercury, would not want to listen to advice. He would either radically transform the English monarchy or radically transform the English expectations of himself. He probably made the better choice.

ELIZABETH BARRETT BROWNING

It is September 1844 and Elizabeth is a poet who has just started to develop a name for herself in literary circles. She is a bedridden invalid and, since her brother's accidental death, has developed a morbid fear of meeting anybody new. She is thirty-eight years old, unmarried, and jealously guarded by her despotic father. She has written to you asking you to do two years of predictive work for her. (See Chart 13.)

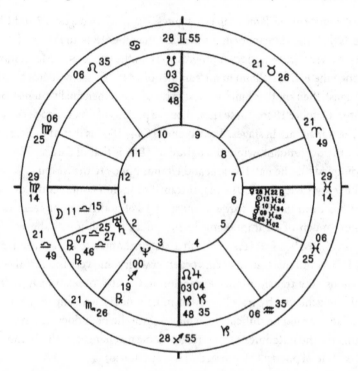

Chart 13. *Elizabeth Barrett Browning, born March 6, 1806, 7:00 P.M. LMT, Kelloe, Northumberland, UK, 56N20, 2W18. Data from* Profiles of Women. *Placidus houses.*

Astrological Background

Elizabeth is in a Third Quarter lunar phase that, by June of 1845, will become Balsamic. The Moon is currently moving through the 5th house and during the course of the next two years, will move over her stellium in Pisces.

The New Moon phase, which is still five years away in 1849, will occur in Aries in the 8th house. By late 1846 or early 1847, the progressed Moon will conjoin the descendant.

In addition, the natal aspect of Saturn conjunct Uranus will become exact by secondary progression in March of 1846, and this whole area of tension that this natal aspect represents is due to undergo a transformation.

The Time Map

The overview of the Time Map (see figures 36 and 37 on pages 177 and 178), reveals that there is activity in the area of December 1844 to February 1845. We see a very active period of progressions, as the progressed Moon moves through the Pisces stellium in the summer of 1845. The active dates are May to August, then another buildup in March 1846, and then finally August, September, October 1846. These should be the periods of events and activities.

The transits are in stages. The flavor of 1844–1845 is that of Jupiter conjunct the descendant, while the nature of 1846 is that of Saturn, Neptune sesquiquadrate the natal Moon, and Uranus opposite the Moon.

Let's start with 1845. The major transit of Jupiter conjunct the descendant has been in effect through most of 1844 and does not seem to be making much of an impression in the poet's life, although she has just recently had a book of verse published. Its final touch to the descendant is in January, and this transit occurs together with some very interesting progressions. The transit implies expansion in the area of relationships. This could be achieved by travel or by forming a new friendship. Such a new friendship would be difficult to achieve, since the poet does not mix with strangers. The outcomes of the transits indicate changes in the home and in her style of poetry (Neptune and the 3rd house).

The progressions for that period, however, are showing ample opportunities, created by her own actions, to encounter a new group of people (progressed Moon forming Yin sextiles to the natal Node and Jupiter). She will meet these new people in her home or where she feels safe, as the 4th house is emphasized by both the transit of Jupiter as well as the progressions being received by the natal Jupiter and Node. It would seem that the young reclusive poet, through her own actions, will be given a chance to broaden her horizons with relationships or friendships.

The advice to Elizabeth at this point is that, due to something that she is doing, she will encounter a new group of people or a person who will

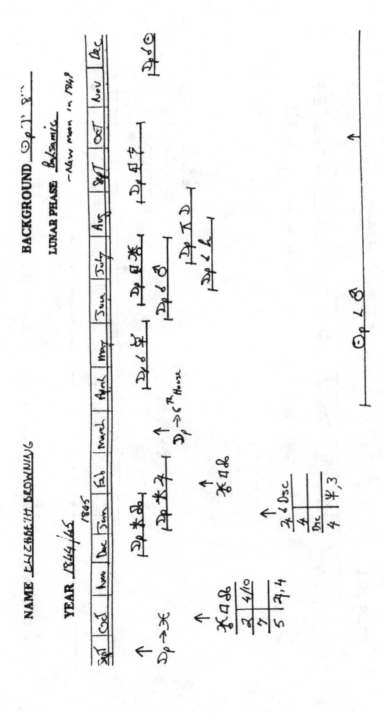

Figure 36. Time Map for Elizabeth Barrett Browning, September 1844–December 1845.

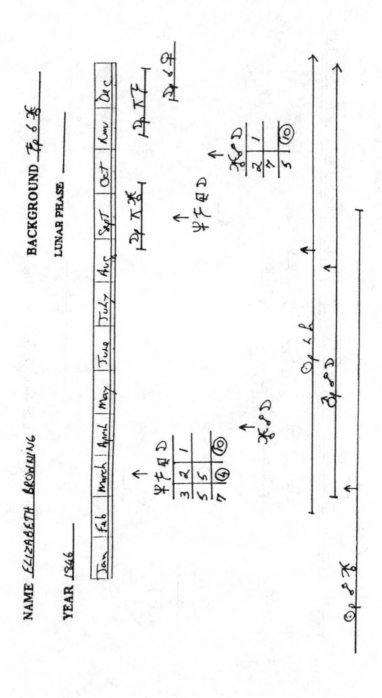

Figure 37. Time Map for Elizabeth Barrett Browning, January 1846–December 1846.

expand her world and to whom she will form some type of bond. It is up to her whether she encourages the opportunity or not, but since change seems to be imminent with the transit of 1846, you advise her to think seriously about being more open to meeting people in this period.

From this opportunity, which hopefully she takes up, she is led into a summer of feelings. When a Time Map shows large numbers of progressions without large transits, generally it is a time of great feeling but not necessarily action.

By April she is writing (progressed Moon conjunct Mercury), by June she is inspired (progressed Moon conjunct Mars), intense (progressed moon conjunct Pluto), frustrated at being an invalid (progressed Moon sesquiquadrate Uranus), and letting go of old emotional concepts or old friends (progressed Moon quincunx Moon). Actions are not being shown on the Time Map (figure 36 on page 177), but her feelings are definitely emphasized.

In September, the intensity of the summer is fading and the progressed Moon sesquiquadrate to Saturn implies frustration with commitments or with authority figures, such as her father. The November–December period is a return of the energy of the previous summer, with the Sun being part of the stellium receiving the progressions.

In January of 1845, Elizabeth had just published a new volume of work and, as a result of its release, received a telegram from a fellow poet, one Robert Browning. In this message he confessed that he loved her work and, although they had not met, he loved her. The 3rd house and Neptune in the bottom row of the Jupiter transit grid is one way to talk of love messages. Elizabeth was fascinated by the message and, heeding her astrologer's advice, opened up a channel of communication to Robert. They met for the first time in the summer of 1845 and fell in love. Needless to say, her father was totally against the relationship.

Moving into 1846, the stage is set for some interesting events. Elizabeth is now in the period of her life where she may successfully rebel against the things that have blocked her (see figure 37). The secondary progressed Saturn is coming to exact conjunction with natal Uranus. Two things have blocked her: first, being an invalid, and second, her father. This is a very important progression and will flavor the whole year.

If Elizabeth comes to you and says that she is in love, but her father is blocking the relationship, you look at the chart and see that progressed Saturn is making an exact conjunction to natal Uranus. In addition, she is about to have transiting Uranus opposite her natal Moon. Would you say that she is going to obey her father and give up her relationship? The chart indicates to the contrary.

The transits of Neptune and Saturn to the Moon are giving evidence of the frustration of keeping her relationship secret and the frustration of not being able to be with Robert. The grid clearly shows the area of activity, as the 5th house implies the lover, and the outcome of the grid is the 7th, 4th, and 10th house. Elizabeth will form a relationship, or vocation, and change residence while changing her social status in some way.

The transit of Uranus opposite her natal Moon serves to emphasize this hypothesis. Due to the influences of another (opposition), she wants to do something. This action or decision is a real break with tradition, coming from emotional tension (Uranus-Moon). The houses in the grid are of no surprise. The emphasis on the 7th (relationships or bonds), 5th (lovers, children, and creativity), and the 10th (how the world sees you) all fit into the same type of energy being described by the other transits to the Moon. The progressed Sun is also forming an opposition to the natal Uranus—breaking with traditions.

It is interesting to note that the creativity of the 5th house was also being expressed in what is considered to be her best period of poetry. *How do I love thee, let me count the ways* is now a household sentence in the English language.[*]

The climax seems to be in the months of August and September 1846. In that period, both transits return, while at the same time, two slow-moving progressions climax. In addition, the natal Saturn-Uranus conjunction receives a quincunx from the progressed Moon.

Breaking this period down into smaller segments, the long-acting Sun progression of the semisquare to Pluto indicates that Elizabeth felt particularly frustrated by her father's nonacceptance of her relationship. Pluto is not necessarily implying father, but it does imply a power struggle. In addition to this climax, a progression of Mars opposite Moon, which has been running for some years, is also reaching a point of transformation: the desire to take personal action—to accept the challenge.

These two together will give Elizabeth the strength to fight for what she wants. That she does fight is shown by the shorter progressions of the Moon,

---

[*] Elizabeth Barrett Browning, "Sonnets from the Portuguese," *A Book of Love Poetry* (Oxford University Press, 1974).

showing change or letting go—the quincunx—through which she utilizes the frustration she has felt all of her life with the Saturn-Uranus aspect.

As her astrologer, you advise her that this is a time of release. She is in a Balsamic Lunar phase: old patterns must be allowed to depart. This is a time to allow changes to come into her life. There will be power struggles about which she can do very little (progressed Sun semisquare Pluto), but she should work around these and make the decisions that bring in the changes. These changes bring a new type of lifestyle that represents a transformation of the blocked and checked life she has been leading.

Elizabeth was secretly married to Robert in September 1846. She was afraid to tell her father and still lived at home for a week after the wedding. She plucked up the courage, told her father she was married, and then left for Italy with Robert. With Robert, she learned to walk again, a physical ability that had been blocked since Saturn had opposed her Saturn-Uranus conjunction when she was fifteen years old. Her father never forgave her for leaving.

An astrologer may not have been able to foresee the marriage and relationship, but the emphasis on the 5th, 7th, and 10th houses all through these two years strongly stresses a physical or religious bond being formed in Elizabeth's life. This strong bond caused her to change her social status by marriage, and these changes also represented the transformation of the very difficult relationship that she had with her father.

A Quick Guide for Using Time Maps

1) Sort the transits that a natal chart is receiving and place on the Time Map only what you considered to be the important transits. (If you choose the wrong transits, at least you will be aware of your error and be able to rectify it next time.) Too much information on the Map is worse than not enough.

2) Use color for the different types of progressions. It's advisable to use the same colors for the progressed aspects as you do natally. I use blue for trines, sextiles, and some conjunctions; green for quincunx; and red for squares, semisquares, sesquiquadrate, and oppositions. This may seem a minor point, but it does make a big difference to the legibility of the Map.

3) Once you have entered the transits and the progressions, then add additional information of Solar Arc, eclipses, and so on if you desire.

4) Pay a great deal of attention to the background information, e.g., Lunar Phase; house position of progressed Sun and Moon; any progressed planet changing sign, house, direction of movement; any natal aspect becoming exact by progression. Consider this carefully; most of the answers will lie in this information, as in the case of Napoleon.

5) Once you have gained a "feel" for the future that you have mapped out or, if you prefer, obtained an overview of the landscape that your client is moving through, then, and only then, start looking at transits. Look for the periods of activity, look to see if transits are occurring at the same time as lunar progression. Define the "timing" of the events of the year. Look to see if there are common houses being emphasized and make a mental note of this.

6) Once you have the theme—given by emphasized houses and types of transit—and the type of terrain that your client is moving into—given by the background information—then start at the beginning of the Map and delineate each transit and progression in order. Take into account what you have just said about one particular transit or progression as you read the next one. The Cosmos has gone to a lot of trouble to lay down the transits and progression in that order, so take notice of it. The order is as much a part of the meaning as the progressions and transits themselves.

7) Get your client or a friend to write notes on the Time Map as things happen. Ask them to bring it back to you next time they see you so that you can "see" how you are doing.

8) Remember that the Cosmos has only the astrological alphabet to communicate the complex patterns of a human life. Put yourself in its (his, her) shoes. Try and write out one of your own years in astrological symbolism, bearing in mind that the geometry of the solar system has to be taken into account. This will give you an appreciation of the Cosmos's problems in communicating information with regards to a single human life.

Don't forget the golden rule (K.I.S.S.): less information is better than too much. Time Maps are like photographs—if you overexpose them, they become unreadable.

Chapter Five

Eclipses and the Saros Cycles

Into the world of predictive astrology, the solar and lunar eclipses fall like gentle rain or hailstones. The approach that most astrologers take to eclipses is to note the date and the zodiacal longitude of an eclipse and then compare it, using some form of aspecting, to a natal chart. Astrologers may also take note of the natal house in which the eclipse will occur. Armed with that information, astrologers then delineate the effect of the eclipse as some type of random, possibly, but not necessarily stressful, event occurring in a particular area of the client's life.

Eclipses

One of the difficulties when reckoning with eclipses is that they appear to be very inconsistent in their expression. We know the timing of the eclipse, and we also know that they tend to be stressful. They can also suddenly expose a hidden problem. What we are not sure of, however, is the nature of the stress. We can look at the natal chart and say that Venus is receiving the eclipse but whether it is good or bad news—even what sort of news it is—can be pure guesswork. The eclipses seem like wild cards stressing emotions or bringing chaotic events or, at times, apparently having little effect. They can sometimes be positive or very exciting and at other times herald a period of difficulties.

Using the metaphor of the lark and the eagle, to work with eclipses, astrologers have often depended upon a good lark, or intuition, to pick the essence of the eclipse.

HOUSE PLACEMENT OF ECLIPSES

One of the ways around this need for a super-lark is to abandon the attempt to predict the effect of any particular eclipse and take greater notice of the natal houses in which eclipses will occur over a given period of time. This is not necessarily the best approach, but it is one that puts the astrologer onto firmer ground.

The eclipses in any one year will occur in a house polarity, e.g., 1st/7th or 2nd/8th, etc. Having stressed a polarity for twelve to eighteen months, the eclipses move retrograde through the chart and will start to stress another set of houses. For example, if you have the 2nd/8th house axis stressed, then in the fullness of time, you will have the 1st/7th stressed, followed by the 12th/6th, and so on.

This stressing of a polarity of houses can be quite a valuable piece of information for the predictive astrologer. What it indicates is where in the person's life he or she will be dealing with unexpected events or, putting it another way, what kinds of issues will be causing the person some concern, whether in a positive or negative way. Astrologers have the problem of not being too sure of the type of energy involved, but now the area of the person's life that will be emphasized is known.

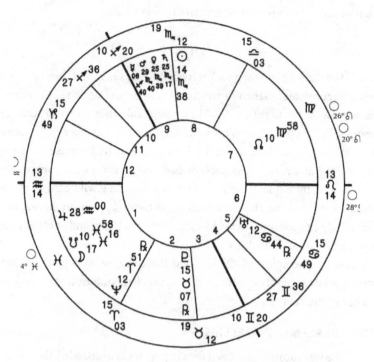

Chart 14. Natal chart of Marie Curie (q.v.) with eclipses for 1906.

Marie Curie, for example, experienced the sudden accidental death of her husband in April of 1906. In looking at Chart 14 (page 184), we can see that the eclipses for 1906 were all falling in her 1st/7th and 6th/12th houses. In other words, the eclipses were crossing over the ascendant/descendant axis of her chart. Her husband did not die on one of these eclipses, nor did any of the eclipses form any conjunctions or oppositions to her natal chart. So even though the eclipses did not aspect her chart in an obvious way, the houses indicate the area of concern for Marie in that period.

Similarly, we can look at Napoleon's chart (Chart 15) and, in March of 1814, when the General is supposedly going to see his astrologer, his astrologer would do well to note that the eclipses are about to move over his natal MC/IC axis, indicating changes and emphasis in his career and social status, as well as in his family or where he is living. This could have been read as wonderful—as an improvement in his position—or, as history states, losing all his power by being caught and exiled from France.

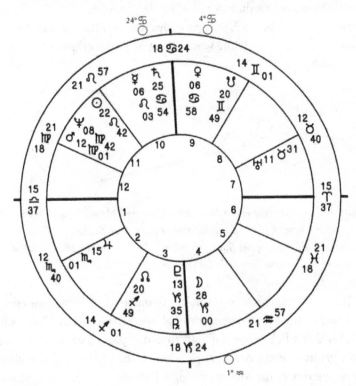

Chart 15. Natal chart of Napoleon I (q.v.) with eclipses for 1814 and 1815.

These are both fairly dramatic examples, and an astrologer should not jump to the conclusion that just because a client is having eclipses in the 1st/7th houses, his or her partner will be killed or, indeed, that the relationship may end. This house information must be read in conjunction with the predictive emphasis entailed in the transits and progressions.

But when do eclipses have big teeth, so to speak, and when are they mild? To start to answer this question, either we can be led back to needing a super-lark, or we can find ourselves needing a better eagle. So let's look at the eagle side of eclipses and examine the mechanics of the situation.

THE GEOMETRY OF ECLIPSES

When we were children, we learned that a solar eclipse is the passage of the Moon across the face of the Sun. Our Moon (as seen from the Earth) appears to be roughly the same size as the Sun, for which reason it has the potential to block out the Sun's light. A solar eclipse, if viewed from the right location on Earth, will cause the darkening of a day. See figure 38. Sometimes the Moon will only partially cross over the Sun and this results in a less dramatic effect. The whole effect of a solar eclipse lasts only for a few minutes.

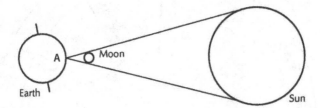

Figure 38. The solar eclipse is a New Moon (Sun and Moon conjunction) converting into a solar eclipse. An individual standing at point A on the Earth will see the Moon blocking out the view of the Sun. Any other individual in any other location on the Earth will not have the view of the Sun obscured.

The eclipse of the Moon is not as dramatic (to the modern eye) and is caused by the Moon passing through the Earth's shadow. The resulting effect is that a Full Moon will darken and appear to go through a whole series of phases in the course of a few hours. The Earth's shadow will sweep across the face of the Moon, causing a Full Moon to darken as shown in figure 39. Unlike solar eclipses, where you have to be in the correct location on the Earth to see the effect of the darkened Sun, the lunar eclipse is visible from all locations where the Moon has risen above the horizon. This means that you should be able to view the darkening of a Full Moon for about half of the total number of lunar eclipses.

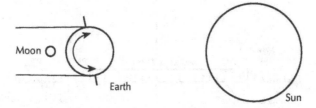

Figure 39. The lunar eclipse is a Full Moon (Sun opposite Moon) converted into a lunar eclipse. The Moon passes through the shadow of the Earth. Any individual standing on the dark side of the Earth (left side) will see the lunar eclipse.

This must have been an awesome sight to the ancients since, for many cultures, the Moon is the life giver, and to see the goddess darken must have been a very strong signal that all may not have been well. It is these lunar eclipses that probably started the earlier astronomers working on understanding eclipses, for they would have been lucky to see even one solar eclipse in a lifetime but would have experienced many lunar eclipses. A solar eclipse can occur only on a New Moon (i.e., a Sun-Moon conjunction), and lunar eclipses can occur only on the Full Moon (i.e., a Sun-Moon opposition). Obviously, the New and Full Moons occur every lunar month, but eclipses are far less frequent. The deciding factor that converts a New or Full Moon to an eclipse is the position of the Nodes.

The Nodes

Imagine two hoops at, say, 45° to each other and then imagine inserting one through the other. There will be two points where both hoops will meet. These two points are called nodes. One point is labeled the North Node and the other the South Node. Indeed, a node is a point where any two circles intersect.

The path of the Earth's orbit around the sun is defined as the ecliptic. We measure planets, or other bodies, as being above or below the ecliptic using celestial latitude. The Sun and the Earth are always at 0° of celestial latitude, and all other bodies in the solar system will have, at different times, north or south celestial latitude.

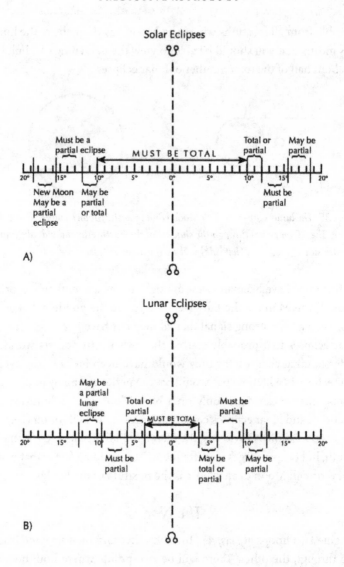

Figure 40. Line graphs showing the orb from the Moon's node where (A) solar
and (B) lunar eclipses can occur.

The points where the other orbiting bodies cross the ecliptic are the
nodes for that particular body. We can have nodes of Venus, Mars, Pluto,
and so on. Halley's Comet has nodes, as do the asteroids. Indeed any orbiting body in our solar system will cross the plane of ecliptic and therefore
have nodes.

The nodes that we plot into natal charts are the Moon's Nodes, that is, the points where the orbit of the Moon will cross the ecliptic. Whenever the Moon conjoins the North or South Node, then it is on the same plane as the Sun and Earth.

Although we have a New Moon and then a Full Moon every fourteen days and the transiting Moon conjoins one of the Nodes every fourteen days, to obtain an eclipse we must have the two events happening at the same time.

Eclipse Orbs for New or Full Moons

The New or Full Moons do not have to be exactly conjunct the North or South Node for an eclipse to occur. The following are the orbs for when a Full or New Moon will convert to an eclipse.

SOLAR ECLIPSES

A New Moon occurring within 18° 31' of the North or South Node can be a partial solar eclipse. Refer to figure 40. If it is within 15° 21' of either Node, then it must be a partial solar eclipse. If the New Moon is between 0° and 9° 55' of either Node, then it must be a total solar eclipse.

If the New Moon occurs between 9° 55' and 11° 15' of either Node, then the eclipse can either be total or partial.

LUNAR ECLIPSES

The orbs are much smaller. See figure 40. If a Full Moon occurs within 12° 15' of either Node, then a partial lunar eclipse can occur. If the Full Moon is within 9° 30' of either Node, there must be a partial lunar eclipse. If the Full Moon is within 0° to 3° 45' of either Node, then it must be a total lunar eclipse. If the Full Moon is within the orbs of 3° 45' to 6° 0' of either Node, the lunar eclipse can be either partial or total.

Frequency of Eclipses and Eclipse Seasons

How often will we get a New or Full Moon occurring within the orbs that we discussed in the previous section? Since the formula for an eclipse is a New or Full Moon conjunct the Nodal axis, then whenever the Sun approaches a conjunction to the Nodal axis, one, two, or three of the New and Full Moons in that period will be eclipses.

The Sun crosses over the Nodal axis twice a year, once over the North Node and six months later over the South Node. Thus, in any given year, there will be two eclipse "seasons" when the Sun moves within an 18° orb to the North or South Node. From that point, the Sun will take approximately 36 days to travel over the Nodal axis and then move a further 18° away from the Nodal axis. So the length of an eclipse season is about 36 days. Any New or Full Moon that occurs during those 36 days, within the orbs given above, will be an eclipse.

These eclipse seasons are not fixed, since the Nodal axis is transiting retrograde through the zodiac at the rate of about one and a half degrees per month. Thus, the eclipse seasons, although always six months apart, can occur in any month of the year, following the transiting node in its retrograde passage through the zodiac.

The eclipse seasons are sometimes noted by astrologers, who may consider the whole 36 days as simply a more chaotic or stressful time, without taking note of the actual placements and frequency of the eclipses within an individual season. When the Sun is in an eclipse season, the following scenarios can occur.

In the next group of figures, I have placed the Nodal axis at 0° Taurus-Scorpio. The circles on the figures show the eclipses.

In figure 41, if a New Moon (Sun and Moon conjunction) occurs at 21° Aries, then there will be a solar eclipse—the New Moon is only 9° away from the Nodal axis.

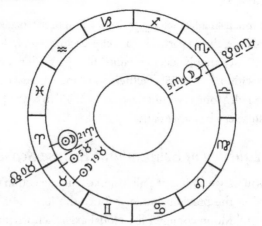

Figure 41. New Moon giving a solar eclipse followed by a lunar eclipse fourteen days later on the Full Moon.

A Full Moon will occur 14 days later. The Sun will have moved from 21° Aries to approximately 5° Taurus (14° further along). Thus the Full Moon (Sun-Moon opposition) will occur within a 5° orb of the Nodal axis, resulting in a lunar eclipse.

Fourteen days later, there will be another New Moon, and the Sun will have moved to approximately 19° of Taurus. This New Moon is just outside the orb for a solar eclipse. Thus, we will experience one solar Eclipse, followed two weeks later by a lunar Eclipse.

In figure 42, a lunar eclipse results from a Full Moon occurring at 21° Aries, only 9° from the Nodal axis.

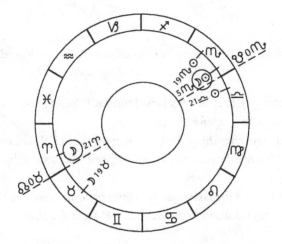

Figure 42. Full Moon giving a lunar eclipse followed by a solar eclipse 14 days later on the New Moon.

Fourteen days later, there will be a New Moon at 5° Scorpio (14° further along), which will result in a solar eclipse (only 5° from the Nodal axis).

The next Full Moon will occur fourteen days later at approximately 19° Taurus; it will have a 19° orb from the Nodal axis, which is far too wide for a lunar eclipse.

Thus we will experience one lunar eclipse followed fourteen days later by a solar eclipse.

In figure 43 (page 192), we have a Full Moon occurring at 17° Aries, too wide an orb for a lunar eclipse (13° from the Nodal axis).

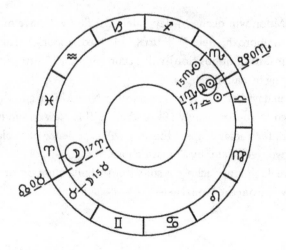

*Figure 43. Full Moon giving no lunar eclipse followed by a solar eclipse
14 days later on the New Moon.*

Fourteen days later, there is a New Moon at 1° Scorpio, only 1° from the
Nodal axis and, thus, a solar Eclipse.

Fourteen days after this, a Full Moon appears at 15° Taurus—too wide
an orb for a lunar eclipse. Thus, we will experience a solar eclipse with no
accompanying lunar eclipses.

Figure 44 shows the last possible eclipse pattern. There is a New Moon
at 12° Aries that results in a solar eclipse (18° from the Nodal axis).

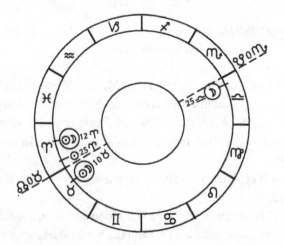

*Figure 44. New Moon giving a solar eclipse followed by a lunar eclipse 14 days later
on the Full Moon with another solar eclipse 14 days later on the next New Moon*

Fourteen days later, the Full Moon at 26° Libra results in a lunar eclipse (only 4° from the Nodal axis).

Fourteen days later, the New Moon appears at approximately 10° Taurus, still within orb for a solar eclipse. Thus, we will experience a solar eclipse followed two weeks later by a lunar eclipse, and then two weeks later again another solar eclipse.

Whichever example the cosmos is playing out, it is clear that if we have a solar eclipse then we may or may not have a lunar eclipse; however, if we have a lunar eclipse then we must have a solar eclipse.

The Saros Cycles

Astrologers have traditionally tended to view eclipses as wild cards whose occurrence can be predicted in timing but whose results vary dramatically from one eclipse to another. Yet, each eclipse does belong to a larger pattern. Each eclipse is a member of a family, and each family has characteristics.

These families or cycles have beginnings, middles, and ends and were first discovered by the Babylonians. Any one cycle will run for well over a thousand years, making the study of individual eclipses equivalent to sitting and watching a giant hardwood tree grow. The tree could be involved in some activity that, because our period of observation is so short compared to the life of the tree, would appear to be a random, unconnected event. However, if we sat there for a thousand years, the random event may well fall into an organized pattern—slowly unfolding over hundreds of years. Or better still, if we understand the nature of the tree, the species, and its characteristics, then the random event could make a lot more sense without the long wait. So what are these "trees"?

By 747 B.C. the Babylonians could accurately predict the timing of an eclipse and, indeed, by the 4th century B.C. had recognized that the eclipses occurred in series. These series were named Saros Series or Cycles by the Greek lexicographer Suidas in the 10th century A.D. (The word "saros" means repetition or to be repeated.)*

What was discovered by the Babylonians was that a lunar eclipse could occur only if there was a solar eclipse and that lunar eclipses may or may not occur within two weeks either side of a solar eclipse. Thus, the solar

---

* *Encyclopedia Britannica,* p. 902.

eclipse was the one to consider mathematically in terms of cycles, the lunar eclipses being mathematical side-shoots of the solar eclipses. This was a big step, since it was the lunar eclipses that were so obvious.

In addition, the solar eclipses were not isolated events. Each solar eclipse belonged to a series or cycle (later named the Saros Series). Each Saros Series produced a solar eclipse every 18 years plus 9 to 11 days (depending on the number of leap years occurring in the 18-year span). Also, each Saros Series would produce a succession of eclipses, each one being a half to a full degree closer to, or further from, the nodal axis.

Each Series starts as a tiny partial eclipse at either the North or South Pole. This eclipse has an orb of between 15° and 18° in front of the nodal axis. During the course of the life span of a Series, each eclipse of the Series will occur closer to the nodal axis, slowly reducing the orb between the eclipse and the axis. As this slow closing of the orb occurs over hundreds of years, the eclipses within a given Series move from being partial to total as they get to within 9° to 11° of the Nodal axis.

After approximately 650 years, the eclipses of the Series will occur conjunct the nodal axis and then continue on their journey, drawing away from the nodal axis until the eclipses in the Series become once again partial at 9° to 11° from the axis.

The end of the cycle is when the Series finally produces a tiny partial eclipse approximately 18° behind the nodal axis. This eclipse will occur on the opposite Pole to where the Series started. If the Saros Series was born, or commenced, with a tiny partial eclipse at the North Pole, then it will finish some 1,300 years later as a tiny partial eclipse on the South Pole.

To figure all this out by the 4th century B.C. when the Earth was thought to be flat (and not even a slide rule or calculator in sight) shows us the caliber of those early astrologers/astronomers.

In figure 45 (page 195), a Saros Series of eclipses starts at the North Pole, let us say, in the year A.D. 1000. This Series would then have an eclipse every 18 years plus a few days. Each eclipse will move across the face of the Earth by 120° of longitude from the previous one, and each eclipse will move a little further south. By 1650, the Saros Series will be halfway through its life span and be producing eclipses around the equatorial region of the globe. As the Series ages, it draws closer to the South Pole and eventually, by approximately the year 2300, the Series will produce a tiny partial eclipse at the South Pole, which will be its last eclipse.

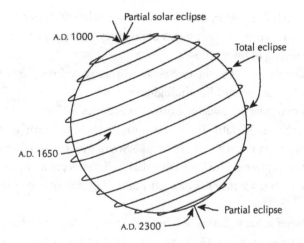

Figure 45. The Saros Cycle moving from the North to the South Pole.

As any one particular Saros Series is running from a Pole, as in the example, then imagine another 19 to 21 Series also running from the same Pole, all at different stages of their lives: as the Saros Series in figure 45 starts, there could be another halfway through its cycle, others started only several hundred years earlier, and still other Series nearly finishing.

Now, duplicate the situation by adding another 19 to 21 Saros Series running at the same time from the South Pole. At any given period there are about 42 Saros Series active, half of them running from the North to South Pole and the other half running from the South to North Pole. All these Series are, as it were, washing over the globe.

As stated earlier, in any given year there are two eclipse seasons, one season at the North Node and the other at the South Node. The Saros Series that are chasing, overtaking, and then pulling away from the South Node originate at the South Pole and are called Saros Series South. The series active around the North Node originate at the North Pole and are called Saros Series North. Therefore, in any one year, we have an eclipse from a North Series and an eclipse from a South Series.

To help distinguish the 19 to 21 Series that originate from the same Pole, each is allocated a number. These numbers are from 1 to 19 and are allocated not by order of birth but by actual years in which the Saros Series will produce an eclipse. For example, the system labels two Saros series as Saros Series 1 South and Saros Series 1 North because they will both be producing eclipses within six months of each other. It does not matter if the two Series are at different stages of their development; what is important is the timing of their eclipses.

For example, in 1965, the two solar eclipses were from Saros Series 3 North and Saros Series 3 South. Eighteen years further on in 1983, there were also two solar eclipses: one from Saros Series 3 North and the other from Saros Series 3 South. These two Saros Series were "born" at different times, 3 North in the year A.D. 991 and 3 South in A.D. 1208, but because their 18-year patterns coincide so that their eclipses occur in the same year, or always within six months of each other, they are allocated the same number.

Sometimes a Saros Series will be ending as another is starting. In the example shown in figure 44 (page 192), we had two solar eclipses with a lunar eclipse in between. The second solar eclipse, being in front of the Node, would belong to a Saros Series that is just starting, maybe only fifty years old. However, the first solar eclipse, being behind the Node, would belong to a Saros Series that had been running for well over a thousand years and was about to finish. When this occurs, the two Saros Series responsible for the solar eclipses are both given the same number. In other words, as a Series finishes, another will be starting and taking its place. There will be an overlapping period of a hundred years or so when the two Saros Series are both producing eclipses within a month of each other. At the moment, there are two Saros Series 9 North producing solar eclipses in one eclipse season. However, one Series would be called Old and the other New. Thus, we have names like Saros Series 9 New North and in the same year Saros Series 9 Old North. Once the transition has occurred between the incoming and the outgoing, then the word *New* is dropped from the name.

The Nature of an Individual Series

Each Saros Series commences at a precise point in time on either the North or South Pole. Thus it has a birth chart. Each Saros Series also contains 71 to 73 "events," or Solar eclipses. Each Solar eclipse and its resulting Lunar eclipse will express the characteristics of the Saros Series to which it belongs.

Imagine the whole concept as a forest. Each Saros Series is a tree in the forest, and each individual eclipse is a leaf from a particular tree.

So we have a forest of trees, each tree at a different stage of development, half the forest originating from the South Pole and growing towards the North Pole, and the other half originating from the North Pole and growing towards the South Pole.

Given that this is a forest of related eclipses, to try and work with them as individual events is like picking up a handful of leaves from our forest floor and trying to work out the history of the tree without knowing that the leaves in your hand belong to more than one tree. At the same time, examining the effects of an eclipse one year and then applying that knowledge to an eclipse happening in the following year is like working with a maple leaf to give you knowledge of a pine tree. No wonder it's super-lark country.

As a Series moves through a chart, it will produce an eclipse very similar in expression every 18 years. You may experience one of these eclipses directly affecting your chart. As an astrologer, you would label that effect as belonging to the eclipse; however, it is very unlikely that you will ever encounter that particular Saros Series again. It will leapfrog a further 10° along in your horoscope and pop up at that new point 18 years later. There is a good chance that your chart does not have any sensitive points in this new location. Meanwhile, you may have experienced other eclipses belonging to a different Saros Series, and you wonder why the effect is not the same.

For each Saros Series has characteristics described by the planetary patterns at its "birth," and each member of a Series expresses those individual characteristics through its eclipses.

It is no wonder that eclipses, looked at as individual units, appear random, chaotic, and as a bit of a joker in the pack. In other words, will what drops on your client's head be a maple leaf or a pine cone? However, if we can sort the leaves and know each tree in the forest, then we stand a much better chance of being accurate in terms of predicting outcomes.

TRANSITING SAROS SERIES

The concept of the transiting Saros Series needs to be considered before we look at the individual Saros Series.

During the course of a Series' life, as it mathematically dances with the Nodal axis, each eclipse member will manifest every 18 years plus 9 to 11 days, at approximately 10° farther along in zodiacal longitude.

Thus a Series can transit a chart. However, this transiting is not achieved in the normal manner for, as figure 46 shows, not every degree of the zodiac is touched. The Series leapfrogs in hops of 10° at a time. It thus misses whole patches of degrees, or sensitive chart points, but lands on others. A bit like playing Monopoly and jumping over Park Place with two hotels only to find yourself sitting on Boardwalk.

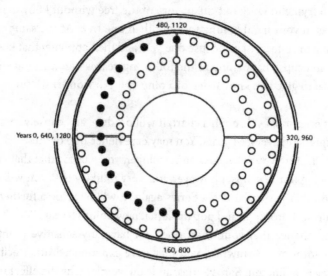

Figure 46. A Saros Series transiting a chart.

For example, in figure 46, the dark circles are total solar eclipses, while the light circles are partial solar eclipses. A Saros Series starts on the supposed ascendant of the hypothetical chart. Each eclipse in the series occurs about 10° farther along in the zodiac. After 160 years, the eclipses will be around the IC, still producing partial eclipses. By the time the series is 360 years old, it will be producing partial eclipses around the descendant of the chart. When it is 480 years old, the eclipses start to be total and would be occurring around the MC of the chart. Halfway through its life, after 640 years, it will be producing total eclipses around the same zodiacal degree from which it started. The Saros Series keeps producing eclipses every 18 years plus a few days, each eclipse taking that leap of about 10° forward through the zodiac. After 800 years, the series will be again producing eclipses around the IC of our pretend chart. Eventually, the Series ends as a partial eclipse, after about 1,280 years, in approximately the same zodiac position at which it started.

As a Saros Series leapfrogs through a chart with its orbital period of approximately 640 years, halfway through its life, its eclipses are total and one of them will be right on the Nodal axis. This midpoint-of-the-Series eclipse will be as total as an eclipse can get and can be considered the most powerful of the whole Series. This particular eclipse, as figure 46 on page 198 shows, will occur approximately at the same zodiacal longitude degree where the Series was born. Another 640 years later, the cycle will be ending—also at approximately the same zodiacal longitude as its birth. Thus, any given Saros Series is born, matures, and dies all around the same zodiacal degree.

One other point concerning the transiting Saros Series is that they have a similar "period" to the supposed planet, Transpluto, whose hypothetical orbital period is 675 years. By coincidence, one particular Saros Series, Saros Series 19 North, is occurring in the same position in the zodiac as this presumptive planet; and, with their periods being very similar, they are also moving forward in a transiting conjunction. This Saros Series was also at its strongest, having its "midpoint eclipses," at the time Transpluto was introduced. This could mean one of two things: the meaning of Transpluto may be affected by this running conjunction with Saros Series 19 North, or Transpluto is actually the transiting Saros Series. Food for thought and food for research.

Working with Saros Series

At this point there are two directions in which an astrologer can travel.

We can explore an individual Saros Series by using long-lived charts, that is to say the charts of countries. Or we can take a theme, like the development of science, art, language, etc., and explore the theme's development through history against the backdrop of Saros Series. There is strong evidence to support the idea that the development of human thought in a particular field is linked to an individual Saros Series.

For example, the year that Gutenberg invented the printing press (1452), the year that Copernicus published his theory that the Sun was the center of the Solar System (1543), the year that Newton published his Laws of Physics (1687), the year that Einstein wrote his "Theory of Relativity" (1905) were all years that Saros Series 14, North and South, were producing eclipses. Whether it is Saros Series 14 North or Saros Series 14 South that is responsible would require further research. However, the years of 1452, 1543, 1687, and 1905 are all connected astrologically and astronomically to one Saros Series and, as we can see, the significant historical theme of these years is that of publications that changed the world.

This first point, although a mouth-watering potential for astrological research, is not within the scope of this book.

The other direction you can take is to examine the individual birth data of the Saros Series that is producing a current eclipse and then apply this knowledge to the delineation of that eclipse in your predictive work.

This last option is the focus that this book takes, and thus in Appendix 6 are the "birth" details of every current Saros Series with a suggested delineation of what that series is about. Also in this appendix is a listing of the years that each Saros Series is active. Armed with this information, you can look up the Saros Series that a particular eclipse belongs to and then look up the data about that particular Saros Series and apply that information to the natal chart that you are working on.

Eclipses do not have to be wild cards. By knowing the trees, we can talk sensibly about the leaves.

By building a better eagle, we now no longer need a super-lark.

SUMMARY OF THE SAROS CYCLE

There are two eclipse seasons every year, one on the South Node and the other on the North Node.

◊ Lunar eclipses are by-products of the geometry of any given solar eclipse.

◊ A solar eclipse is not an isolated incident but rather a member of a particular Saros Series.

◊ A Saros Series will have a birth, or first eclipse, at either the North or South Pole, and once a Series starts, it will travel at a regular rate to the opposite Pole.

◊ Any given Saros Series will produce an eclipse every 18 years and 9 to 11 days.

◊ The total number of eclipses in one Series is between 70 and 72.

◊ Each Saros Series will take approximately 1,280 years to complete.

◊   Each Saros Series is named for the Pole of origin and numbered from 1 to 19 based on years of occurrence.

◊   Each Saros Series will produce an eclipse approximately 10° further along in the zodiac every 18 years.

◊   A given Saros Series transits a chart in roughly 650 years.

Practical Questions about Eclipses

Having untangled the meaning of an individual eclipse, there is a set of questions that any thinking astrologer will then pose. The answers to these questions are important, for they will significantly affect the overall use of eclipses in your predictive work. Therefore, be aware of the answers that you formulate. If you find that you are off the mark, check to see if you need to change one of your answers to correct the situation. Remember, this continuous, productive feedback is the essential ingredient in predictive work.

Is there a difference in the effect of a solar eclipse and a lunar eclipse? The difference between the solar and lunar eclipse, as a rule of thumb, seems to be that solar eclipses are more external, dealing with events around the person, and lunar eclipses are more emotional and internal—pondering the problems of life, and so on. However, sometimes this pondering can lead to external events generated by the actions of the individual. So, in summary, we can hypothesize that the solar eclipse will bring in events that we have not consciously precipitated, and the lunar eclipses will be associated with events brought about by our own thoughts or feelings.

What aspects should be used in relating an eclipse to a natal chart? Every astrologer will probably have a different answer to this question. Since eclipses are interjections in one's life, I feel it is best to use only major aspects. In fact, in my own work, I tend to look only for conjunctions and oppositions. The use of the square is optional, and I tend to use it if the eclipse is squaring a natal luminary.

What orbs should be used for those preferred aspects? Using orbs of, at the most, 2° for oppositions and up to 2.5° for conjunctions seems to yield the best results. If you choose to use the square, I would suggest an orb of only 1°.

How long will the effect of the eclipse last? This is a particularly interesting question and perhaps brings us to the point of pondering a more philosophical question:

What purpose do eclipses serve in astrology? If we decide that eclipses have very little purpose and they tend to be like a fly in one's soup—halting the proceedings but having very few major consequences—then the effect of the eclipse could be considered to last for just the period of the eclipse season. If, on the other hand, our definition of the purpose of eclipses is that they have a profound effect on the person's life, then although the tension may last for only a few weeks, the effect may be considered to last a lifetime.

Let us imagine eclipses like spotlights shining on the pathway of your life. These lights are not on all of the time but they switch on, catching you in mid-action, so to speak. As this spotlight shines, it will illuminate an area of your life. Whatever has been pushed to one side or shoved under the carpet will become obvious. This bringing to the surface of hidden problems can be dramatic and emotional. However, it is an opportunity to become aware of issues that may need some work. You can, of course, choose not to work on the problems that have come to the surface; you could choose to blame it all on someone else, and so on. But, this may not lead to a healthy future. If you do choose to accept the challenge offered by the events of the eclipse, then although it may be a hard struggle—or possibly just an easy ride, depending on the Saros Series involved—the effect of the eclipse could be very long-term. It can change your life.

Another way of looking at eclipses is to think of them as earthquakes. Earthquakes are the movements of Mother Earth as She settles Herself. If She hasn't moved for a long time, then She needs to do quite a lot of flexing very quickly, with possibly disastrous results to all concerned. However, if She shuffles along a little at a time, then it is much easier for everyone. If we shuffle, as the eclipses happen in our charts, making the necessary changes that are being spotlighted by the eclipse, then we are keeping our life in balance—changing on our feet, so to speak. So, although the tension of an eclipse may last only for the length of the eclipse season, the effect can be profound. You are being allowed to see the issues in your life that are holding you back, or hindering the fulfillment of your chosen destiny or (dare I say) your fate. Your decisions about how you deal with those issues will have major consequences.

A Case Study of Eclipses

A client (Chart 16) is coming to see you at the beginning of 1979 and, apart from setting up her transits and progressions for the year, you note that the following eclipses are approaching:

February 26th, solar eclipse 7° Pisces S.S. 17 South; March 13th, lunar eclipse 4° Libra;

August 22nd, solar eclipse 29° Leo S.S. 18 North; September 6th, lunar eclipse 13° Pisces.

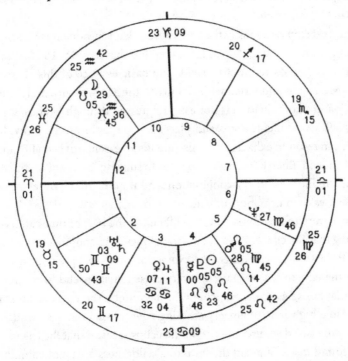

Chart 16. Client chart for case study of eclipses. Data withheld for confidentiality.

The only eclipse directly affecting a natal point or planet is the solar eclipse at 29° Leo in August. This is forming an opposition to the natal Moon in the 11th house.

In addition, the eclipses for the year are emphasizing the 5th/11th houses, so there will be issues about friends and lovers, children, and other 5th/11th house issues.

The solar eclipse directly affecting the 11th house Moon suggests that there will be events concerning a female friend or a friend toward whom the client feels very nurturing. This friend may even be connected to the household or be "family" in some way, as the Moon is ruling the 4th house in the client's chart.

In checking for other times that the natal Moon has received an eclipse, we can look up both 29° Leo and 29° Aquarius (plus or minus a degree) in Appendix 6. This is an important step because if there has been previous eclipse activity on the Moon (although this would belong to other Saros Series), we could at least start to judge, by the client's history, how his or her natal Moon reacts to eclipses.

The next step is to look at the Saros Series that is producing this eclipse. Once again referring to Appendix 6, you find that it is S.S. 18 North and that this Series started in A.D. 1060. The basic essence of this chart is a Pluto-Mercury conjunction with Uranus on the Mars/Saturn midpoint. A Mars/Saturn combination is not easy. Expressed through Uranus, it portends sudden, difficult times and places a large drain on the individual, which can result in exhaustion. It also entails an essence of brutality about it and, indeed, Ebertin even goes so far as to suggest, "a case of death." Add to this the Pluto-Mercury conjunction, and it points to an obsessiveness about news or information, or engenders intense worry.

The nature of this Saros Series is difficult at the best of times and, considering that the client is also having transiting Pluto conjunct her descendant, the astrologer can expect the expression of this eclipse to be heavy.

As the eclipse season started, a very close female friend, who lived in the same house as the client, could not be found. The client spent some weeks in a high state of anxiety awaiting news of the missing friend. The news came two days after the end of the eclipse season that the friend had been found dead. She had driven into a wilderness area and committed suicide. S.S. 18 North is a very difficult Saros Series.

The following year, 1980, for the same client, the eclipses were as follows:

February 16th, solar eclipse 27° Aquarius S.S. 18 South; March 1st, lunar eclipse 11° Virgo;

August 10th, solar eclipse 18° Leo S.S. 19 North; July 27th, lunar eclipse 5° Aquarius.

Two of these eclipses are affecting the chart. The solar eclipse in February is just in orb to form a conjunction with the natal Moon. The lunar eclipse in July will be opposing her natal Sun-Pluto conjunction.

The eclipses of 1980 are now starting to emphasize her 4th/10th houses, so the background issues of the year relate to home, family and career, social status, and so on.

Now, any astrologer working with this client would be concerned about another solar eclipse affecting the natal Moon, given the result of the last eclipse. However, this eclipse belongs to a different Saros Series, so it will have a totally different expression.

In looking up S.S. 18 South, this picture is described by a Venus-Jupiter quincunx with the Node sitting on the midpoint of the New Moon, Neptune, and the Venus/Saturn midpoint. This whole Saros Series is about partings and separations. Although upsetting, they express Venus-Jupiter flavor, which suggests that they are occurring for a positive reason.

At the time of the eclipse, 1979, the client was in a state of depression concerning the death of her friend. A female friend who lived in another city suggested that the client visit her for a vacation. At the end of the eclipse season, the client went on the vacation and, while there, met and fell in love with someone in the healing profession. She decided to move to this new city. This caused her some distress, since she would be parting from a lot of good friends.

The lunar eclipse of late July, opposing her Sun-Pluto conjunction, belongs to S.S. 19 North.

This Series concerns Neptune conjunct the South Node and a Venus-Jupiter-Saturn T-square with Saturn at the apex. Neptune on the South Node is focusing energy onto old issues, while the T-Square with Saturn at its apex denotes realism, being practical, and putting things into action.

In late July, the client, involved in a new relationship and living in another city, was still marking time, not working. She was still recovering from the events of 1979. By early August, she returned to where she had once lived to see old friends. She realized that her life was no longer in that city. On returning to her new home, she decided to start training for a new career and to get on with her life.

The above case study is a simple example of how the different eclipses will express different energies. I have not included the transits and progressions, but these would, of course, be very necessary to reveal the overall picture.

So now we have a better eagle, and our lark does not have to work so hard.

Born on an Eclipse

In 1982, the world was atwitter with the birth of a future king of England. The first child of Prince Charles had been born. The date was June 21, 1982. Astrologers knitted their brows because, also on that day, a solar eclipse occurred. Prince William, the heir to the British throne, was born with the Sun in his natal chart conjunct a solar eclipse. See Chart 17. Being born on a solar eclipse is not unusual, since these eclipses happen at least twice a year, but having a future king with such a natal event brought eclipses to greater astrological attention.

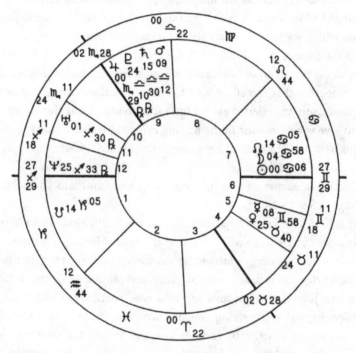

Chart 17. Prince William, heir to the throne of Great Britain, June 21, 1982, 9:03 P.M. BST, London, England, 51N31, 0W10. Data from Astro-Data 111. Placidus houses.

If you are born on a solar or lunar eclipse, your life is going to encapsulate that particular Saros Series that produced the eclipse at your birth.

Thus, you are deeply connected to that Saros Series, and you will act as a vehicle for the Series' expression.

Prince William was born into Saros Series 2 Old North. We know that, given his social position, he is not fated to have an ordinary life and that events in his life are now, and ever will be, intimately bound to the history of Britain. If there is a drama in his life, particularly in adulthood, then there is a good chance that there will be some drama in the monarchy.

Saros Series 2 Old North is finishing. It is in its last stages and just a few more tiny partial eclipses around the South Pole are yet to occur. It started its life in A.D. 792 and will end in July 2036, when the Prince is fifty-four years old.

The Series (as given in Appendix 6) is one of separation or ending of unions. Issues of separation and parting must be reckoned with for those born with this Saros Series prominent. In fact, lives touched by this Series often symbolize schism, rift, or disunion. Life's challenges will highlight the ability to act quickly, allowing old structures to crumble while learning how to create new forms from the collapse of the old ones.

Thus for Prince William, a future King of England, to be part of this Series is to presuppose that he may well be the last British monarch in the current style. There could be a sudden collapse of the monarch's role in the community while William is king. He would then find himself faced with the choice of either adapting very quickly or being swept away with the old structure.

This presages the end of an era. The years around 2036 are the most likely for these events to manifest. To add extra weight to this theory, this Series started in A.D. 792 at about the beginning of the tradition of the monarchy. The first recognized King of England who could truly claim that title was the Anglo Saxon, Ecgberht. He came to power in A.D. 802.

WHEN IS A PERSON BORN UNDER AN ECLIPSE?

This is a tricky point as so little work has been done on this subject. One would like to think that, once the Sun, Moon, Earth, and Nodes were within the orbs given for the formation of Solar and Lunar eclipses, then the person is born on an eclipse. Like any aspecting, the closer the birth is to the actual eclipse, the stronger the eclipse's effect should be felt in the natal chart.

However, rarely are rules in astrology so cut and dried. A good example of this is Hsuan-T'ung P'u-i, better known as the last Emperor of China. He was born on February 7, 1906, technically "out of orb" of the Lunar eclipse occurring on February 9th, 1906. This Lunar eclipse belonged to Saros Series 16 South, whose major aspecting was Neptune on the New Moon/Node midpoint, while Mars was on the midpoint of Neptune and Uranus.

Living an ineffectual life as an abdicated Emperor and a prisoner in his own palace, existing in a fantasy of splendor that was no longer viable, is very much the essence of the Neptune-Node-New Moon combination. Going from that point of illusion and wasted energy, P'u-i was deceived into being a puppet emperor for the Japanese in Manchuria—Mars/Neptune/Uranus. He eventually lost all of his illusory power and became an ordinary citizen of the Republic of China. This is almost a textbook delineation of Saros Series 16 South.

Chapter Six

Older Systems

From time to time, we encounter a client or friend whose natal chart does not respond to transits, or possibly even to progressions. This can be baffling, as well as a blow to the astrologer's confidence. This failure happens to a very small percentage of the community—about 5 percent or five of every 100 charts. At least this is the case for what I define as the community; your community may be different and the group may not seem so small or so large.

You discover this small group of people when your eagle totally and utterly fails you. Take, for example, the client who has had transiting Pluto conjunct Venus (Venus will be at that degree regardless of the birth time) and there is no manifestation of this transit, whether in dreams, with acquaintances and friends, or in his or her personal life. The client does not change in any way and thinks that you're probably crazy because you spent so long discussing the possible expression of the forthcoming transit.

Or, you may discover the opposite case, which can be even more rattling, of the client in whose chart the transits and progressions show a fairly normal year with no transiting outer planets forming significant aspects and no major progressions occurring, yet who experiences the world falling apart. Once again, the eagle has let you down rather badly.

With such clients, you are left with no alternative but to accept that what works for others—transits and progressions—does not work for them. This is after you have eliminated the possibility of a failed lark and you have checked and rechecked your work. Therefore, a totally different eagle is required for what appears to be a totally different astrological group. So let's look at some other systems of predictive astrology.

Predictive Systems

MUNDANE ASTROLOGY

There are three major systems of predictive astrology. The first system, Mundane astrology, does not involve individual charts. It is based on Ingresses, Eclipses, Lunations, and transiting planetary aspects. This astrology is for the masses or for countries. It rules over all the events that are "in the lap of the gods"—earthquakes, global disasters, weather patterns, and so on.

The modern-day astrologer—very much like the astrologers of old—makes a note, for example, of a forthcoming planetary configuration and produces predictive work. No other input is required. The beginnings of this system are lost in antiquity, for it was the first type of astrology. The shaman of the tribe would note the movement of Mars next to a Full Moon or the conjunction of Saturn to Venus, and so on, and make predictions for the whole tribe based on this data.

Our ancestors' relationship to the heavens, or to the gods, or to fate was very one-sided. They saw themselves at the whim of the gods; at no time did they feel that they had any influence or rights (with regard to the gods). This is the time of sacrifices, the time of the hunter-gatherer, when we considered ourselves the lowest of the low and would grovel at the feet of the gods for a little mercy. Here there was no court of appeal—no complaint department.

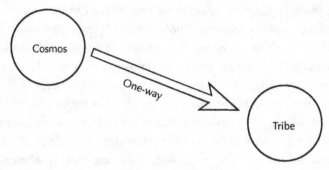

Figure 47. Mundane astrology.

But astrology is about humankind's relationship to the Cosmos, so the astrology of the day reflected this one-way relationship (figure 47). The natal chart was not even imagined, and all predictive work was for the group or the tribe. However, as we changed our relationship to the Cosmos, we changed our astrology, so that nowadays this is not the only astrological system used. But it is interesting to note that these old systems are still used for any phenomenon that we consider to be beyond human control.

STATIC ASTROLOGY

Around the time of cultivation, humans started to change their relationship to the "gods." We were not so vulnerable. If Mars occurred next to a Full Moon, implying a bad hunt, then what was once of major concern to a tribe, which survived on hunting, was now a much smaller worry for the cultivators. We were starting to gain control over parts of our lives and were less susceptible to the "whim of the gods."

It is in this period that the horoscope came into astrology. The individual—and individual events—started to be recognized and, therefore, needed to be reflected in the astrology of the day. The old systems of Mundane astrology still worked, but now the individual had to be incorporated.

Thus, the ancient astrologers started to construct charts for important times—the birth of key individuals, the winning of a battle, the death of a king, or the beginning of a king's reign. These charts were important, and astrologers would watch to see if any of the astrological events were repeated. For example, they would note the Sun's return to where it was when the king started his reign. Or they would monitor two planets in the same configuration as they had been for an earlier event. When these astrological phenomena occurred, more charts would be created, and these charts were then considered as "episodes" of the original event. Now we find predictive work being done that had some small involvement with a horoscope, so the predictive work became more individual and less generalized.

Now if the metaphysical tool that measures fate's involvement in a human life—astrology—changes its systems to allow individual predictive work, then the individual must be changing his or her relationship to fate.

Indeed the study of the development of astrological predictive systems through history will also be a study of the development of humans and their relationship to fate.

The individual was now "choosing" moments in the dance of the heavens that would be relevant to them. Data was taken from horoscopes and used as a method of choosing the time for the plotting of an episode chart. At times, a horoscope was not even used. The individual would choose the moment by asking a question, at a point in time, and the resultant chart would give an answer.

Fate can be considered as a weaver with a cloth. In the beginning—the hunter-gatherer stage—fate contributed all the threads, and we took whatever was produced. Then with the recognition of the individual, humans started to contribute a few chosen threads to the weave of their lives, and the natal chart became increasingly important.

Over thousands of years, different predictive techniques have been developed, all of them using more and more of the natal chart to plot the outcomes—more and more threads to the cloth. However, techniques involving the single-thread stage gave rise to what can be considered static predictive astrological methods.

These methods all give horoscopes that can be read for outcomes and, for example in the case of returns, produce a series of charts where each chart is valid for a given period of time. So, this type of predictive work is like working with a series of still photographs. The old layer of Mundane astrology was still in the astrologers' psyche, but now this new layer of static systems is laid on top of it. In the same way, we still have in our chromosome structure genes we no longer need that are now overridden by other genetic codes; we still have times of a bad hunt, but now the hunt is not that important.

Mars appearing next to a Full Moon may still imply a difficult month for a hunt, but we no longer need to go on the hunt. We can stock up at the supermarket instead. These Static systems are as follows:

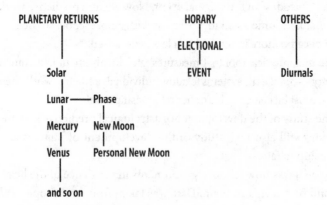

212

I believe that because these systems are static—each one producing a chart derived from only one piece of natal data—these charts represent a more fated relationship with the Cosmos and they can be read as "stand only charts," in other words independent of the natal chart.

DYNAMIC SYSTEMS

In comparison, we have the dynamic systems of transits and directions that came into being from a collective need for greater involvement in the weave of our lives. These systems involve the whole natal chart and therefore imply, by this total involvement, a greater contribution by humans to the nature and color of the cloth of their lives. Or, putting it simply, they imply greater free will in the outcomes of our lives.

This layer of dynamic astrology can be thought of as a layer over, firstly, the mundane systems, and secondly, static systems with each layer representing a greater involvement of the natal chart and thus an easing of the hand of fate.

Most of us function from this top layer of dynamic astrology. If we strip off this layer, we move backward in time, where astrology was more "black and white," less humanistic, fate seeming to have a greater hand in things. All of these ancient layers still function in the modern human, just like our unmanifested tails, but the modern layer may be more applicable to our consciousnesses and, therefore, more useful to the astrologer.

The Failed Eagle

However, back to our 5 percent or so of people for whom, when we apply modern techniques of predictive astrology, we come up with zero results. These people are obviously, for reasons that I can't even try to fathom, not attuned to the modern collective unconscious, at least not with regard to the indicators of their fate and life path. They respond to a different eagle. In this search for a different eagle, we are naturally led to the older principles of the static systems.

The individuals of this group, who respond only to an older layer of predictive astrology, don't look like gorillas, nor do they seem to have any special features. They do not lack the ability to cope in the modern world; they simply "are." They come from all walks of life and appear no different from anybody else. Nor does this characteristic seem to be inherited or restricted to any particular group in the community. The only thing they seem to have in common is that the more chart-involved techniques of predictive astrology just do not work for them.

We can take this small group and "strip off" the most recent/personalized predictive methods, then we "strip off" transits, but there may still be some directions with which we can work. If these prove unsuccessful, then we must "strip off" this whole layer, thereby removing the veneer of natal chart-related movement, and start working with static systems. This means that you reduced the number of threads that your client is contributing to the cloth. Thus you should be changing the model of fate that you are working with. Fewer threads from the chart mean potentially less free will, or, more importantly for the predictive astrologer, more fate involved, and a higher level of predictability.

If the static charts do not work (and I have never encountered this situation), then you would need to peel off this layer and arrive at the area of non-individually related predictive astrology, i.e., mundane astrology. Here, no factor of the individual's chart is considered, the individual has no input to the timing of any charts, and the resultant predictions will affect the whole tribe or community. Of course, this would be of little personal use to your client, as it does not acknowledge the individual.

SUMMARY

The three layers of predictive astrology are:

◊   Mundane: Non-chart-related predictive astrology. The earliest form and very fatalistic. Still used today for events over which we have no control.

◊   Static: Limited chart-related predictive astrology. Less fatalistic than Mundane astrology. Very useful for working with clients who do not respond to dynamic methods.

◊   Dynamic: Total natal chart involvement. Gives the individual many options and, therefore, is less fatalistic.

With these points in mind, the best approach to take if transits don't work is to look more closely at progressions.

If progressions don't work, then move back one layer into the world of static astrology and examine return charts. I suggest that you use the natal chart only to give the position of the planets for which the returns are to be constructed. You can still delineate the natal chart. Only for predictive work for this client, whose transits do not work, must we abandon it.

A human's connection to the cosmos is in layers: the more layers you strip off, the less power the individual has to influence the outcomes. In other words, the further back you go, the less subtle will be the astrology.

Returns (Planets or Luminaries)

The basic principle of returns is that of personalized cycles. At a given moment, when a planet returns to its natal position—i.e., the transiting planet forms a conjunction to its birth position—a new horoscope can be erected. This chart is an event chart just like an Ingress chart (a chart constructed for the time when a planet enters a new zodiac sign) except that the event is meaningful for that particular individual.

These charts were first used in connection with the Sidereal zodiac: the return measured back to the fixed star position of the natal placement. Nowadays, they are also used with the Tropical zodiac: the return being measured back to its appropriate position in relation to the Northern Hemisphere's Spring Equinox. The debate is still going on as to what zodiac to use, with no solution coming from the ancient methods, as the Sidereal and Tropical zodiac were so closely aligned back then that the ancients did not even recognize the difference, the Northern Hemisphere Spring Equinox occurring in the stars of early degrees of Aries. If you choose to use the

Sidereal zodiac then you will need to precess the return. See Appendix 2 for the method of constructing returns with or without precession. All the returns presented in this book are Tropical returns.

The main planet, or luminary, used for this concept of returns was that of the Sun, resulting in what we know today as the solar return. Since the Sun was watched to measure the seasons, it was not too much of a leap to look at its relationship to other planets at the time that it returned to the place it occupied at a previous major event. The resultant chart was then considered to give information about the forthcoming period, lasting until the next return. This principle can be applied to any planet or luminary, with the resultant information being viewed or read through the meaning of the planet on which the return was based.

To read these return charts within the parameters of the old system of predictive astrology, we can use the modern planets. However, there are a few very basic guidelines:

1) The return chart can be read on its own without referral to the natal chart. This is a strong statement that seems to fly in the face of the normal rules for reading returns. But if your client's chart does not respond to transits, then I strongly advise that you ignore the natal chart for predictive information and read your static charts as "stand-alone" charts.

2) If the principal planet, i.e., the planet that is being returned to its natal position, is conjunct one of the angles (Rising, Setting, Culminating, or at the Nadir), then whatever that planet symbolizes will be acutely emphasized throughout the period of the return.

3) Use the Mean Node, the one that the ancients used. If any planet at the time of the return is in the same degree as the Node, then that planet will be acutely emphasized throughout the period of the return. For example, if the Node is at 10° Aries 52', then *any* planet which is at 10° of *any* zodiac sign is said to be in "the degree of the Node." If a planet was at 11° of a zodiac sign then, even though it will be within 1° of a possible aspect to the Node, it is not considered to be "in the degree of the Node."

4) The most important statements made by a return chart, apart from the above-mentioned emphases, are the big statements. This is to say: the stellium in a house, the planet on an angle, and so on.

5) The rulers of the 8th house and the 12th house can be considered to be difficult planets in that particular return. Also the 5th and 9th house rulers are beneficial. This concept of house rulers works well in both the Equal and Placidus house systems.

6) Analyze the chart for the tightest possible aspects, or planetary patterns, and delineate them simply: planets, and/or points, in each other's degrees regardless of the type of aspect involved. Any aspect with an orb of less than 1°.

7) Return charts should be located for where a person is at the time of the return, and then relocated as they travel around the world. When returns were used as the main system of predictive astrology, the astrologer was not expecting the client to travel to another country for business or a holiday. So if you are midway through a return and you change your location, relocate the return to that new location.

8) For planetary returns: always delineate a return chart through the lens of the symbolic meaning of the principal planet. Venus return charts talk about Venus events, not Mars events, and so on. Which leads us to the next section.

SOLAR RETURNS

The solar return is by far the most frequently used return. The chart for the return of the Sun to its natal placement will be concerned with everything related to the Sun: your life force and health, your social position, your authority and power—the lack of or changes to—and your desire to interact with the world around you. It is no wonder that this is the major return used in astrology.

Reading these returns very, very simply, using the points mentioned above, let's look at a few interesting examples and, as we look at them, put on an older hat. We are working with a system where the hand of fate is much stronger, so allow yourself to get into some old-fashioned, predictive astrology.

A Local Government Politician

This case is from my own files. A client, whom I will call Steven, came to see me in late 1985. I haven't given his natal chart for we don't need it (and "Steven" would not appreciate it being published), but in looking into 1986 there was nothing in either progressions or transits that would indicate the sort of year that lay ahead of him. Little did I realize at the time that he was one of those clients belonging to that elusive 5 percent.

During the course of 1986, he traveled to Scotland for a vacation. While he was there, his wife bought a haggis and packed it into one of his bags, unable to fit it into her own luggage.* Due to other commitments, she returned to Australia earlier than Steven and forgot to tell him about the haggis. Steven completed his holiday, picked up the "haggis" bag from his Scottish club, and flew back into the country. In the course of his flight, he filled out his customs card, signing it in the belief that he had nothing to declare. As he entered the country, he again stated that he had nothing to declare. Now haggis, for quarantine reasons, is an illegal import in Australia and, of course, the customs found it in his luggage.

Steven was fined for making a false customs declaration. The dust had just settled for Steven when an anonymous letter was sent to the powers that be in local government, pointing out that Steven had a felony against his name—false customs declarations being a federal offense—and was therefore ineligible to hold any form of political office. Steven's life was about to go down the drain, all because of his wife's haggis and the devious mind of a hidden enemy who sent the anonymous letter.

Not being a man to take things lying down, he fought the courts of the land to have the criminal charge of the false customs declaration declared invalid. Over the course of the year Steven ended up in the High Court employing a Q.C. (Queens Counsel) in the attempt to clear his name. He was eventually victorious, but at a huge cost of not only money but also energy and health.

Steven returned to me, politely complaining about the complete inadequacy of my predictive work. I could not blame him. I was stunned at the lack of any indication of these events by transits and progressions.

At my earliest convenience, I pounded the eagle to death. Using an IBM computer and the latest in software, I tore Steven's chart apart, knowing

---

* Haggis is a Scottish dish in which a sheep's stomach is stuffed with minced meat, heart, liver mixed with suet, and oatmeal, and heavily seasoned. It can be eaten boiled or fried.

that I was not looking for some minor semisquare or some obscure aspect to a regressed planet. I had to find a system that would give a big statement about that year.

There was nothing in the transits, nothing in the progressions, nothing in the Solar Arc. Tear off that layer of astrology and throw it away. And there it was. The solar return (Chart 18) beaming out its message.

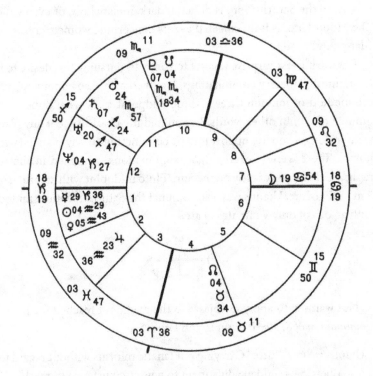

Chart 18. Solar return chart for Steven. Data withheld for confidentiality.

The Sun, Neptune, MC, and Node are *all* in the same degree: a threat to his life/social status/authority that will affect his career through the lens of Neptune. Neptune expressed its energy first, via the holiday to Scotland (Neptune loves the escapism of travel), then through the lack of knowledge of the haggis and the ensuing confusion, and, third, by way of the anonymous letter that exposed his felony. And it was his wife—Moon conjunct the descendant—who bought the haggis. The confusion over the signed customs declaration was indicated also by the critical degree of Mercury ruling the 9th house. Any ancient astrologer's eyebrows would have shot up to the ceiling at the sight of that return.

In then examining the solar return for any exact or very tight aspecting, apart from the obvious Node, MC, Neptune, Sun pattern, we can see that Pluto is in the same degree as Saturn. The Moon is forming a quincunx to Uranus with an orb of less than 1°. These charts must be read simply, so the Saturn-Pluto is difficult, dark, melancholy, or even violent. The Moon-Uranus is unexpected events concerning women, children, or (dare I say) food.

But the biggest surprise was yet to come. In pursuing this desire to find the tightest planetary combinations, I applied a little cosmobiology using the method of midpoint trees. These midpoint trees were done using a module of 90°. In other words, I examined the chart to see if any planets were making a square, opposition, or conjunction to any planetary midpoints. There were two very tight combinations contained in the solar return: Uranus was exactly on the Sun/Pluto midpoint with an orb of only 7 minutes of arc. Uranus was also conjunct the Saturn/Neptune midpoint with an orb of only 9 minutes of arc.

Not wanting to apply my biases to the reading, I reached for Ebertin's *Combination of Stellar Influences,* and I quote:

Uranus = Sun/Pluto: "Carrying out fanatic reforms without regard for oneself.—Sudden adjustment to new circumstance (arrest)."

Uranus = Saturn/Neptune: "... a weakness or illness manifesting itself suddenly."*

Here was the whole story laid out, very simply, very openly, and so easy that one could actually look up the tight planet combination in a reference book. Indeed, it was so straightforward even a computer could have delineated the solar return chart if it were programmed with the basic rules.

In working with his solar return to examine the tightest aspects, I took no notice of the angles—Ascendent and MC. With all solar returns, I now

---

* R. Ebertin, *The Combination of Stellar Influences.*

work with only the two tightest planetary patterns. This normally means that I work with orbs of less than 12 minutes of arc, so that a few seconds change in the birth time, or a rounding off of the longitude or latitude, would place the angle in incorrect focus.

Abraham Lincoln

Abraham Lincoln was a president of the United States who desired an end to slavery. As we are all aware, this fairly heated debate was one of the seeds of the American Civil War, and this war over slavery and other issues is considered the motivation behind his assassination in 1865. The assassination occurred on April 15, 1865—just days after the Union victory.

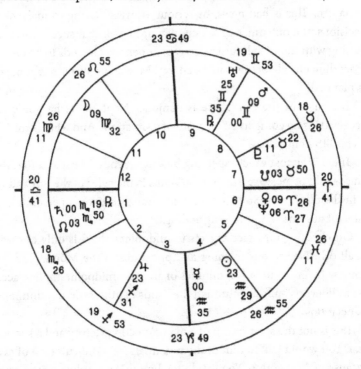

Chart 19. Solar return chart for Abraham Lincoln, born February 12, 1809, "sun up" (7:40 A.M. LMT used by author), Hodgenville, Kentucky, 37N33, 85W45. Data from Circle Book of Charts. Return chart calculated for February 12, 1865, the year of his assassination. Washington, D.C., 38N54, 77W2. Placidus houses.

By using a very simple approach, we can examine the solar return for the year of his death. As already stated, the Sun is the life force, so when the life force is violently challenged, there should be some statement of violence in the return.

He is coming to see you, an astrologer, early in 1865. He is confident of victory by the Union and is generally expecting a good year. Chart 19 is Lincoln's solar return chart, relocated for Washington, DC, in 1865. There are no planets in the degree of the Node. However, there is a very strong Saturn rising and close to the Node.

If we considered this Saturn statement, there is a sense of greater responsibility; as president of the Union, we would expect this to show up in his return.

The ruler of the 12th house is Mercury, and it is making an exact square to Saturn. This is bad news, or serious worries: having to make serious decisions, the outcomes of which may not be all that successful. We are dealing with the 12th house ruler, remember, which tends to produce the more difficult side of the planet's energy. Maybe the War is not going to go as planned?

The ruler of the 8th house is conjunct Neptune. Is he going to be deceived? Is he going to be unaware of a situation? And what is this Pluto on his 8th house cusp?

There is almost exact aspecting between Venus, Mars, and the Moon. This would be positive except that Venus is the ruler of the 8th and Mars is in the 8th house. So this strong emotional time on a personal level is difficult in some way, involving endings.

On checking for exact aspects to midpoints, there is only one with a small orb: Neptune is forming an opposition to the Moon/Node mid-point with an orb of only 6 minutes of arc. This midpoint implies, according to Ebertin, "suffering through the hands of others; disappointments in associations."

This is not the solar return of a man expecting victory and a successful year. You would talk to him of the potentials for a difficult turn of events because of a deception. You would tell him that an ending was approaching, and it was not necessarily going to happen the way he had planned it.

You would note with relief that the Sun was in an exact sextile to Jupiter (only a 3' orb) so that, no matter what happened, he would be given an opportunity to expand his world or image somehow. I doubt very much that you would share the president's optimism for his future year, and you would be warning him to be very cautious.

You would not have picked his assassination in a theater, even though the Neptune is emphasized by the 8th house ruler; those types of delineations are easy in hindsight. The Jupiter sextile Sun was still working, however, as it indicated the high profile that he would, and still does, hold in American history. At least your eagle was giving you the right information.

Marie Curie

This is an interesting case, as we know that Marie's chart works on the higher layers of predictive astrology; but to examine her solar return in the same manner shows how older layers are still functioning in all of us. Marie's birth details are given in an earlier section (see figure 31, page 153), so here now (Chart 20) is her solar return for that fateful year of her husband's death, located in Paris.

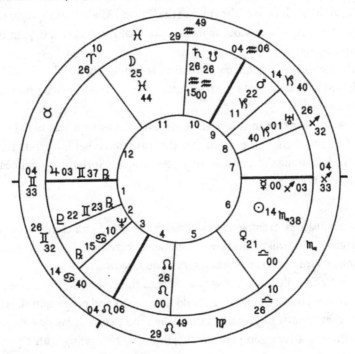

Chart 20. *Solar return chart for Marie Curie (q.v.) calculated for November 7, 1905. Paris, 48N52, 2E20. Placidus houses.*

The first thing we notice is that Saturn is in the degree of the Node. In addition, if you had set up her transit work, you would also note that she was having transiting Saturn conjunct her natal Nodal axis. For this statement to be echoed by the solar return chart is to indicate that it is a very strong message indeed.

Saturn, in this very highly stressed position, indicates that she will be forced to take on greater responsibilities—to stand on her own two feet, so to speak. The eventual outcomes are very positive, for Saturn is ruling the 9th house. However, Saturn is not only in the degree of the Node but is also conjunct the South Node. Remember the South Node—associations of family and tribe. Is this increase in responsibilities going to be caused by issues to do with her family and tribe?

There is also a Mars-Pluto-Venus pattern, all within a 1° orb. This configuration is intense, passionate, emotional, and bound up with relationships. The rulerships of these three planets are also exclusively to do with the 6th/12th house axis. Jupiter is rising at the time of the return, but is just into the 12th house. The ruler of the 7th and 8th being emphasized in the 12th house is so obvious in its meaning that I will leave it to your own interpretation.

The tightest midpoint configuration is Jupiter square the Sun/Pluto midpoint with an orb of only 6 minutes of arc: success corning from dramatic change.

Considering that in this year Marie Curie's husband was killed in an accident and then, by a twist of fate, she was offered her husband's job—thereby becoming the first woman professor at the Sorbonne—your eagle has served you well.

These are just a few examples. You will find that by doing your clients' or friends' solar returns, you will be giving the transits and progressions a greater depth, for the solar return can act as a backup, giving you a "second opinion."

What normally occurs is very similar to the case of Marie Curie: the solar return gives a similar story as do the transits and progressions. However, what is most important is that, when the two systems *do not* agree, then there is a very good chance that you may be dealing with a person who does not respond to transit work, and so on. This can act as an early warning device, so to speak, for you, the astrologer. When this occurs, you would be wise to believe the solar return rather than the transits.

There are many variations on a theme for solar returns. Apart from the variations caused by the question of whether to use the Sidereal zodiac or the Tropical zodiac, one can also construct a solar return for when the transiting Sun is exactly opposite the natal Sun, or when the transiting Sun is exactly square the natal Sun. Another system is to produce a solar "return" chart for when the Sun gets to the same natal degree, minute, and second of any zodiac sign, thus giving twelve solar "returns" a year. There is also the concept of kinetic solar returns where the Sun is returned to a progressed Sun's position—different types of progressions can be used. All these attempts are to give some element of timing to the principle of the solar return. For a solar return is effective for one year and the events in that return could manifest at any stage throughout that year. These variations on a solar return do not seem all that successful when using this more fatalistic approach to reading returns; however, a more modern approach to them may or may not be rewarding.

LUNAR RETURNS

Using the same principles and rules as the solar return, one can, of course, produce a lunar return. The motivation for doing so is to give a better system of timing to the expression of the energies of the solar return. Returns are static. The lunar return, producing a chart for a period only 27 days long, is the shortest planetary return that astrology can produce and thus, for astrologers doing predictive work through returns, it gives them a month-by-month description. This return can be precessed in the same manner as a solar return.

There are quite a few different types of lunar returns. (The Eskimos have many words for snow.) The understanding is that the greater number of words that a language has for a given subject or object, then the greater importance that object has in peoples' lives. If we consider astrology as a language and its various processes as its parts of speech, the fact that there are more types of lunar returns than of any other planetary return is an indication of the Moon's importance in astrology. The different types are shown in figure 48.

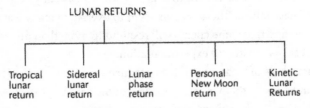

Figure 48. Various types of Lunar returns.

The Tropical Lunar return is a standard lunar return based on the moment when the transiting Moon forms a conjunction with the natal Moon. This is returning the Moon to the precise Tropical zodiac position it occupied at birth. This return will occur every 27 days. This is probably the most popular type of lunar return.

The Sidereal Lunar return is achieved by precessing the return in the same manner as for solar return charts. This implies that you are returning the Moon to the precise position it occupied at your birth in relationship to the fixed stars. If you were born with your Moon conjunct a fixed star, then the return would be measured to this fixed star. This method is just as valid as the one above.

The Lunar Phase return is based on the repetition of a precise lunar phase. A chart is erected for every time the Moon returns to the exact lunar phase under which you were born. This type of return occurs every 29-and-a-half days. This is a very ancient system, as the lunar phase was the most obvious feature of the Moon. We still use Full and New Moon charts for predicting global events. The lunar calendar was also based on the lunar phases, and the vestiges of this remain in the celebrations of Easter and Passover. The disadvantage of these returns is that you do need a computer to calculate them.

The Personal New Moon chart is a return chart erected for every time the transiting Moon conjoins the zodiac position of your natal Sun. Very similar to the standard lunar return, but this time you are returning it to the natal Sun's position rather than the natal Moon's position.

The Kinetic Lunar return is a chart erected for the time that the transiting Moon conjoins the position of the progressed Moon. The type of progression used can vary.

Take your pick; play around with the different types. You will find that one particular type will function consistently for a particular client. Some clients or friends may respond to the Lunar return, while others resonate to the PNM return, and yet another group will consistently respond to the Lunar Phase return. These returns seem to overlap in many ways, and you may also find that some clients will respond to more than one type of return. It really is a matter of experimentation.

The normal use of lunar returns is to produce a set of them, six to twelve months, and look at them as one month leading into the other. As you work with them, look at them very simply—even more simply than the solar returns. Use the guidelines already given for returns, but look for the obvious statement. The following are some examples of different lunar returns for a few of the case studies that have already been used.

The Accession of Elizabeth

Elizabeth I seems to respond quite well to both the Tropical Lunar return and the Personal New Moon return. Chart 21 is the lunar return that encompassed the period when she came to the throne, which was November 17, 1558. The lunar return for Elizabeth occurred on October 26, 1558, and this return will be valid until the end of November 1558. The returns were both located in London.

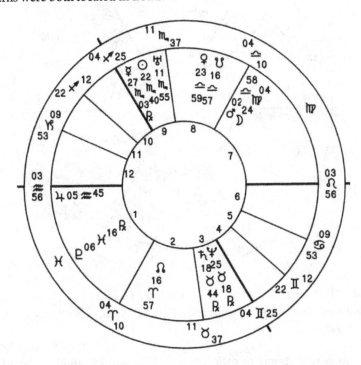

Chart 21. Lunar return for Queen Elizabeth I (q.v.) calculated for October 26, 1558, the period of her accession to the English throne. London, 51N31, 0W10. Placidus houses.

Probably the strongest feature of this chart is the Sun-Uranus conjunction, with the involvement of a tightly aspected Venus. This shows a sudden event. Uranus is also the ruler of the MC and is conjunct the ruler of the IC. So the sudden event could well do with family and social status.

There is a tight Pluto-Moon aspect and, since the young Princess has a half sister who is dying, this does tend to imply that the death will occur during this period.

Elizabeth's personal New Moon Chart (Chart 22) occurred on the 5th of November and will be valid until early December 1558. This is the chart for the time that the transiting Moon will exactly conjoin Elizabeth's natal Sun in Virgo.

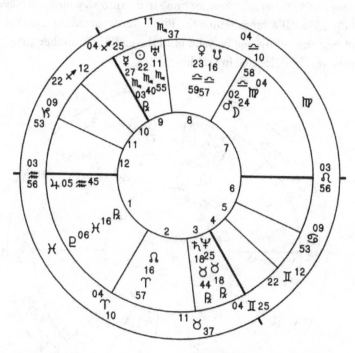

Chart 22. Personal New Moon return for Queen Elizabeth I (q.v.) calculated for November 5, 1558, the period of her accession to the English throne. London, 51N31, 0W10. Placidus houses.

This is very simple to delineate. Jupiter is forming an exact sextile to the MC and at the same time rising in the chart to conjoin the ascendant. It is also the ruler of the MC. Obviously this is the major planet of the return—very strong indications of the raising of Elizabeth's status. If this were a normal client in our modern-day world, you would suggest that it would be a good time to apply for that job promotion, or to try to achieve something that feels out of reach.

There are other aspects, of course, but don't pull the chart apart. Let it give the simple message that it offers.

Marie Curie

Looking once again at the difficult March and April in 1906 when Marie Curie's husband was killed in an accident, the following returns are located in Paris. Chart 23 is the lunar return for Marie that was active at the time of her husband's accidental death. Mercury is in the degree of the Node and, in addition, it is the ruler of both the 10th and 1st houses. This is an important month regarding career, writing, or news. Mercury is in the 8th house, so this news is about an ending and could be a little abrupt. Pluto is in the 10th house, but don't leap to conclusions as it is not being emphasized.

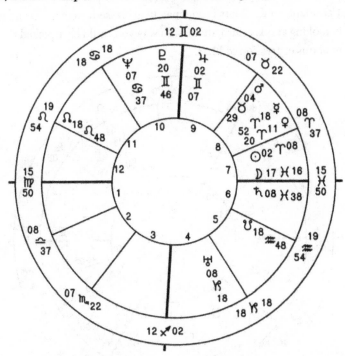

Chart 23. Lunar return for Marie Curie (q.v.) calculated for March 23, 1906, the period of her husband's accident and her promotion to professor at the Sorbonne. Paris, 48N52, 2E20. Placidus houses.

The lunar return contains a Balsamic phase (yes, you can use the phase of the Moon in the lunar return chart). This Balsamic phase of release is in the 7th house, with the Moon conjunct the descendant. So there will be changes in the relationship. The astrologer may surmise that Pierre, her husband, will get news that will mean that he will have to travel—or maybe she will receive news that will mean she has to travel.

Moving to the Personal New Moon chart that was applicable for that time (see Chart 24), this chart is quite ominous. Now Mars is in the degree of the Node, ruling the 4th house. Mercury, ruler of the 7th house, is conjunct the 4th house cusp in Aries. Horary astrology often refers to the 4th house as the "end of the matter" and, since these return charts function more on horary rules than on humanistic principles, this 4th house emphasis is not surprising. So, in this chart, we would surmise that there is some event that is Mars in nature, born from anger, or very energetic, or an accident that directly affects the role of the partner in the family or at home. Pierre was killed in a street accident, so the Mars is adequately expressed. Remember, however, that in looking at this return, there is no way you could have picked the fatal nature of this expression of Mars.

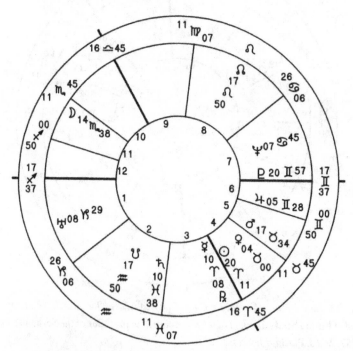

Chart 24. *Personal New Moon return for Marie Curie (q.v.) calculated for April 10, 1906, the period of her husband's accident and her promotion to professor at the Sorbonne. Paris, 48N52, 2W20. Placidus houses.*

Avoid reading too much into these charts from the wisdom of hind-sight. Set up a batch for yourself, predict from them, and then let them give you your feedback.

The Duke of Windsor

Edward VIII abdicated in December of 1936, and his chart seems to respond better to the principle of lunar phase returns than any other type. Edward announced his decision to the powers that be at the end of October 1936. It then took a little time to sort out the necessary paperwork, since this involved more than the common bureaucratic form that the public service could supply.

Chart 25 is the lunar phase return that was current for the time that Edward made his decision. This chart is constructed for London, and the lunar phase in the chart is the exact lunar phase under which the King was born, to within a second of arc.

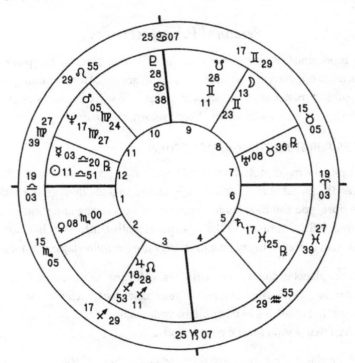

Chart 25. Lunar Phase return for Edward VIII (q.v.) calculated for October 5, 1936, the period of his decision to abdicate the British throne. London, 51N31, 0W10. Placidus houses.

The chart is almost self-explanatory. If you were the court's astrologer, and given that the rumors were thick on the ground that the king could abdicate, Chart 25 confirms your worst suspicions: Pluto is in the 10th house, and emphasized, for it is not only conjunct the MC but is also in the same degree as the Node—the dramatic transformation of one's life path. There is a T-Square involving Jupiter on the apex and Saturn-Neptune opposition—the successful resolution to a sorrowful situation. This decision was not taken lightly.

The exact opposition between Venus and Uranus from the 1st to the 7th house leaves us no doubt as to the motivation for the career change, indicated by the very strong Pluto.

In summary, read any type of lunar return even more simply than solar returns. They should be constructed six or so at a time so you can see any recurring themes. And most importantly, as with any type of return, use very tight orbs for your aspects.

Personal Planet Returns

The more unusual returns are those of the other planets. The planetary returns, as opposed to the luminary returns, are a tool for examining a precise subject matter in the person's life. That is to say, for matters of money or the heart, one should use the Venus return, and so on.

RULES FOR THE RETROGRADE RETURN

Probably the major difference to be kept in mind is that, unlike the luminaries, the planets move both directly and retrograde through the zodiac. Therefore, you can have three Venus returns occurring in a short period of time. Which return to take is a question that astrology has not yet answered; however, in my own practice, I use the following guidelines:

If the planet is direct at birth, then take the first direct return. For example, if your Mars is direct in your natal chart, then the *first* time that transiting Mars conjoins your natal planet is the return chart that is valid for the next period of time.

If the planet is retrograde in the natal chart, then use the retrograde return. For example, if your Mars is retrograde in your natal chart, then the true "repeat of the natal situation" will not occur until Mars is in that position.

If the planet makes only one pass over its natal position, then regardless of the direction of movement of the planet at the time of birth, this single touch will be the return.

These are just guidelines. The best approach is to backtrack on some of your own returns and see for yourself which touch of the return is the best description of that period.

MERCURY RETURNS

You would use a Mercury return to examine issues of writing, studying, talking, body movement, short journeys, issues with younger people. If a person is taking up a course of study, the Mercury return will show the ease or difficulty encountered during the period of the return. Duration is approximately twelve months.

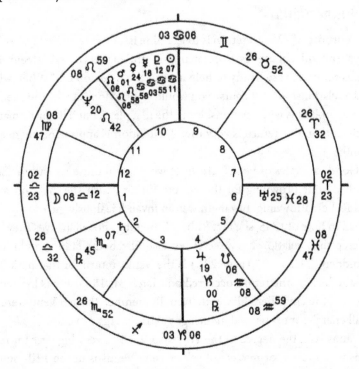

Chart 26. Mercury return for George Bernard Shaw, born July 26, 1856, 12:40 A.M. LMT, Dublin, Ireland, 53N20, 6W15. Data from Circle Book of Charts. Return chart calculated for June 29, 1925, London, 51N31, 0W10. Placidus houses.

George Bernard Shaw struggled for many years before finding his true niche in literature as a playwright. After a brilliant career in this field, he was awarded, in 1925, the Nobel Prize for Literature. Chart 26 (page 233) is the Mercury return that was current for him when he received this prize. The chart is located in London, the city in which he was living at the time.

The chart is a stunning example of a very important successful Mercury year: half the solar system is in the 10th house. Huge public recognition for writing or any other Mercurial subjects—remember, this is a Mercury return.

There are no planets or points in the degree of the Node, but there is a Sun, Saturn, Moon, Node statement. Maybe recognition through long hard struggle. The Moon is rising in the chart and is ruler of the 10th house, adding extra strength to the 10th house emphasis.

VENUS RETURNS

The purpose of a Venus return is to examine issues of relationships, either private or with colleagues, issues of money, and matters of self-esteem. The Venus return is very handy to help answer the question of: "When will I find a relationship?" Of course you would want to look at why the client is having problems with relationships in the first place, but if it's just a matter of time, then this return is very useful. Duration is approximately twelve months.

Good examples of Venus returns at work are in those returns for Elizabeth Barrett Browning for the period during which she met and married Robert Browning. Elizabeth was an invalid, jealously guarded by her father. In June of 1845, she met Robert Browning and fell in love. They had to keep their relationship a secret because Elizabeth's father would have forbidden it. Chart 27 (page 235) is the Venus return for that period in Elizabeth's life. The return occurred on March 31, 1845, and is located in London, the city where Elizabeth lived. Remember, this is a Venus return, so all energies must be read in the light of the energy of Venus.

Venus is in the degree of the Node, so this is a very big year for relationships, money, or matters of self-esteem. Venus is in the 12th house, pointing to a secretiveness or hidden quality to the situation.

Uranus is right on the ascendant, so these matters of relationship or money happen very suddenly. The very large 1st house implies that Elizabeth takes personal action. Elizabeth and Robert fell in love upon meeting;

indeed, Robert had already said that he loved her in a letter before they met. Speed of events is a quality of Uranus.

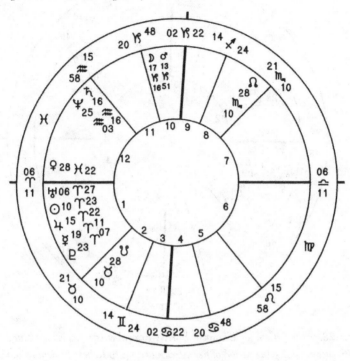

Chart 27. Venus return for Elizabeth Barrett Browning (q.v.) calculated for March 31, 1845, the period when she met her future husband, Robert Browning. London, 51N31, 0W10. Placidus houses.

The second chart, Chart 28 on page 236, is the following Venus return, which occurred on May 5, 1846, located once again in London. It is in September of 1846 that Elizabeth secretly married Robert and fled from her father's house without telling him. Here we have the same packed 1st house as the previous return, the continuation of personal action. Now, the Venus is exactly conjunct the ascendant and so becomes the biggest statement in the chart. Mars conjunct the IC indicates the change of home or, because it is a Venus return, being motivated to live with a lover.

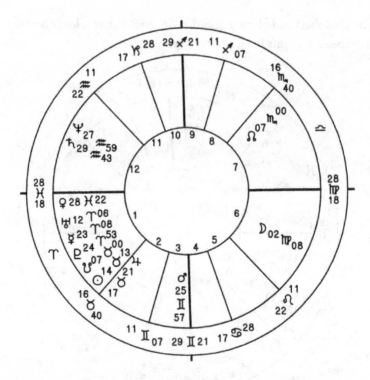

Chart 28. Venus return for Elizabeth Barrett Browning (q.v.) calculated for May 5, 1846, encompassing the period of her secret marriage to Robert Browning and subsequent rift with her father. London, 51N31, 0W10. Placidus houses.

MARS RETURNS

The purpose of a Mars return is to examine vigorous undertakings, matters of war, important times of achievement for athletes, years of high sexual activity, years of giving birth. The Mars return would be useful if your clientele consisted of people very much engaged in some form of physical expression. In the static systems, Mars also has a slight Pluto essence.

Duration of this return is about two-and-a-half years.

One of the best examples of Mars return charts that I have ever seen is the Mars return chart for when Joan of Arc was captured. Chart 29 (page 237) is the Mars return chart that started for Joan on October 16, 1430. This is located for Rouen, where she was being held prisoner at the time the return began. During this Mars return Joan is executed.

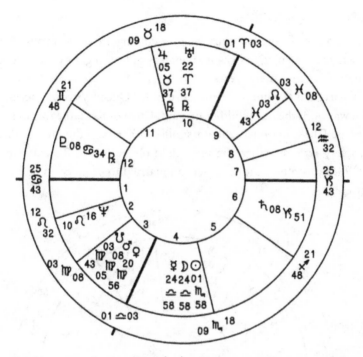

Chart 29. Mars return for Joan of Arc (q.v.) on the occasion of her capture and execution. October 16, 1430, Rouen, 49N26, 1E05. Placidus houses.

In this Mars return we have Mars, the principle planet, in the same degree as a Saturn-Pluto opposition. Capture, violence, mistreatment, fighting for one's life are key terms. Indeed, Ebertin actually mentions "to be martyred." Also note the Balsamic Lunar phase in the chart endings.

Outer Planet Returns

Once we go beyond Mars, we move into the area of long-lived returns. A Jupiter return is current for twelve years, and a Saturn return chart for approximately twenty-nine years.

Since these returns are current for such a long time, they tend to talk more about life directions, or purpose, rather than emphasizing a particular subject. In addition, because of the length of time that these returns are applicable, they can be read at a greater depth, and it is advisable to increase aspect orbs to about two or three degrees.

JUPITER RETURNS

The purpose of a Jupiter return is for examining the areas of your life into which you are going to expand, the areas of learning, or exploration. Its duration is about twelve years.

Chart 30 is the Jupiter return current for Queen Victoria's accession. She was born the only child of Edward, Duke of Kent, the fourth son of George III. At her birth, the possibility of her ascending to the throne was very remote. When the only child of the Prince Regent (George IV) died, his other three brothers all married to produce an heir to the throne.

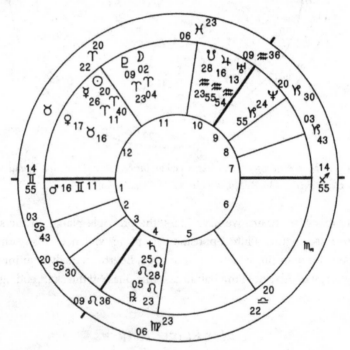

Chart 30. Jupiter return for Queen Victoria, born May 24, 1819, 4:15 A.M. GMT, Kensington Palace, London, England, 51N31, 00W10. Data from Fowler's Compendium of Nativities. The chart is calculated for her 12th year of life, April 11, 1831, London, 51N31, 0W10. Placidus houses.

When George IV died with his daughter already dead, he left the throne to his next-oldest brother, William IV. Now William IV had many children, but only two were legitimate and, unfortunately, these two children died in infancy. Thus, William was not producing any heirs. Upon his death, the throne went to the next-oldest brother. This brother had long since died, but had produced a legal offspring. This child was Victoria. At eighteen years of age, she ascended the throne.

Chart 30 is a return for when Victoria was twelve years old, twelve years being the period of Jupiter. Strangely enough, according to the *Encyclopedia Britannica*, there was a legend that Victoria did not know she was heir to the throne until she was twelve years old. Within six years of the commencement of this return, she was on the throne.

The obvious statement in this chart is the Jupiter-Uranus conjunction on the MC. The area of expansion and growth is going to be in the area of the public eye. What is of great interest in this chart is Saturn conjunct the North Node in the 4th house. This is where effort is exerted with regard to this expansion—home, family, tribe. She knew she had to have children to secure and stabilize the British throne.

SATURN RETURNS

Saturn returns are a comment on what it is that you are building with your life. What are the structures into which you are going to put your energy—consciously or unconsciously. This can be a very interesting return. The duration is about 29 years.

Continuing with Queen Victoria, Chart 31 on page 240 is her first Saturn return chart. This shows what she is building. This was not necessarily conscious, for Victoria was delighted to be a mother and wife and was quite happy for Albert to carry a great many of the royal responsibilities. However, as she went about her preferred role of mother, she, of course, built not only the "Victorian Age" but also a family dynasty.

The big 10th house in the chart contains the Saturn that, by ruling the 7th house, shows that she is quite grateful for the help of Albert. Neptune conjunct the MC, and ruling it, perhaps implies that this empire-building was unconscious or not sought by Victoria. During her reign, the British Empire grew. She became Queen of Ireland and also Empress of India—nice Saturn titles.

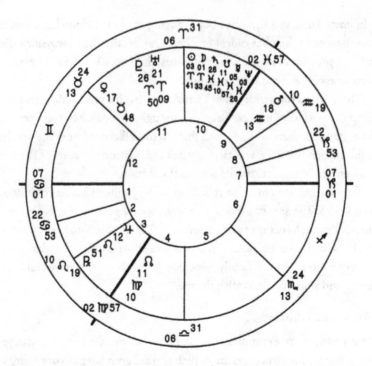

Chart 31. Saturn return for Queen Victoria (q.v.) upon her first Saturn return, March 24, 1849, London, 51N31, 0W10. Placidus houses.

Summary and Additional Comments

◊ When transits or progressions are not producing results, use Luminary or Planetary returns for your predictive work.

◊ Read the charts simply, using the guidelines given.

◊ The shorter the period of the return, the more simply you should read the chart. Put yourself in the place of the Cosmos: if the chart is a Lunar return chart, then the Cosmos does not have too much choice in where it places the outer planets. Indeed it is more concerned with angles and the rulers of houses. So if Pluto is in the 10th, for example, it is only relevant if it is being highlighted in some way.

◊ The most personal information in a return are the angles and thus the rulerships of the houses.

◊ In the case of returns involving the Moon, experiment with what type of Lunar return is working best for your client. The difficulty here is that for any given month one of the types of returns will work, with the others being pale echoes, and although there is a certain degree of consistency for a given person, it can and will change.

◊ When using planetary returns, make a decision about whether to use the 1st, 2nd, or 3rd hit of the return.

◊ Planetary returns of Jupiter outwards need to be done on a computer to get accurate angles.

Luminary and Planetary Arcs

Imagine a wooden wheel. On that wheel, paint some spots around the edge and make them all different colors. As the wheel slowly turns, the spots are going to move around, but they will never change their relationship to each other. A chart is like this wheel, and we can move the chart around. No matter how much we spin it, the planets and angles will always be in the same relationship to each other. However, imagine turning your whole chart around just a little, then laying it back over the top of your original unturned chart. As you keep turning the top natal chart, there will be times when, for example, the Pluto of the top chart is conjunct the Venus of the bottom chart as in figure 49. Although on your natal chart and on the top turning chart, the planets never change their relationship to each other, if we compare the top turning chart to the bottom natal chart, then we have changing relationships.

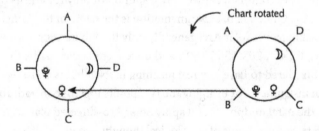

Figure 49. Movement of a chart by a planetary arc. Pluto moved onto the natal Venus.

How much we turn the top chart, and how quickly, is decided by the progressed movement of one planet. If it's a lunar arc, then the top chart is progressed at the rate of movement of the secondary progressed Moon, about 12° per year, and so on. Although this system of planetary arcs is a dynamic system, it only takes into account one facet of the natal chart, the movement of one progressed planet or luminary, and moves the whole chart at that rate of movement.

So, for example, if we use the Sun, we are moving the whole chart by the rate of movement of the progressed Sun and then examining this "solar-moved natal chart" against the original natal chart. In a strange sort of way, it is similar to a solar return; for in both cases, we are predicting events from the energy expressed by one planet or luminary. See figure 50.

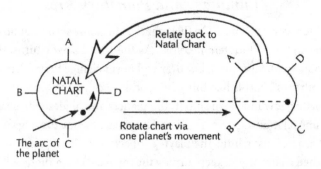

Figure 50. Planetary arcs. The natal chart is rotated via the movement of one planet or luminary, and then that rotated chart is compared back to the natal chart.

Thus the method of planetary arc falls halfway between the static and the dynamic systems, and it is for this reason that clients whose charts do not respond to transits will probably respond not only to returns but also to Solar Arc. Once again, experimentation is the name of the game.

In working with Solar Arc, generally only the 8th harmonic aspects are used, i.e., 0°, 45°, 90°, 135°, 180°; and once a contact is made, the aspect is not considered to have any real meaning in itself but is considered simply as an instrument for bringing the two points together. In addition, you can use the natal midpoints and apply Solar Arc–directed planets to those midpoints. Some schools of astrological thought also use Half Solar Arc or even Double Solar Arc. This is achieved by simply halving or doubling the amount of movement you are going to apply to the natal chart.

In a brief look at Abraham Lincoln's life through the lens of Solar Arc, we can see interesting planetary combinations. For example, when Abraham Lincoln, as a young man, suddenly broke off his engagement to Mary Todd in January of 1841, his Solar Arc–directed Venus had moved into an exact opposition with his natal Uranus.

VENUS (SA) = URANUS

In the following year, they patched up their differences and were married in early November 1842. Lincoln's Solar Arc at the time was:

MOON (SA) = SUN/JUPITER

meaning that the Solar Arc–directed Moon was forming a relationship to the natal Sun/Jupiter midpoint.

Looking at his public life: Lincoln became a Republican upon the disintegration of the old Whig Party due to internal party disagreement on slavery issues. Lincoln's Solar Arc was:

JUPITER (SA) = URANUS

His election to the Presidency was indicated by:

ASCENDANT (SA) = SATURN

The beginning of the Civil War, indicated in Lincoln's predictive work because he was the President of the Union:

SATURN (SA) = MARS

And his assassination in April 1865:

PLUTO (SA) = URANUS

When a Solar Arc planet is forming a relationship to a natal planet or point, then you can consider it effective for three to four months. When the Solar Arc–directed planet is forming a relationship to a natal midpoint, then it is effective for about six weeks.

Predictive techniques have evolved in layers. See figure 51 (page 244). Each layer responds to the development of the human psyche in its relationship to the cosmos. If the top layer is not working, peel it off.

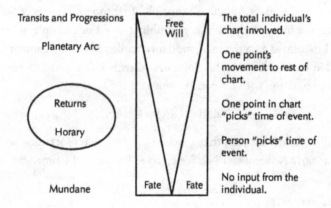

Figure 51. The development of the human relationship to the cosmos.

Once you have found that a client's chart works with Solar Arc directions, there is a good chance that you can keep applying this method successfully. Work with both the Solar Arc planets to the natal points and to natal midpoints. However, you may find that some people's charts don't respond at all to Solar Arc. If it is not functioning for big events in their lives, then I suggest that you use other predictive techniques for that person. In reverse, if the transits do not function for the person, then there is a good chance that the Solar Arc will.

Chapter Seven

Once the Lark Sings

A long, long time ago, one of the older gods of the ancient Greeks had two sons. These sons were Epimetheus and Prometheus. The two boys were quite distinct in their personalities. One son, Prometheus, had a gift and could see the future; whereas his brother Epimetheus was blind to the future and could only see and understand the event once it had happened. One son could look forward and the other only backwards in time.

One day Prometheus foresaw a terrible event and that event involved his brother. The ominous signal was to be a gift from Zeus, the king of the gods, and this gift would turn into a curse. So Prometheus warned his brother and then went about his own business, and Epimetheus promised his brother he would be careful.

Time passed, and unbeknown to Epimetheus, Zeus became enraged with Prometheus and wished to hurt his latest creation—the human race. So Zeus created a beautiful woman and bestowed on her all the gifts of the gods. She was charming, beautiful, and curious. Zeus called his creation "Pandora" and sent her to Epimetheus as a gift. This wondrous gift was accepted with joy.

Now in Epimetheus's house was a jar, discarded by his brother, that contained the leftovers of creation, all the things that Prometheus considered the human race did not need: plagues, illness, spite, revenge, envy, and other such gremlins. All these lived in this jar, and the jar was carefully sealed to prevent their escape. Epimetheus had never bothered to dispose of the jar for, having no forward vision, he couldn't foresee any problems occurring. The jar was safe, so let it be.

But now the lovely Pandora filled his life, and as she explored Epimetheus's house, out of curiosity she inquired about the jar. Epimetheus did not explain the contents of the unwanted and, up till now, forgotten jar and simply ordered her to leave it be. Time passed, and with it Pandora's curiosity grew. Unable to contain herself any longer, she removed the seals on the jar and opened the lid. Thus Epimetheus, to his great regret, now understood the prophecy of his brother.

But what good was his brother's prediction since it had come to pass? What good is a prophecy if it comes true? Of what use had Prometheus been to his brother? What use was his future sight?

If Prometheus had helped his brother with understanding the shape of the future, helped him by giving him awareness of his own ability to shape his future, then maybe Epimetheus would have been able to alter the progression of events. But Prometheus could only *see* the future—he had no real ability to use this knowledge.

If as astrologers we copy the example of Prometheus—issue forth the prophecy as if it were chiseled into stone—then there is no point in our predictions. What is the point of knowledge if it cannot be used to advantage?

Life is like a journey down a stream; sometimes the stream is calm, sometimes it is white-water rapids. If you know where the rapids are, you can prepare. There are times when the Cosmos wants us to push forward and times when it wants us to retreat. Good predictive work connects us to the rhythm of fate in our lives—puts us in step, so that we become conscious of our own timing. With that consciousness, we can then explore the options and understand the consequences of our future—of actions that we may be taking.

The poet Elizabeth Barrett Browning needed to rebel. It was a time of rebelling. By flowing with that energy, she became fulfilled in her life. What would have happened to her if she hadn't rebelled against her father?

The Duke of Windsor was going to transform either the monarchy or himself. It was a time of transforming a structure; he chose to transform himself.

Napoleon needed to let go of his ambitions, but he decided not to, hence his difficult end. What if he had taken your advice? What new creative ground would he have discovered in the much more hospitable environment of the island of Elba with his own men?

The future is not totally formed. Fate gives us the marble with which to work, and it is the individual, like a sculptor, who creates the final shape. Indeed, it is the sculptor who dictates the final outcome.

Calculating Secondary Progressions

The principle of Secondary progressions is that each day after your birth is equivalent to one year of your life.

USING A MIDNIGHT OR NOON EPHEMERIS

Pretend that you were born at midnight (0 hours) GMT (if using a noon Ephemeris, pretend that you were born at noon GMT) on January 1, 1950.

The positions, as listed in the ephemeris, on the 1st of January would be the natal positions of your planets, luminaries, and so on. On January 2nd, the position of the planets, as listed in the ephemeris, would be the exact position of your secondary progressed planets for your first birthday or the beginning of your second year of life.

If we leap to January 10, 1950, the position of the planets and luminaries, as listed in the ephemeris, will be the position of your secondary progressed planets on your birthday—the beginning of your tenth year of life. Remember, every *day* in the ephemeris is a *year* in your life.

The daily movement of the planets and luminaries is shown as the difference in the positions at midnight (or noon) on the tenth of January to midnight (or noon) of the 11th of January. That movement represents the movement of your secondary progressed planets between your ninth birthday (January 1, 1959) and your tenth birthday (January 1, 1960) because it represents the movement of the planets from your ninth day after birth to your tenth day after birth. See figure 52 (page 248).

These progressed planets can be compared back to your natal chart by aspecting.

As shown in the ephemeris, the progressed planets do not remain stationary (unless they are actually making a station shown). During the course of the day (January 10, 1950), they will be moving—the Moon quite rapidly, the Sun only about a degree, and the other planets at their own different rates. This 24-hour movement is stretched out and becomes the movement of the progressed planets for the entire 12 months between your 9th birthday on January 1, 1959, and your 10th birthday on January 1, 1960, as illustrated in figure 52.

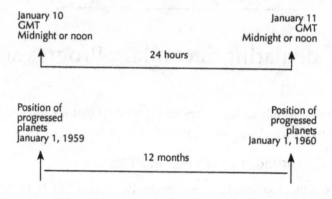

Figure 52. A day for a year method.

So, since there is this movement, the secondary progressed planets and luminaries will move in and out of orb and form aspects back to your natal chart.

It is important that you know precisely when, in a given year, the progressed Moon, or any other progressed body, is going to be forming exact aspects to the natal chart.

For example, we subtract the position of the Moon on January 10, 1950, from the position of the Moon on January 11, 1950, and armed with this information, we can find out how much the Moon has moved over the course of the day. This movement is the movement of the secondary progressed Moon from the birthday in 1959 to the birthday in 1960.

Using a midnight ephemeris, the lunar positions are:

Position of Moon on January 11, 1950 = 14° 29′ 12″ ♎

Position of Moon on January 10, 1950 = 0° 30′ 05″ ♎

Movement of the Moon   13° 59′ 07″

Thus, the movement of the secondary progressed Moon from the 9th birthday (January 1st) in 1959 to the 10th birthday (January 1st) in 1960 is 13° 59' 07".

We now take this progressed Moon's motion and divide it by 12, to obtain the monthly rate of movement for the progressed Moon between January 1, 1959 and January 1, 1960.

Yearly movement of progressed Moon   =   13° 59' 07"

_____

12 months in a year   = 12

In this example, the Moon's monthly movement is 1° 09' 56". So, continuing with the above example, your progressed Moon on your 9th birthday is 0° 30' 05" Libra (actually, the position of the Moon at midnight on January 10, 1950, in the ephemeris). If you are using a noon ephemeris, substitute the noon figures. So, the progressed Moon's rate of motion per month is 1° 09' 56". One month later, on February 1, your secondary progressed Moon will be:

Progressed Moon's position on January 1:   0° 30' 05" ♎

Rate of progressed lunar monthly motion: + 1° 09' 56"

_____

Progressed Moon's position on February 1:   1° 40' 01" ♎

The progressed Moon on March 1 (don't worry about the differences in lengths of the months) will be:

Progressed Moon's position on February 1:   1° 40' 01" ♎

Rate of progressed lunar monthly motion: + 1° 09' 56"

_____

Progressed Moon's position on March 1:   2° 49' 57" ♎

Continue in this fashion, adding the lunar monthly motion to the previous month's position to obtain the monthly positions of the progressed Moon as follows:

| January 1, 1959 | 0° ♎ 30' 05" |
| February 1, 1959 | 1° ♎ 40' 01" |

March 1, 1959	2° ♎ 49′ 57″
April 1, 1959	3° ♎ 59′ 53″
May 1, 1959	5° ♎ 09′ 49″
June 1, 1959	6° ♎ 19′ 45″
July 1, 1959	7° ♎ 29′ 41″
August 1, 1959	8° ♎ 39′ 37″
September 1, 1959	9° ♎ 49′ 33″
October 1, 1959	10° ♎ 59′ 29″
November 1, 1959	12° ♎ 09′ 25″
December 1, 1959	13° ♎ 19′ 21″

These progressed Moon positions can be compared back to the natal chart to find out when certain aspects are going to be made. The other progressed planets will be moving at a much slower rate than the Moon, so it is not normally necessary to compile a monthly table for them.

If, in our above example, the person had been born instead at midnight GMT (or noon) on July 17, 1950, then we could find the position of the planets ten days after birth (July 27, 1950), calculate the movement, divide the movement by 12 to find the monthly movement, and then construct a table starting from July 17, then going to August 17, September 17, and so on.

Thus, if you were lucky enough to be born at midnight GMT (or noon GMT if using a noon ephemeris), you could take the planetary positions as given in the ephemeris and read them as the secondary progressed planets for your birthday in any given year you were examining: 20th year of life equals 20th day after birth, and so on.

Very few of us are born at exactly midnight GMT (or noon GMT). Most of us are born at some other time.

THE ADJUSTED CALCULATED DATE OR ACD

If we took our GMT birth time and calculated the position of the planets for the GMT on a particular date being examined for progression, i.e., the 20th day after birth, and so on—in exactly the same manner as if you were constructing a new natal chart, pretending that you were born 20 days later—then the progressed position of the planets would be for your birthday in your 20th year of birth. You could then do the same process for the 21st day after life, find the difference between the first set of progressed planetary positions and the second, divide those by 12 to get the monthly movement, and construct the table as given above.

Planets calculated for the GMT of your birth on a prescribed day after your birth will always equate to your exact secondary progressed planets on your birthday of that particular prescribed year.

In figure 53, the 24 hours from one midnight (or noon) to the next is symbolized by the length of the top line. By the principle of secondary progressions, one day (24 hours) represents one year of your life. The second line represent one year in your life. The point on the 24 hour line that is your GMT of birth is equivalent to your birthday on the second line.

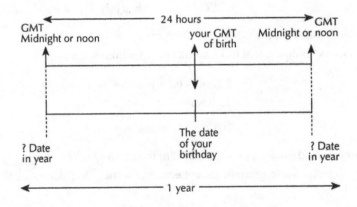

Figure 53. The adjusted calculated date.

What would be the calendar date on the bottom line whose midnight (or noon) would be equivalent to birth GMT? If we knew this date in the year, then we could look up the midnight (or noon) position from ephemeris, and the positions of the planets would be the exact progressed planets for *that* date in any given prescribed year. The position of the planets at midnight (or noon) for the following day would be the exact secondary progressed planetary position for *that* date in the following year, and so on.

The major advantage of knowing that date is that you would no longer need to calculate the planet's positions from your GMT of birth, thereby finding the progressed planetary positions for your birthday on that particular year. Now, you could just use the midnight (or noon) positions for any day with which you wanted to work, and these midnight (or noon) positions would be the exact secondary progressed planets on, not your birthday, but rather that date.

That date is known as the Adjusted Calculated Date or abbreviated to the ACD. Once you work it out for yourself, it never changes because your birth time never changes. The ACD of any year will be the calendar date that the midnight (or noon) ephemeris position will be the exact secondary progressed positions in that year. The calculation of the ACD is as follows:

Step 1: Find the GMT of birth.
(Remember: the GMT, *not* the local birth time)
Example: GMT of birth is 1:43 P.M.
              GMT date of birth is July 17, 1950.

Step 2: Subtract the GMT from 24 hours.
1:43 P.M. is equivalent to 13 hours and 43 minutes, thus,

$$24 \text{ hours } 00 \text{ minutes}$$
$$\underline{-13 \text{ hours } 43 \text{ minutes}}$$
$$10 \text{ hours } 17 \text{ minutes}$$

Step 3: Add the answer from Step 2 to the midnight (or noon) Sidereal Time, given in the ephemeris, for the GMT date of birth.

Continuing the example and using a midnight ephemeris, the Sidereal Time at midnight for the GMT date of birth is:

17 July 1950	=	19h 37' 0"
Answer from Step 2	=	10h 17' 0"
Total	=	29h 54' 0"

Step 4: If the answer to Step 3 is greater than 24 hours, then subtract 24 hours.

$$29\text{h } 54' \ 00''$$
$$\underline{- \ 24\text{h}}$$
$$5\text{h } 54' \ 00''$$

Step 5: Find this time listed in your ephemeris as a Sidereal Time. The date that the ephemeris gives for this Sidereal Time will be the ACD.

It does not matter if you go forward or backwards in the ephemeris, as any given calendar date will always have the same midnight (or noon) Sidereal Time—give or take a few minutes.

Using a midnight ephemeris:

5h 54'0" is the Sidereal Time for December 20th or 21st of *any* year.

You could use either December 20th or 21st as the ACD.

Step 6: If the ACD is later in the year than your birthday, then your progressions will be for that date *the year before.*

To explain, if we look at the above example, the ACD is in December and the birthday is in July, so the ACD is later than the birthday.

In the year of birth, on July 17, 1950, when December 20th came around, you were only five months old. So, if we took the midnight (or noon) positions on July 18, 1950 (the day after your birth), those positions would not be equivalent to December 20, 1951 (1950 plus 1 year)—when you were 18 months old—but rather December 20, 1950—when you were just five months old.

(1950 plus 1 year = 1951, put date back a year = 1950)

On the other hand, if we have worked out that the ACD for a person born on July 17, 1950, was March 14, then the ACD is earlier in the year than the birth date. Thus when we look at the midnight (or noon) positions for July 18, 1950 (the day after birth), then we are looking at the exact secondary progressed planets for March 14, 1951.

(1950 plus 1 year = 1951)

ACD OCCURRING LATER THAN THE BIRTHDAY

Once the ACD date has been found, the next step is to find the date in the ephemeris after birth that corresponds to the year of the client's life that you want to examine.

Staying with the same example, let us say that your client, Jane, was born on July 17, 1950, and her ACD is December 20th. She is coming to see you in 1988.

1988 − 1950 = 38 years

That means you will need to examine the situation 38 days after she was born. However, if we work with the data from 38 days after she was born we are NOT going to get the progressed planets for December 20, 1988. As Step 6 denotes, her ACD is later than her birthday:

Year of birth + 38 years, and then put date back a year.

This means the progressed positions after 38 days will be for December 20, 1987.

Using Table 1 on page 255:

July 17 =   198th   day of the year

    plus   38   days (number of years from 1950 to 1988)

            236th day of the year.

The 236th day of the year is August 24.

Therefore the position of the planets on August 24, 1950, will be her secondary progressed planets for December 20, 1987.

ACD OCCURRING EARLIER THAN THE BIRTHDAY

Use the same birth date, but now let the ACD be March 14. The client is coming to see you in 1988.

1988 – 1950 = 38 years

Therefore we need to look at the position of the planets 38 days after she was born.

July 17 =   198th   day of the year

    plus   38   days

            236th day of the year.

The 236th day of the year is August 24.

Therefore, if we look up the midnight (or noon) planetary positions for August 24, 1950, these will be the exact secondary progressions for March 14, 1988.

Table 1. Number of Days between Two Dates*

January	February	March	April	May	June	July	August	September	October	November	December
1	32	60	91	121	152	182	213	244	274	305	335
2	33	61	92	122	153	183	214	245	275	306	336
3	34	62	93	123	154	184	215	246	276	307	337
4	35	63	94	124	155	185	216	247	277	308	338
5	36	64	95	125	156	186	217	248	278	309	339
6	37	65	96	126	157	187	218	249	279	310	340
7	38	66	97	127	158	188	219	250	280	311	341
8	39	67	98	128	159	189	220	251	281	312	342
9	40	68	99	129	160	190	221	252	282	313	343
10	41	69	100	130	161	191	222	253	283	314	344
11	42	70	101	131	162	192	223	254	284	315	345
12	43	71	102	132	163	193	224	255	285	316	346
13	44	72	103	133	164	194	225	256	286	317	347
14	45	73	104	134	165	195	226	257	287	318	348
15	46	74	105	135	166	196	227	258	288	319	349
16	47	75	106	136	167	197	228	259	289	320	350
17	48	76	107	137	168	198	229	260	290	321	351
18	49	77	108	138	169	199	230	261	291	322	352
19	50	78	109	139	170	200	231	262	292	323	353
20	51	79	110	140	171	201	232	263	293	324	354
21	52	80	111	141	172	202	233	264	294	325	355
22	53	81	112	142	173	203	234	265	295	326	356
23	54	82	113	143	174	204	235	266	296	327	357
24	55	83	114	144	175	205	236	267	297	328	358
25	56	84	115	145	176	206	237	268	298	329	359
26	57	85	116	146	177	207	238	269	299	330	360
27	58	86	117	147	178	208	239	270	300	331	361
28	59	87	118	148	179	209	240	271	301	332	362
29		88	119	149	180	210	241	272	302	333	363
30		89	120	150	181	211	242	273	303	334	364
31		90		151		212	243		304		365

*Add a day for leap years.

Calculating Returns

TROPICAL RETURNS

Using the solar return as an example:

Step 1: Find the natal position of the Sun to the nearest second of arc. You more than likely know the position of your natal Sun to the accuracy of degree and minute. But for a return we need to know the seconds of arc. If you do not know this information then recalculate your natal Sun, taking the seconds of arc into account.

Step 2: Find the GMT date in the year that the Sun is going to return to this natal position.

For a solar return, this will always be your birthday plus or minus a day.
For example, if the natal position of your Sun is 12° 15′ 34″ Gemini and we wanted to calculate the solar return in 1985, then the date on which the Sun was going to return to that position will be June 2, 1985.

Step 3: Find the daily movement of the Sun on the day given in Step 2.

June 3, 1985, the Sun	= 12° 30′ 34″
June 2, 1985, the Sun	= 11° 32′ 23″
Daily movement of Sun	= 0° 58′ 11″

Step 4: Find out how much the Sun has to move from its earlier position to be in the return, or natal, position.

On June 2, 1985, the Sun was at 11° 32′ 23″. During the course of the day it will pass over the natal position of 12° 15′ 34″ and by midnight it will be at 12° 30′ 34″ Gemini. How much does it have to move from its earlier position (11° 32′ 23″) to its return position (12° 15′ 34″)?

Return position   =   12° 15′ 34″

Earlier position   =   11° 32′ 23″

Movement required   =   0° 43′ 11″

Step 5: Use the following formula:

$$\text{GMT of Solar Return} = \frac{\text{Movement required}}{\text{Daily movement}} \times 24 \text{ hours}$$

Using our example:

$$\frac{0° \, 43′ \, 11″}{0° \, 58′ \, 11″} \times 24 \text{ hours}$$

Do this using a calculator, and the answer is: 17 hours 48 minutes 46 seconds. This time is the GMT of the solar return.*

Step 6: Calculate the solar return, for any given location, using the GMT date and time worked out in Steps 1 to 4.

If you were in Adelaide, South Australia, you would calculate a chart for the following data:

> June 2, 1985
> 17h 48′ 46″ GMT
> Adelaide, South Australia
> Longitude 138E34
> Latitude 34S55

If you were in London you would calculate a chart for the following data:

> June 2, 1985
> 17h 48′ 46″ GMT
> London, UK
> Longitude 0W10
> Latitude 51N31

and so on, for any given location.

Using these steps, you can calculate the returns of the Sun, Moon, Personal New Moon, Mercury, Venus, and Mars. However, a word of caution: if Mercury, Venus, or Mars is moving very slowly on the date of the return,

---

*   This is much simpler to do if your calculator has keys for degrees, minutes, and seconds. Otherwise, you have to convert from base 60 to decimal.

then your angles could be out because you may need to work with units smaller than a second of arc, and the ephemeris does not give planet data to such a degree of accuracy.

SIDEREAL RETURNS

These returns are for the moment that the Sun, or any orbiting body in the solar system, returns to a particular position with regards to the fixed stars.

The fixed stars appear to move forward at a rate of 50.25″ arc per year, thereby making the 0° Aries point appear to move backwards against this belt of "fixed" stars.

Thus in our above example, if we had wanted to calculate the Sidereal solar return we would do the first step:

Step 1: Find the natal position of the Sun to the nearest second of arc.

In our example that was 12° 15′ 34″ Gemini.

However, before we go to Step 2, this natal position is altered to take into account the moving "fixed" stars. The stars are moving at a rate of 50.25″ per year.

Let's pretend that the person was born in 1950. We are doing the return for 1985.

$$1985 - 1950 = 35 \text{ years}$$

The stars are moving at a rate of 50.25″ per year. Therefore: 35 years × 50.25″ = how much the stars have moved since the person was born.

$$35 \times 50.25'' = 0° 29' 19''$$

So in 1950 the stars that were at 12° 15′ 34″ Gemini have now, by the birthday in 1985, moved on by 0° 29′ 19″.

Thus to get the Sun returning to these stars, we must return the Sun to its natal position plus this star movement.

$$12° 15' 34'' + 0° 29' 19'' = 12° 44' 53''$$

The position of the Sun used for a Sidereal return is the natal position plus 0° 0′ 50.25″ for every year of life.

Thus we will use the position of 12° 44′ 53″ Gemini. Armed with this new position, we can go on with steps 2 through 6 as given for the Tropical returns. The same methodologies apply to all other previously mentioned returns.

Appendix 3

Planetary Arcs

For a given date that you wish to examine by Solar Arc:

Step 1: Find the position of the progressed Sun.

Step 2: Subtract the natal Sun from this new progressed Sun position.

This will give you the distance traveled by the progressed Sun from birth to the date that you are examining. This movement is called the Solar Arc. (We could do the same process for the progressed Moon and that would give us the Lunar Arc, and so on.)

Step 3: Add this Solar Arc to all the natal planetary and point positions. This will give you the Solar Arc directed chart.

Step 4: Compare this Solar Arc directed chart back to the natal chart using the following aspects: 0°, 45°, 90°, 135°, 180°.

We will use Abraham Lincoln as an example:

On the day of Lincoln's assassination, his secondary progressed Sun was 19° 24′ Aries. Subtract his natal Sun from this new position:

$$
\begin{array}{rl}
\text{Natal Sun} \quad = & 23° 27′ \text{ Aquarius} \\
- & 19° 24′ \text{ Aries} \\
\hline
= & 55° 57′
\end{array}
$$

Thus Lincoln's Solar Arc for the date of his death was: 55° 57′

This Solar Arc is then added to every point in his chart shown in the following table on page 260.

Natal Position	plus 55° 57'	Solar Arc
Sun: 23° 27' Aquarius	55° 57'	19/24 Aries
Moon: 27° 06' Capricorn	55° 57'	23/03 Pisces
Mercury: 10° 19' Pisces	55° 57'	6/16 Taurus
Venus: 7° 28' Aries	55° 57'	3/25 Gemini
Mars: 25° 29' Libra	55° 57'	21/26 Sagittarius
Jupiter: 22° 06' Pisces	55° 57'	18/03 Taurus
Saturn: 3° 08' Sagittarius	55° 57'	29/05 Capricorn
Uranus: 9° 40' Scorpio	55° 57'	5/37 Capricorn
Neptune: 6° 41' Sagittarius	55° 57'	2/38 Aquarius
Pluto: 13° 37' Pisces	55° 57'	9/34 Taurus
North Node: 6° 56' Scorpio	55° 57'	2/53 Capricorn
Ascendant: 26° 27' Aquarius	55° 57'	22/24 Aquarius
MC: 10° 17' Sagittarius	55° 57'	6/14 Aquarius
Vertex: 15° 09' Virgo	55° 57'	11/06 Scorpio

In comparing the Solar Arc position back to the natal, you will notice that the SA directed Pluto is at 9° 34' Taurus and the natal Uranus is at 9' 40' Scorpio. Keep your orbs less than 1°.

Planetary Conjunctions (1900–2050)

JUPITER-SATURN (ABOUT EVERY 20 YEARS)

1901	November 28	14° ♑ 00'
1921	September 10	26° ♍ 36'
1940	August 8	14° ♉ 27'
1940	October 20	12° ♉ 28'
1941	February 15	9° ♉ 07'
1961	February 19	25° ♑ 12'
1980	December 31	9° ♎ 30'
1981	March 3	8° ♎ 06'
1981	July 24	4° ♎ 56'
2000	May 28	22° ♉ 43'
2020	December 21	0° ♒ 29'
2040	October 31	17° ♎ 56'

JUPITER-URANUS (ABOUT EVERY 14 YEARS)

1900	October 20	10° ♐ 06'
1914	March 4	9° ♒ 32'
1927	July 15	3° ♈ 24'
1927	August 11	3° ♈ 00'
1928	January 25	0° ♈ 24'
1941	May 8	25° ♉ 38'
1954	October 7	27° ♋ 23'
1955	January 7	26° ♋ 04'
1955	May 10	24° ♋ 15'
1968	December 12	3° ♎ 39'
1969	March 11	2° ♎ 27'
1969	July 20	0° ♎ 40'

1983	February 18	8° ♐ 52'
1983	May 14	7° ♐ 44'
1983	September 25	5° ♐ 49'
1997	February 16	5° ♒ 56'
2010	June 8	0° ♈ 18'
2010	September 19	28° ♓ 43'
2011	January 4	27° ♓ 02'
2024	April 21	21° ♉ 50'
2037	September 8	23° ♋ 03'
2038	February 19	20° ♋ 39'
2038	March 30	20° ♋ 05'

JUPITER-NEPTUNE (ABOUT EVERY 13 YEARS)

1907	May 22	10° ♋ 50'
1919	September 24	10° ♌ 49'
1920	March 8	9° ♌ 12'
1920	April 24	8° ♌ 45'
1932	September 19	8° ♍ 25'
1945	September 22	5° ♎ 54'
1958	September 24	3° ♏ 18'
1971	February 1	2° ♐ 47'
1971	May 22	1° ♐ 44'
1971	September 16	0° ♐ 37'
1984	January 19	0° ♑ 01'
1997	January 9	27° ♑ 09'
2009	May 27	26° ♒ 29'
2009	July 10	26° ♒ 02'
2009	December 21	24° ♒ 18'
2022	April 12	23° ♓ 59'
2035	March 24	21° ♈ 21'
2047	July 22	21° ♉ 19'
2047	November 16	20° ♉ 05'
2048	February 24	19° ♉ 01'

JUPITER-PLUTO (ABOUT EVERY 13 YEARS)

1906	June 26	22° ♊ 31'
1918	August 10	6° ♋ 03'

1931	May 27	19° ♋ 16'
1943	August 1	6° ♌ 53'
1955	November 2	28° ♌ 25'
1956	February 8	27° ♌ 36'
1956	June 16	26° ♌ 28'
1968	October 13	23° ♍ 40'
1981	November 2	24° ♎ 53'
1994	December 2	28° ♏ 26'
2007	December 11	28° ♍ 24'
2020	April 5	24° ♑ 53'
2020	June 30	24° ♑ 06'
2020	November 12	22° ♑ 52'
2033	February 5	14° ♒ 50'
2045	April 12	3° ♓ 32'

SATURN-URANUS (ABOUT EVERY 45 YEARS)

1942	May 3	29° ♉ 20'
1988	February 13	29° ♐ 55'
1988	June 26	28° ♐ 47'
1988	October 18	27° ♐ 49'
2032	June 28	28° ♊ 01'

SATURN-NEPTUNE (ABOUT EVERY 36 YEARS)

1917	August 1	4° ♌ 45'
1952	November 21	22° ♎ 47'
1953	May 1	22° ♎ 39'
1953	July 22	21° ♎ 12'
1989	March 3	11° ♑ 55'
1989	June 24	11° ♑ 14'
1989	November 13	10° ♑ 22'
2026	February 20	0° ♈ 45'

SATURN-PLUTO (ABOUT EVERY 33 YEARS)

1914	October 4	2° ♋ 14'
1914	November 1	2° ♋ 04'
1915	May 19	0° ♋ 54'
1947	August 11	13° ♌ 07'

| 1982 | November 8 | 27° ♎ 36' |
| 2020 | January 12 | 22° ♑ 46' |

URANUS-NEPTUNE (ABOUT EVERY 171 YEARS)

1993	February 2	19° ♑ 34'
1993	August 20	18° ♑ 48'
1993	October 24	18° ♑ 33'

URANUS-PLUTO (ABOUT EVERY 127 YEARS)

1965	October 9	17° ♍ 10'
1966	April 4	16° ♍ 28'
1966	June 30	16° ♍ 06'

NEPTUNE-PLUTO (ABOUT EVERY 492 YEARS)

(LAST CONJUNCTION)

1891	August 2	8° ♊ 38'
1891	November 5	8° ♊ 19'
1892	April 30	7° ♊ 42'

Appendix 5

Outer Planet Conjunctions

Year	Conjunction	Year	Conjunction
1900	Jupiter-Uranus	1942	Saturn-Uranus
1901	Jupiter-Saturn	1943	Jupiter-Pluto
1906	Jupiter-Pluto	1945	Jupiter-Neptune
1907	Jupiter-Neptune	1947	Saturn-Pluto
1914	Jupiter-Uranus	1952	Saturn-Neptune
1914	Saturn-Pluto	1953	Saturn-Neptune
1915	Saturn-Pluto	1954	Jupiter-Uranus
1917	Saturn-Neptune	1955	Jupiter-Uranus
1918	Jupiter-Pluto	1955	Jupiter-Pluto
1919	Jupiter-Neptune	1956	Jupiter-Pluto
1920	Jupiter-Neptune	1958	Jupiter-Neptune
1921	Jupiter-Saturn	1961	Jupiter-Saturn
1927	Jupiter-Uranus	1965	Uranus-Pluto
1928	Jupiter-Uranus	1968	Jupiter-Uranus
1931	Jupiter-Pluto	1968	Jupiter-Pluto
1932	Jupiter-Neptune	1969	Jupiter-Uranus
1940	Jupiter-Saturn	1971	Jupiter-Neptune
1941	Jupiter-Saturn	1981	Jupiter-Saturn
1941	Jupiter-Uranus	1981	Jupiter-Pluto

Year	Conjunction	Year	Conjunction
1982	Saturn-Pluto	2020	Jupiter-Pluto
1983	Jupiter-Uranus	2020	Saturn-Pluto
1984	Jupiter-Neptune	2022	Jupiter-Neptune
1988	Saturn-Uranus	2024	Jupiter-Uranus
1989	Saturn-Neptune	2026	Saturn-Neptune
1993	Uranus-Neptune	2032	Saturn-Uranus
1994	Jupiter-Pluto	2033	Jupiter-Pluto
1997	Jupiter-Uranus	2035	Jupiter-Neptune
1997	Jupiter-Neptune	2037	Jupiter-Uranus
2000	Jupiter-Saturn	2038	Jupiter-Uranus
2007	Jupiter-Pluto	2040	Jupiter-Saturn
2009	Jupiter-Neptune	2045	Jupiter-Pluto
2010	Jupiter-Uranus	2047	Jupiter-Neptune
2011	Jupiter-Uranus	2048	Jupiter-Neptune
2020	Jupiter-Saturn		

Appendix 6

The Saros Cycles

What follows is a detailed look at each individual Saros Series current at the time of writing. They are listed in order by their number, starting with Saros Series 1 and ending with Saros Series 19.

The birth data, or commencement date, of each Series is given, as well as the planetary positions at that moment. The tightest aspects are then listed. You may want to consider more unconventional aspects, so the full planetary listing with degrees and minutes has been provided. I have not included the angles because the eclipse occurs at 90° of northern or southern latitude, making the concept of angles meaningless.

In addition the planetary pattern has been delineated—but through the lens of my own ideas, experience, and research. If you feel that you would delineate some of these patterns differently, please feel free to go ahead. Feedback over the years will eventually sharpen up these, or your, delineations. Browse through this forest of trees; the diversity between different Saros Series will show you that eclipses can have a whole range of expression. Each Series has its own precise planetary patterns, some difficult, some easy.

After each delineation, I have listed the years between 1900 and 2050 when that particular Series will be occurring. A more detailed listing is given later in the book.

S.S. 1 NORTH

Starts: January 4, 1639, 5:12:37 GMT North Pole
Ends: February 2, 2883

Planets:

☉ & ☽ 13° ♑ 48′	☿ 17° ♑ 42′
♀ 2° ♑ 47′	♂ 17° ♓ 39′
♃ 27° ♏ 44′	♄ 6° ♒ 22′
♅ 27° ♎ 46′	♆ 22° ♏ 30′
♇ 28° ♉ 43′	☊ 27° ♐ 0′

Aspects: There is a Jupiter-Pluto opposition that is directly on the Uranus/Node midpoint. The Jupiter/Saturn midpoint is also on the Venus axis. Mars squares the New Moon/Neptune midpoint.

Jupiter = Pluto = Uranus/Node

Venus = Jupiter/Saturn

Mars = New Moon/Neptune

Unexpected events involving friends or groups place a great deal of pressure on personal relationships. These relationship issues may loom large as the eclipse affects the chart. The individual would be wise not to make any hasty decisions since information is distorted and possibly false. The eclipse also has an essence of tiredness or health problems attached to it.

Eclipses 1950–2050:

1909, 1927, 1945, 1963, 1981, 1999, 2017, 2035

S.S. 1 SOUTH

Starts: August 24, 1729, 14:04:17 GMT South Pole

Ends: September 22, 2973

Planets: ☉ & ☽ 1° ♍ 15'   ☿ 15° ♌ 09'

☿ 15° ♋ 26'   ♂ 26° ♋ 27'

♃ 27° ♋ 36'   ♄ 5° ♓ 57'

♅ 23° ♏ 02'   ♆ 12° ♊ 51'

♇ 8° ♎ 51'   ☊ 13° ♒ 59'

Aspects: Mercury conjunct South Node. The Node is on the midpoint of the Mars/Jupiter conjunction and the New Moon.

Node = Mercury = New Moon/Mars, Jupiter

This family of eclipses is concerned with ideas and their enthusiastic expression. If this eclipse affects your chart, you will be flooded with ideas or options. There may seem to be an element of haste, but if you can go with the new ideas, they will have positive outcomes.

Eclipses 1900–2050:

1909, 1927, 1946, 1964, 1982, 2000, 2018, 2036

S.S. 2 OLD NORTH

Starts: June 24, 792 o.s., 6:03:26 GMT North Pole

Ends: July 23, 2036

Planets: ☉ & ☽ 5° ♋ 49'   ☿ 25° ♊ 56'

♀ 16° ♌ 10'   ♂ 29° ♈ 24'

♃ 6° ♋ 53'   ♄ 6° ♉ 58'

♅ 11° ♍ 13'   ♆ 18° ♍ 21'

♇ 24° ♑ 49'   ☊ 19° ♊ 47'

Aspects: The New Moon conjuncts Jupiter and this conjunction sits directly on the Mars/Uranus midpoint. Mercury is on the Venus/Saturn midpoint.

New Moon = Jupiter = Mars/Uranus

Mercury = Venus/Saturn

This is a difficult eclipse family, as its members bring unfortunate news concerning friendships or relationships. You will be dealing with ideas of separation or the ending of a union. However, although the picture may look glum as the eclipse takes effect, the actual results are quite positive. You will quickly grasp what has to be done, and fast action can bring good results. The theme of this eclipse is action concerning personal relationships.

Eclipses 1900–2050:

1910, 1928, 1946, 1964, 1982, 2000, 2018, 2036 Series ends

S.S. 2 NEW NORTH

Starts: June 17, 1928, 20:41:45 GMT North Pole

Ends: July 16, 3172

Planets: ☉ & ☽ 26° ♊ 21'   ☿ 12° ♋ 27'

♀ 22° ♊ 36'   ♂ 23° ♈ 51'

♃ 2° ♉ 42'   ♄ 15° ♐ 02'

♅ 7° ♈ 09'   ♆ 26° ♌ 51'

♇ 16° ♋ 09'   ☊ 8° ♊ 43'

Aspects: Uranus squares the New Moon/Pluto midpoint. The New Moon is also on the Mercury/Node midpoint. The Jupiter/Pluto midpoint is on the Nodal axis, and the Saturn sits on the Venus/Node midpoint.

New Moon = Mercury/Node

Uranus = New Moon/Pluto

Node = Jupiter/Pluto

Saturn = Venus/Node

If this family of eclipses affects a chart, the person will experience the sudden collapse of plans or lifestyles. Confusion may reign, but the long-term effects are those of rebuilding and transformation. After the dust has settled, the rebuilding starts and the consequences of this reshaping will have far-reaching effects. This eclipse family changes a person's direction through the sudden collapse of an existing structure.

Eclipses 1900–2050:

1928, 1946, 1964, 1982, 2000, 2018, 2036

S.S. 2 SOUTH

Starts: April 17, 991 o.s., 9:38:39 GMT South Pole
Ends: May 19, 2235

Planets:

☉ & ☽ 1° ♉ 47′	☿ 16° ♈ 33′
♀ 0° ♈ 19′	♂ 14° ♐ 39′
♃ 12° ♈ 59′	♄ 8° ♒ 59′
♅ 3° ♒ 42′	♆ 7° ♐ 27′
♇ 10° ♎ 57′	☊ 14° ♎ 24′

Aspects: The Nodal axis is on the midpoint of Mercury/Jupiter. The Jupiter is on the Pluto/Node midpoint. The Mercury is on the New Moon/Venus midpoint. The Neptune is on the Uranus/Pluto midpoint.

Node = Mercury/Jupiter

Jupiter = Pluto/Node

Mercury = New Moon/Venus

Neptune = Uranus/Pluto

This eclipse is concerned with unusual groups and the individual's involvement with those groups. This could be the time when the individual notices or suddenly desires to find a particular group whose concerns would be with healing, the arts, or the love of humanity. The individual will feel that, through involvement with such a group, he or she will gain a great deal.

Eclipses 1900–2050:

1910, 1928, 1946, 1964, 1982, 2000, 2019, 2037

S.S. 3 NORTH

Starts: October 10, 991 o.s., 14:11:40 GMT North Pole

Ends: November 11, 2235

Planets:

☉ & ☽ 22° ♊ 06'	☿ 1° ♏ 34'
♀ 6° ♏ 49'	♂ 17° ♑ 42'
♃ 26° ♈ 01'	♄ 2° ♒ 59'
♅ 29° ♑ 53'	♆ 6° ♐ 04'
♇ 13° ♎ 13'	☊ 5° ♎ 04'

Aspects: The New Moon is on the midpoint of Mercury/Pluto. Jupiter is on the midpoint of Venus/Pluto.

New Moon = Mercury/Pluto

Jupiter = Venus/Pluto

This is an over-excessive eclipse family. Its main theme is either news involving young people or news that transforms a situation. This information can cause worry or can cause the person to become obsessive. The individual may want to undertake large plans or activities, which can be very positive as long as the individual doesn't get carried away.

Eclipses 1900–2050:

1911, 1929, 1947, 1965, 1983, 2001, 2019, 2037

S.S. 3 SOUTH

Starts: August 13, 1208 o.s., 8:24:13 GMT South Pole
Ends: September 17, 2452

Planets: ☉ & ☽ 27° ♌ 10'   ☿ 26° ♌ 58'
☉ & ☽ 19° ♋ 19'   ♂ 19° ♋ 33'
♃ 13° ♌ 13'   ♄ 5° ♋ 14'
♅ 0° ♍ 50'   ♆ 5° ♈ 27'
♇ 10° ♌ 15'   ☊ 10° ♒ 57'

Aspects: Mercury is conjunct the New Moon. There is a Venus-Mars conjunction and Pluto is conjunct the Nodal axis. The Node-Pluto conjunction is on the midpoints of both the Mars/Uranus and the Venus/Uranus.

Mercury = New Moon

Node = Pluto = Uranus/Mars = Venus/Uranus

This family of eclipses brings with it the sudden ending of associations or of a relationship, possibly with a younger person. There is a large emotional component, as the Pluto is involved, and a sense of traumatic transformation. This can be through news received or short journeys undertaken.

Eclipses 1900–2050:

1911, 1929, 1947, 1965, 1983, 2001, 2019, 2038

S.S. 4 NORTH

Starts: May 25, 1389 o.s., 16:53:11 GMT North Pole
Ends: June 29, 2633

Planets: ☉ & ☽ 12° ♊ 08'   ☿ 1° ♋ 44'
♀ 13° ♉ 47'   ♂ 16° ♋ 04'
♃ 24° ♎ 44'   ♄ 20° ♌ 48'
♅ 0° ♏ 33'   ♆ 13° ♉ 21'
♇ 24° ♉ 47'   ☊ 24° ♉ 21'

Aspects: Jupiter is quincunx a Pluto-Node conjunction. Venus conjuncts Neptune. The New Moon is also on the Mercury/Node midpoint while Saturn is on the New Moon/Uranus midpoint.

New Moon = Mercury/Node

Saturn = New Moon/Uranus

Jupiter (quincunx) Pluto = Node

Neptune = Venus

Restriction, inhibition, restraint, separation, and illusions are the trademarks of this family of eclipses. Events can occur that seem to block the individual. In this blocking, the individual is very prone to misjudge his or her strengths or the situation and is best advised to wait until the eclipse passes before taking any real action. This is a difficult Saros Series.

Eclipses 1900–2050:

1912, 1930, 1948, 1966, 1984, 2002, 2020, 2038

S.S. 4 SOUTH

Starts: March 19, 1624, 4:25:46 GMT South Pole
Ends: May 15, 2868

Planets:

☉ & ☽ 29° ♓ 0'	☿ 26° ♓ 13'
♀ 14° ♒ 29'	♂ 16° ♉ 52'
♃ 21° ♌ 55'	♄ 12° ♌ 27'
♅ 13° ♌ 10'	♆ 19° ♎ 40'
♇ 14° ♉ 45'	☊ 13° ♎ 10'

Aspects: The New Moon is on the Venus/Pluto midpoint. There is a Mars-Pluto conjunction, and Venus is in opposition to the Saturn-Uranus conjunction.

New Moon = Venus/Pluto

Mars = Pluto

Venus = Saturn = Uranus

The series carries with it very strong emotional feelings concerning relationships and/or money. There could be anger or lust. There is a sense of fatedness, and individuals may find themselves caught up in relationship events that are beyond their control. There could also be the sudden desire to finish a relationship. These emotions may be blocked or checked in some way, leading to a great deal of frustration. The best approach to this eclipse is to avoid rash action until the issues settle down.

Eclipses 1900–2050:

1912, 1930, 1948, 1966, 1984, 2002, 2020, 2038

S.S. 5 NORTH

(The starting date of this series may be incorrect.)

Starts: October 12, 1624, 9:08:29 GMT North Pole
Ends: 2868

Planets:

☉ & ☽ 19° ♎ 26′	☿ 11° ♏ 19′
♀ 24° ♎ 39′	♂ 0° ♎ 43′
♃ 19° ♍ 30′	♄ 29° ♌ 11′
♅ 20° ♌ 42′	♆ 20° ♎ 13′
♇ 16° ♌ 42′	☊ 2° ♎ 11′

Aspects: The New Moon is conjunct Neptune, and Mars is on the Mercury/Uranus midpoint.

New Moon = Neptune

Mars = Mercury/Uranus

A very unusual Saros Series involving sudden flashes of ideas that seem to have a psychic or unconscious flavor to them. Hunches, visions, prophetic dreams are the essence of this family of eclipses. A truly creative series that should leave the individual enriched. The ideas or hunches that come from this eclipse can be acted upon.

Eclipses 1900–2050:

1913, 1931, 1949, 1967, 1985, 2003, 2021, 2039

S.S. 5 NEW SOUTH

Starts: July 14, 1787, 23:03:14 GMT South Pole

Ends: August 12, 3031

Planets: ⊙ & ☽ 22° ♋ 16'   ☿ 17° ♌ 17'

♀ 27° ♊ 10'   ♂ 22° ♉ 05'

♃ 15° ♊ 15'   ♄ 27° ♒ 50'

♅ 25° ♋ 38'   ♆ 16° ♎ 15'

♇ 15° ♒ 33'   ☊ 4° ♑ 21'

Aspects: The New Moon is on the midpoint of Mercury/Venus, and the Node is on the New Moon/Jupiter midpoint.

New Moon = Mercury/Venus

Node = New Moon/Jupiter

This is a very joyful, happy family of eclipses. There is a sense of good news, falling in love, a peak experience that is joyful in some way. The benefits that appear in the individual's life under this eclipse Series can be expected to continue well after the eclipse has passed.

Eclipses 1900–2050:

1913, 1931, 1949, 1967, 1985, 2003, 2021, 2039

S.S. 6 NORTH

Starts: May 15, 850 o.s., 12:14:28 GMT North Pole

Ends: June 15, 2094

Planets: ⊙ & ☽ 27° ♉ 55'   ☿ 19° ♊ 44'

♀ 12° ♈ 22'   ♂ 14° ♑ 43'

♃ 24° ♉ 40'   ♄ 22° ♈ 19'

♅ 17° ♉ 41'   ♆ 27° ♑ 35'

♇ 6° ♈ 30'   ☊ 10° ♉ 05'

Aspects: The Node is on the New Moon/Saturn midpoint, and there is a New Moon-Neptune quincunx.

Node = New Moon/Saturn

New Moon quincunx Neptune

This family of eclipses is concerned with the individual's relationship to father figures, authority figures, or the need to take responsibility and control. This is a time to accept the commitments that are presented, commitments that could occur due to another person's illness or another person's unreliability.

Eclipses 1900–2050:

1914, 1932, 1950, 1968, 1986, 2004, 2022, 2040

S.S. 6 SOUTH

Starts: March 6, 1049, 15:45:55 GMT South Pole
Ends: April 8, 2293

Planets:
☉ & ☽ 21° ♓ 55'   ☿ 15° ♓ 51'
♀ 20° ♓ 30'   ♂ 13° ♌ 25'
♃ 27° ♒ 33'   ♄ 27° ♑ 19'
♅ 10° ♎ 10'   ♆ 13° ♈ 03'
♇ 12° ♒ 30'   ☊ 4° ♍ 45'

Aspects: There is a Pluto-Mars opposition and the eclipse is conjunct Venus with this conjunction sitting on the Uranus/Node midpoint.

Pluto = Mars

New Moon = Venus = Uranus/Node

This eclipse series is about being forceful and taking power. It has a manic flavor about it, with great force or strength manifesting in the relationship area. Individuals experiencing this Saros Series may experience sudden events, like falling in or out of love or sudden sexual encounters. The individual may also exert a huge effort in some group activity.

Eclipses 1900–2050:

1914, 1932, 1950, 1968, 1986, 2004, 2022, 2040

S.S. 7 NORTH

Starts: October 3, 1103 o.s., 3:08:03 GMT North Pole
Ends: November 5, 2347

Planets: ☉ & ☽ 15° ♎ 29'   ☿ 22° ♎ 55'

                        ♀ 6° ♏ 47'   ♂ 23° ♍ 56'

                        ♃ 4° ♎ 25'   ♄ 1° ♐ 52'

                        ♅ 27° ♉ 59'   ♆ 16° ♌ 45'

                        ♇ 14° ♈ 44'   ☊ 29° ♍ 11'

Aspects: The eclipse occurs while being in opposition to Pluto and at the same time sits on the Venus/Mars midpoint.

New Moon = Pluto = Venus/Mars

A very sensual family of eclipses, ranging from sudden sexual passions and lust to birth and procreative drives. This series is not subtle; it can catch people off guard and confront them with their own very deep passion, which may have been hidden for many years.

Eclipses 1900–2050:

1915, 1933, 1951, 1969, 1987, 2005, 2023, 2041

S.S. 7 SOUTH

Starts: June 22, 1248 o.s., 19:07:18 GMT South Pole
Ends: July 26, 2492

Planets: ☉ & ☽ 8° ♋ 03'   ☿ 0° ♌ 52'

                        ♀ 23° ♉ 42'   ♂ 8° ♌ 34'

                        ♃ 5° ♐ 37'   ♄ 5° ♏ 09'

                        ♅ 26° ♒ 38'   ♆ 3° ♋ 24'

                        ♇ 8° ♏ 09'   ☊ 20° ♐ 01'

Aspects: Pluto trines the eclipse and Mars forms a square to the Pluto.

(Mars = Pluto) trine New Moon

The immense power, anger, and force of the Mars square Pluto are channeled into this family of eclipses via the trine. The individual experiencing this series will find that huge obstacles will suddenly and easily clear or, on the negative side, a pending potential crisis will suddenly manifest and move through his or her life very rapidly. Either way, the individual will feel that everything is moving at great speed.

Eclipses 1900–2050:

1915, 1933, 1951, 1969, 1987, 2005, 2023, 2041

S.S. 8 NORTH

Starts: May 17, 1501, 3:39:06 GMT North Pole

Ends: June 23, 2745

Planets:

☉ & ☽ 4° ♊ 51′	☿ 26° ♊ 47′
♀ 12° ♉ 18′	♂ 27° ♓ 14′
♃ 24° ♈ 08′	♄ 8° ♊ 07′
♅ 4° ♓ 00′	♆ 19° ♑ 04′
♇ 26° ♏ 12′	☊ 18° ♉ 32′

Aspects: The New Moon squares Uranus and is also on the midpoint of Mercury/Venus. Pluto holds a powerful position as it occupies the midpoint of Venus/Saturn as well as the New Moon/Node. In addition, there is a Mars-Mercury square with Mars on the New Moon/Neptune midpoint.

New Moon = Uranus = Mercury/Venus

Pluto = Venus/Saturn = New Moon/Node

Mars = Mercury = New Moon/Neptune

Inventiveness and flashes of genius are the hallmark of this Saros Series. The individual will have intuitive leaps, insights, good ideas, visions, or vivid dreams. This newfound inspiration will pull the person away from his or her social life or relationship, thereby causing strain in the private life. This is a time when the person needs to be free, if only for a few weeks.

Eclipses 1900–2050:

1916, 1934, 1952, 1970, 1988, 2006, 2024, 2042

S.S. 8 SOUTH

Starts: April 1, 1718, 0:15:02 GMT South Pole

Ends: April 30, 2962

Planets: ☉ & ☽ 10° ♈ 54'   ☿ 19° ♓ 52'

                       ♀ 23° ♈ 21'   ♂ 20° ♉ 19'

                       ♃ 24° ♋ 27'   ♄ 29° ♎ 42'

                       ♅ 3° ♎ 16'   ♆ 14° ♉ 25'

                       ♇ 12° ♍ 45'   ☊ 24° ♍ 27'

Aspects: Saturn is on the New Moon/Mars midpoint.

Saturn = New Moon/Mars

Separation and loss. To be parted. To finish something and to feel sad at its completion. Physical injury is also possible through overstraining one's strength. This is not the time to undertake strenuous physical activities.

Eclipses 1900–2050:

1916, 1934, 1952, 1970, 1988, 2006, 2024, 2042

S.S. 9 NEW NORTH

Starts: August 21, 1664, 9:12:03 GMT North Pole

Ends: September 18, 2908

Planets: ☉ & ☽ 28° ♌ 50'   ☿ 22° ♌ 05'

                       ♀ 23° ♌ 17'   ♂ 20° ♎ 54'

                       ♃ 8° ♑ 07'   ♄ 21° ♐ 13'

                       ♅ 13° ♒ 40'   ♆ 15° ♑ 21'

                       ♇ 26° ♊ 14'   ☊ 11° ♌ 17'

Aspects: A Venus-Mercury conjunction is on the Mars/Pluto midpoint, and Mars is on the Uranus/Pluto midpoint.

Venus = Mercury = Mars/Pluto

Mars = Uranus/Pluto

This is a very physically expressive Saros Series: accidents, great physical effort, violence, or any sudden physical events. These can be experienced positively as, for example, the first time skiing, or it can be felt negatively in terms of accidents and so on. The approach to take when this Series is affecting a chart is not to hide away but to undertake some physical activity, with an ever-watchful eye to safety.

Eclipses 1900–2050:

1917, 1935, 1953, 1971, 1989, 2007, 2025, 2043

S.S. 9 NEW SOUTH

Starts: July 19, 1917, 2:59:41 GMT South Pole
Ends: August 17, 3161

Planets:

☉ & ☽ 25° ♋ 51'	☿ 3° ♌ 13'
♀ 18° ♌ 18'	♂ 23° ♊ 54'
♃ 3° ♊ 48'	♄ 3° ♌ 04'
♅ 22° ≈ 45'	♆ 4° ♌ 16'
♇ 4° ♋ 28'	☊ 9° ♑ 49'

Aspects: There is a Mercury-Saturn-Neptune conjunction. The New Moon is on the Venus/Pluto midpoint.

Mercury = Saturn = Neptune

New Moon = Venus/Pluto

This Saros Series appears to be concerned with the bringing to the surface of long-term worries about loved ones, health, or issues to do with paperwork or communication. This could manifest as a worrying piece of news about a loved one or responsibilities with paperwork coming home to roost. Any news will have a sense of destiny or fatedness about it.

Eclipses 1900–2050:

1917, 1935, 1953, 1971, 1989, 2007, 2025, 2043

S.S. 9 OLD SOUTH

Starts: June 23, 727 o.s., 21:45:03 GMT South Pole
Ends: July 23, 1971

Planets:

☉ & ☽ 4° ♋ 16'	☿ 7° ♋ 30'
♀ 1° ♊ 05'	♂ 1° ♌ 54'
♃ 2° ♑ 18'	♄ 18° ≈ 21'
♅ 7° ♐ 48'	♆ 28° ♈ 16'
♇ 27° ♌ 55'	☊ 17° ♐ 04'

Aspects: Mars is on the midpoint of the New Moon/Pluto and the Node is on the midpoint of the New Moon/Venus. In addition, Venus occupies the midpoint of the New Moon/Neptune.

Mars = New Moon/Pluto

Node = New Moon/Venus

Venus = New Moon/Neptune

Great energy is contained in this Saros Series via the Mars-Pluto combination. However, this energy is constructive and seems to be focused on the reuniting of loved ones, or the expression of love to a person, or some artistic endeavor. There is also a touch of idealism in this family of eclipses.

Eclipses 1900–2050:

1917, 1935, 1953, 1971 Series ends

S.S. 10 NORTH

Starts: April 25, 944 o.s., 10:31:03 GMT North Pole
Ends: May 27, 2188

Planets:

☉ & ☽ 9° ♉ 53′	☿ 10° ♉ 04′
♀ 24° ♊ 17′	♂ 24° ♐ 13′
♃ 26° ♈ 55′	♄ 0° ♋ 53′
♅ 28° ♊ 55′	♆ 22° ♌ 31′
♇ 10° ♋ 14′	☊ 23° ♈ 00′

Aspects: The New Moon is conjunct Mercury, and Saturn is on the midpoint of the New Moon/Neptune.

New Moon = Mercury

Saturn = New Moon/Neptune

There is a very strong emphasis on communication and, at the same time, frustrating or inhibiting events may come into the person's life via news, paperwork, or a young person. The person may feel tired and drained, and this is therefore a good time to take things quietly and work through the difficulties one at a time.

Eclipses 1900–2050:

1917, 1935, 1954, 1972, 1990, 2008, 2026, 2044

S.S. 10 SOUTH

Starts March 10, 1179 o.s., 7:36:20 GMT South Pole

Ends: April 13, 2423

Planets:	☉ & ☽ 26° ♓ 01'	☿ 2° ♓ 21'
	♀ 8° ♉ 37'	♂ 12° ♏ 40'
	♃ 16° ♒ 03'	♄ 23° ♊ 24'
	♅ 20° ♈ 25'	♆ 0° ♒ 40'
	♇ 27° ♊ 56'	☊ 10° ♍ 10'

Aspects: Mars is on the midpoint of the New Moon/Pluto, and the New Moon is on the midpoint of Mercury/Uranus. In addition to this, Mercury is on the Mars/Saturn midpoint.

Mars = New Moon/Pluto

New Moon = Mercury/Uranus

Mercury = Mars/Saturn

This Saros Series concerns itself with breaking out of a very negative situation where no hope can be seen to a more positive space containing many options. A worry that may have been affecting a person will suddenly clear. The solution is shown by the Cosmos and needs to be taken up without too much delay.

Eclipses 1900–2050:

1900, 1918, 1936, 1954, 1972, 1990, 2008, 2026, 2044

S.S. 11 NORTH

Starts: August 1, 1125 o.s., 5:03:55 GMT North Pole

Ends: September 4, 2369

Planets: ☉ & ☽ 14° ♌ 33'   ☿ 3° ♌ 19'
            ♀ 14° ♋ 22'   ♂ 11° ♊ 31'
            ♃ 10° ♌ 24'   ♄ 6° ♍ 20'
            ♅ 3° ♍ 35'   ♆ 1° ♎ 18'
            ♇ 6° ♉ 55'   ☊ 26° ♋ 58'

Aspects: The New Moon is on the Uranus/Node midpoint, and Jupiter is on the midpoint of Venus/Saturn.

New Moon = Uranus/Node

Jupiter = Venus/Saturn

Under the influence of this family of eclipses, individuals may suddenly change the groups with which they are mixing, either through travel or ideas. However, the separation implied by the Venus-Saturn would produce very positive outcomes. This whole eclipse Series could also talk of suddenly deciding to make greater commitments in a relationship. Either way, the eclipse is gentle and individuals can trust the situations that arise and allow themselves to be led along by their momentum.

Eclipses 1900–2050:

1900, 1918, 1936, 1954, 1973, 1991, 2009, 2027, 2045

S.S. 11 SOUTH

Starts: June 14, 1360 o.s., 6:01:54 GMT South Pole
Ends: July 20, 2604

Planets: ☉ & ☽ 0° ♋ 48'   ☿ 19° ♋ 53'
            ♀ 19° ♉ 53'   ♂ 26° ♈ 34'
            ♃ 5° ♊ 50'   ♄ 27° ♌ 24'
            ♅ 19° ♊ 40'   ♆ 9° ♓ 40'
            ♇ 28° ♈ 08'   ☊ 14° ♐ 12'

Aspects: There is a Mars-Pluto conjunction, and Uranus is on the midpoint of Mercury/Venus.

Mars = Pluto

Uranus = Mercury/Venus

This family of eclipses is concerned with the need to make sudden reforms. Old ideas or methods will fail and new systems are required to deal with the events brought by the eclipse. As a consequence, the person will need to think of new ways of handling the issues. Any blocks could be violently or tragically removed.

Eclipses 1900–2050:

1901, 1919, 1937, 1955, 1973, 1991, 2009, 2027, 2045

S.S. 12 NORTH

Starts: May 19, 1613, 17:58:33 GMT North Pole
Ends: June 17, 2857

Planets:

☉ & ☽ 28° ♉ 38'	☿ 21° ♊ 05'
♀ 12° ♉ 26'	♂ 29° ♋ 06'
♃ 16° ♍ 40'	♄ 28° ♓ 09'
♅ 24° ♊ 52'	♆ 23° ♍ 47'
♇ 5° ♉ 51'	☊ 12° ♉ 40'

Aspects: Saturn is forming a sextile to the New Moon, and Venus is conjunct the Node. The New Moon is also on the midpoint of Mars/Saturn and Mercury/Pluto.

Saturn sextile New Moon

Venus = Node

New Moon = Mars/Saturn = Mercury/Pluto

Opportunities to accept greater responsibilities can come suddenly into the person's life. These new commitments will most likely come as a result of another individual being unable to carry on. Although the events that herald these opportunities may be difficult, the outcomes in terms of harmony or self-esteem are good.

Eclipses 1900–2050:

1901, 1919, 1937, 1955, 1973, 1992, 2010, 2028, 2046

S.S. 12 SOUTH

Starts: September 19, 1541 o.s., 20:45:11 GMT South Pole
Ends: October 27, 2785

Planets: ☉ & ☽ 6° ♎ 10'   ☿ 14° ♌ 52'
            ♀ 20° ♎ 28'   ♂ 26° ♌ 32'
            ♃ 16° ♍ 24'   ♄ 26° ♎ 58'
            ♅ 23° ♌ 34'   ♆ 17° ♈ 17'
            ♇ 13° ♒ 13'   ☊ 18° ♓ 13'

Aspects: Jupiter is on the midpoint of the New Moon/Mars, and Neptune is on the New Moon/Saturn midpoint.

Jupiter = New Moon/Mars

Neptune = New Moon/Saturn

This Saros Series will bring successful outcomes to long-term worries or illness. An issue that has worried or drained the individual for some time will at first seem worse and then clear, with successful outcomes.

Eclipses 1900–2050:

1902, 1919, 1938, 1956, 1974, 1992, 2010, 2028, 2046

S.S. 13 NORTH

Starts: August 14, 1776, 5:40:33 GMT North Pole
Ends: September 12, 3020

Planets: ☉ & ☽ 21° ♌ 52'   ☿ 9° ♌ 52'
            ♀ 22° ♌ 46'   ♂ 18° ♋ 13'
            ♃ 14° ♋ 40'   ♄ 17° ♎ 12'
            ♅ 10° ♊ 33'   ♆ 23° ♍ 28'
            ♇ 26° ♑ 38'   ☊ 5° ♌ 28'

Aspects: There is a New Moon-Venus conjunction and, in addition, the Node is on the midpoint of the New Moon/Mars. Pluto is also on the midpoint of Mars/Node.

New Moon = Venus

285

Node = New Moon/Mars

Pluto = Mars/Node

This is an eclipse family of groups and associations. Its energy is about large, ambitious group projects. These group projects will require a separation or the breaking of a bond that already exists. The individual may well experience this eclipse initially as a separation and then as joint achievement.

Eclipses 1900–2050:

1902, 1920, 1938, 1956, 1974, 1992, 2011, 2029, 2047

S.S. 13 SOUTH

Starts: May 24, 803 o.s., 12:56:24 GMT South Pole
Ends: June 23, 2047

Planets: ☉ & ☽ 5° ♊ 56'   ☿ 0° ♋ 26'
              ♀ 11° ♋ 54'   ♂ 27° ♑ 11'
              ♃ 7° ♊ 55'   ♄ 19° ♍ 49'
              ♅ 2° ♏ 52'   ♆ 12° ♎ 19'
              ♇ 11° ♒ 59'   ☊ 18° ♏ 41'

Aspects: There is a Jupiter-New Moon conjunction, and Mars is on the midpoint of the New Moon/Saturn.

Jupiter = New Moon

Mars = New Moon/Saturn

This family of eclipses has a very similar energy to its North Node cousin: expansive energy under which lies a more sinister flavor. An urge to expand is experienced, but the expansion contains frustration, inhibitions, and loss or separation.

Australia's chart seems to be very sensitive to this 13 Series. The first time it affected Australia's chart was 13 South in 1939—the year when Australia went to war. It occurred again in 1975, and that was a year of constitutional crises climaxing in the dismissal of Prime Minister Whitlam. The three times that 13 North affected Australia's chart were: first in

1938—The Empire Games in Sydney; second in 1956—The Olympic Games in Melbourne; and third in 1974—Cyclone Tracy. Darwin, the only city in Australia to be bombed in WW2, was devastated by a cyclone. This event caused the biggest peacetime evacuation that Australia had ever seen. Australia seems to be experiencing this family of eclipses as a striving for group endeavors, in a positive or negative fashion.

Eclipses 1900–2050:

1903, 1921, 1939, 1957, 1975, 1993, 2011, 2029, 2047

S.S. 14 NORTH

Starts: April 29, 1074 o.s., 1:11:42 GMT North Pole
Ends: June 1, 2318

Planets:	☉ & ☽ 13° ♉ 54′	☿ 5° ♊ 54′
	♀ 4° ♈ 57′	♂ 0° ♓ 30′
	♃ 15° ♈ 30′	♄ 8° ♐ 11′
	♅ 0° ♒ 47′	♆ 9° ♊ 09′
	♇ 14° ♓ 48′	☊ 28° ♈ 24′

Aspects: Neptune is forming an opposition to Saturn, and Venus is on the Uranus/Neptune midpoint.

Neptune = Saturn

Venus = Uranus/Neptune

A most peculiar eclipse family, heralding an acute time of confusion in personal relationships, unexpected happenings in financial matters, and possible illness. Unrequited love, despair, confusion, a draining of energy, a peculiar turn of events. No important decisions should be made concerning incoming events, as there is too much confusion and possible delusion to make clear judgments.

Eclipses 1900–2050:

1903, 1921, 1939, 1957, 1975, 1993, 2011, 2029, 2047

S.S. 14 SOUTH

Starts: August 29, 984 o.s., 8:13:10 GMT South Pole
Ends: September 30, 2228

Planets: ☉ & ☽ 10° ♏ 59'   ☿ 25° ♌ 47'

♀ 25° ♋ 28'   ♂ 5° ♋ 40'

♃ 16° ♍ 48'   ♄ 14° ♏ 46'

♅ 1° ♑ 02'   ♆ 20° ♍ 10'

♇ 24° ♍ 34'   ☊ 22° ♒ 39'

Aspects: Jupiter is on the midpoint of New Moon/Pluto as the New Moon is on the midpoint of firstly Mercury/Pluto and secondly Mars/Saturn.

Jupiter = New Moon/Pluto

New Moon = Mercury/Pluto = Mars/Saturn

This eclipse family will tend to bring success. There may have been long periods of hard work from which the success has grown. With the Mercury-Pluto content, there is also the potential for an obsessive idea to finally be accepted, which then leads to the promised success of the Jupiter. During this eclipse period, individuals should push for the acceptance of their ideas or methodologies, as this eclipse can bring the long-awaited breakthrough.

Eclipses 1900–2050:

1904, 1922, 1940, 1958, 1976, 1994, 2012, 2030, 2048

S.S. 15 NORTH

Starts: July 13, 1219 o.s., 8:21:39 GMT North Pole
Ends: August 17, 2463

Planets: ☉ & ☽ 26° ♋ 42'   ☿ 27° ♋ 46'

♀ 19° ♊ 42'   ♂ 24° ♉ 03'

♃ 15° ♋ 16'   ♄ 9° ♏ 56'

♅ 19° ♎ 00'   ♆ 0° ♉ 34'

♇ 29° ♌ 01'   ☊ 9° ♋ 52'

Aspects: The New Moon is conjunct Mercury, while Venus is on the Mars/Jupiter midpoint. There is also a trine between the Node in Cancer and Saturn in Scorpio.

Node trine Saturn

New Moon = Mercury

Venus = Mars/Jupiter

There is a sense of joy through commitment about this Saros Series. When this family affects a chart, it is a time of good news that entails responsibilities or commitments, but ones in which there is joy in the undertaking. Pregnancy, birth, parenthood are just some of this eclipse family's possible expressions.

Eclipses 1900–2050:

1904, 1922, 1940, 1958, 1976, 1994, 2012, 2030, 2048

S.S. 15 SOUTH

Starts: June 6, 1472 o.s., 20:31:36 GMT South Pole
Ends: July 12, 2716

Planets: ☉ & ☽ 24° ♊ 38'   ☿ 9° ♋ 54'
          ♀ 18° ♉ 33'   ♂ 20° ♌ 52'
          ♃ 24° ♎ 37'   ♄ 16° ♊ 08'
          ♅ 26° ♎ 34'   ♆ 13° ♏ 36'
          ♇ 12° ♍ 38'   ☊ 8° ♐ 20'

Aspects: There is a Jupiter-Uranus conjunction that is trine the New Moon, and Pluto is on the midpoint of Saturn/Node.

(Jupiter = Uranus) trine New Moon

Pluto = Saturn/Node

This series is about the release of tension. A situation that has been lingering will suddenly clear. In the clearing of the problem, there is also a sense of grief or loss that is not so much personal as belonging to a group or collective.

Eclipses 1900–2050:

1905, 1923, 1941, 1959, 1977, 1995, 2013, 2031, 2049

S.S. 16 NORTH

Starts: February 15, 1599 o.s., 1:50:18 GMT North Pole

Ends: March 25, 2843

Planets:	☉ & ☽ 6° ♓ 02'	☿ 2° ♓ 52'
	♀ 4° ♓ 26'	♂ 16° ♒ 48'
	♃ 10° ♋ 08'	♄ 15° ♎ 35'
	♅ 24° ♈ 24'	♆ 24° ♌ 05'
	♇ 20° ♈ 47'	☊ 17° ♒ 54'

Aspects: Uranus forms a trine to Neptune, and Venus is on the mid-point of the New Moon/Mercury.

Uranus trine Neptune

Venus = New Moon/Mercury

A gentle family of eclipses that bring a sense of inspiration or the illumination of ideas. The presence of the Uranus-Neptune combination talks of the sudden release of material from the unconscious that brings with it a great deal of insight. These ideas are good, and the individual would be wise to act upon them.

Eclipses 1900–2050:

1905, 1923, 1941, 1959, 1977, 1995, 2013, 2031, 2049

S.S. 16 SOUTH

Starts: September 21, 1653, 16:12:13 GMT South Pole

Ends: October 20, 2897

Planets:	☉ & ☽ 28° ♏ 58'	☿ 16° ♎ 23'
	♀ 19° ♎ 36'	♂ 24° ♐ 18'
	♃ 7° ♒ 37'	♄ 21° ♌ 32'
	♅ 26° ♐ 56'	♆ 21° ♐ 03'
	♇ 15° ♊ 05'	☊ 12° ♓ 24'

Aspects: Neptune is on the New Moon/Node midpoint, while Mars is on the midpoint of Uranus and Neptune.

Neptune = New Moon/Node

Mars = Uranus/Neptune

Under the influence of this family of eclipses, individuals will find themselves dealing with issues of wasted energy or misdirected motivation, particularly when dealing with groups. There can be sudden inspiration but this is potentially unfulfilling. No real action should be taken.

Eclipses 1900–2050:

1906, 1924, 1942, 1960, 1978, 1996, 2014, 2032, 2050

S.S. 17 NEW NORTH

Starts: July 28, 1870, 11:18:04 GMT North Pole

Ends: August 26, 3114

Planets:	☉ & ☽ 5° ♌ 07′	☿ 6° ♌ 33′
	♀ 2° ♋ 01′	♂ 2° ♋ 35′
	♃ 17° ♊ 50′	♄ 22° ♐ 35′
	♅ 23° ♋ 05′	♆ 21° ♈ 50′
	♇ 18° ♉ 52′	☊ 18° ♋ 20′

Aspects: Venus is conjunct Mars, while the Node occupies the midpoints of the New Moon/Venus and the New Moon/Mars as well as the Mercury/Venus.

Venus = Mars

Node = New Moon/Venus =

New Moon/Mars = Mercury/Venus

This Series brings an impulsive energy to events. Socializing becomes hectic and issues emerge that motivate the individual. This motivation may be concerned with financial projects or relationship issues. Whatever the motivation, it is impulsive, passionate, and exciting. Have fun, enjoy it.

Eclipses 1900–2050:

1906, 1924, 1942, 1960, 1978, 1996, 2014, 2032, 2050

S.S. 17 SOUTH

Starts: May 27, 933 o.s., 3:46:29 GMT South Pole

Ends: June 28, 2177

Planets:	☉ & ☽ 9° ♊ 56′	☿ 20° ♊ 05′
	♀ 27° ♈ 38′	♂ 0° ♈ 42′
	♃ 27° ♉ 31′	♄ 19° ♒ 29′
	♅ 15° ♉ 22′	♆ 29° ♋ 00′
	♇ 27° ♊ 32′	☊ 24° ♏ 05′

Aspects: Jupiter occupies the midpoint of the New Moon/Uranus as well as the midpoint of Venus/Pluto. In addition, the Node is on the midpoint of Mercury/Venus.

Jupiter = New Moon/Uranus = Venus/Pluto

Node = Mercury/Venus

The issues with this family of eclipses are of sudden success in group projects or personal relationship matters. Happiness in love, thinking of love matters, good news concerning relationships, or creative expression with a group.

Eclipses 1900–2050:

1907, 1925, 1943, 1961, 1979, 1997, 2015, 2033

S.S. 18 NORTH

Starts: February 4, 1060 o.s., 21:06:29 GMT North Pole

Ends: March 8, 2304

Planets:	☉ & ☽ 21° ♒ 34′	☿ 27° ♒ 19′
	♀ 25° ♑ 09′	♂ 28° ♉ 34′
	♃ 26° ♑ 57′	♄ 3° ♊ 52′
	♅ 1° ♐ 26′	♆ 6° ♉ 20′
	♇ 26° ♒ 15′	☊ 3° ♒ 37′

Aspects: There is a Pluto-Mercury conjunction, and Uranus is on the midpoint of Mars/Saturn.

Pluto = Mercury

Uranus = Mars/Saturn

A high stress level accompanies the energy of this series, and individuals will experience a taxing of their strength. Events will occur that require the expenditure of effort; this can also manifest as illness or accident. The whole flavor of this eclipse is one of physical concern, as well as worry or obsessive thinking.

Eclipses 1900–2050:

1907, 1925, 1943, 1961, 1979, 1997, 2015, 2033

S.S. 18 SOUTH

Starts: August 20, 1096 o.s., 18:24:19 GMT South Pole
Ends: September 22, 2340

Planets: ☉ & ☽ 3° ♏ 29'   ☿ 25° ♌ 32'
☿ 20° ♋ 59'   ♂ 22° ♎ 16'
♃ 20° ♒ 53'   ♄ 13° ♍ 23'
♅ 28° ♈ 54'   ♆ 0° ♌ 31'
♇ 8° ♈ 21'   ☊ 16° ♒ 50'

Aspects: Jupiter forms a quincunx to Venus, and the Node sits on the midpoint of the New Moon/Neptune as well as the Venus/Saturn midpoint.

Jupiter quincunx Venus

Node = New Moon/Neptune = Venus/Saturn

This family of eclipses is concerned with endings or separations. Thus when it affects a chart, individuals will find themselves dealing with a parting. This parting can be anything from a friend traveling overseas and the saying of goodbyes to the ending of a relationship with a loved one, which could bring much anguish or grief. However, the pain of the separation is lessened by encountering new situations that lead to very positive outcomes.

Eclipses 1900–2050:

1908, 1926, 1944, 1962, 1980, 1998, 2016, 2034

S.S. 19 NORTH

Starts: July 5, 1331 o.s., 22:51:35 GMT North Pole
Ends: August 10, 2575

Planets: ☉ & ☽ 20° ♋ 32'   ☿ 16° ♋ 23'
 ♀ 5° ♊ 37'   ♂ 13° ♍ 05'
 ♃ 4° ♐ 32'   ♄ 4° ♍ 41'
 ♅ 23° ♒ 14'   ♆ 3° ♑ 41'
 ♇ 28° ♓ 58'   ☊ 4° ♋ 00'

Aspects: Neptune is conjunct the South Node, and there is a T-square of Venus opposition Jupiter, both squared by Saturn.

Neptune = Node

(Venus = Jupiter) square Saturn

This Saros Series is about realism, a coming down to earth. The individual will become aware of an old situation and see it for what it is rather than what he or she thought it was. This can be a constructive time for tackling the truth.

Eclipses 1900-2050:

1908, 1926, 1944, 1962, 1980, 1998, 2016, 2034

S.S. 19 SOUTH

(The starting date of this series may be incorrect.)

Starts: April 16, 1512 o.s., 6:32:37 GMT South Pole
Ends: May 2772

Planets: ☉ & ☽ 5° ♉ 27'   ☿ 9° ♈ 56'
 ♀ 21° ♓ 50'   ♂ 26° ♐ 57'
 ♃ 22° ♓ 53'   ♄ 28° ♎ 38'
 ♅ 15° ♈ 07'   ♆ 13° ♒ 32'
 ♇ 23° ♐ 15'   ☊ 17° ♎ 24'

Aspects: There is a Venus-Jupiter conjunction, and Uranus is on the midpoint of the New Moon/Jupiter.

Venus = Jupiter

Uranus = New Moon/Jupiter

This is a family of eclipses that brings with it the element of the pleasant surprise. Sudden happiness, a joyful event, the lucky break, the lucky win. The events that will be occurring can be believed and can positively change the person's life.

Eclipses 1900–2050:

1908, 1927, 1945, 1963, 1981, 1999, 2017, 2035

Eclipses (1900–2050)

The following section is a listing of every year from 1900 to 2050 with the dates and zodiacal placement of both Solar and Lunar eclipses, as well as the Saros Series to which the Solar eclipses belong. The use of this table is to enable any year to be examined for the timing and placement of eclipses, as well as, most importantly, the particular Saros Series that is active. With this knowledge, the particular Saros Series involved can be examined using Appendix 6.

This section has been compiled using Michelsen's 20th-century ephemeris. Michelsen lists some Lunar eclipses that are possibly just out of range of the orbs given above; however, they have been included in the tables.[*]

Solar			Lunar	
1900	MAY 28	7° ♊ 10′ South	JUN 13	22° ♐
	NOV 22	0° ♐ 11′ North	DEC 6	14° ♊
1901	MAY 18	27° ♉ 11′ South	MAY 3	13° ♏
	NOV 11	18° ♏ 12′ North	OCT 27	3° ♉
1902	APR 8	18° ♈ 12′ Old South	APR 22	2° ♏
	MAY 7	16° ♉ 12′ New South		
	OCT 31	7° ♏ 13′ North	OCT 17	23° ♈

---

[*]   N. F. Michelsen, *The American Ephemeris for the 20th Century: 1900 to 2000 at Midnight.*

Solar			Lunar	
1903	MAR 29	7° ♈ 13′ South	APR 12	21° ♎
	SEP 21	27° ♍ 14′ North	OCT 6	26° ♎
1904	MAR 17	26° ♓ 14′ South	MAR 31	10° ♎
	SEP 9	17° ♍ 15′ North	SEP 24	1° ♈
1905	MAR 6	15° ♓ 15′ South	FEB 19	0° ♍
	AUG 30	6° ♍ 16′ North	AUG 15	22° ♒
1906	FEB 23	4° ♑ 16′ South	FEB 9	20° ♌
	JUL 21	28° ♋ 17′ Old North	AUG 4	11° ♒
	AUG 20	26° ♌ 17′ New North		
1907	JAN 14	23° ♑ 17′ South	JAN 29	9° ♌
	JUL 10	17° ♋ 18′ North	JUL 25	1° ♒
1908	JAN 3	12° ♑ 18′ South	JAN 18	27° ♋
	JUN 28	7° ♋ 19′ North	JUN 14	23° ♐
	DEC 23	1° ♑ 19′ South		
1909	JUN 17	26° ♊ 1′ North	JUN 4	13° ♐
	DEC 12	20° ♐ 1′ South	NOV 27	4° ♊
1910	MAY 9	18° ♉ 2′ North	MAY 24	2° ♐
	NOV 2	9° ♏ 2′ South	NOV 17	24° ♉
1911	APR 28	7° ♉ 3′ North	MAY 13	21° ♏
	OCT 22	28° ♎ 3′ South	NOV 6	13° ♉

Solar			Lunar	
1912	APR 17	27° ♈ 4' North	APR 1	12° ♎
	OCT 10	17° ♎ 4' South	SEP 26	3° ♈
1913	APR 6	16° ♈ 5' North	MAR 22	1° ♎
	AUG 31	8° ♍ 5' Old South	SEP 15	22° ♓
	SEP 30	6° ♎ 5' New South		
1914	FEB 25	6° ♓ 6' North	MAR 12	21° ♍
	AUG 21	28° ♌ 6' South	SEP 4	11° ♓
1915	FEB 14	24° ♒ 7' North	MAR 1	10° ♍
	AUG 10	17° ♌ 7' South	AUG 24	1° ♓
1916	FEB 3	14° ♒ 8' North	JAN 20	29° ♋
	JUL 30	7° ♌ 8' South	JUL 15	22° ♑
	DEC 24	3° ♑ 9' Old North		
1917	JAN 23	3° ♒ 9' New North	JAN 8	17° ♋
	JUN 19	28° ♊ 9' Old South	JUL 4	12° ♑
	JUL 19	26° ♋ 9' New South		
	DEC 14	22° ♐ 10' North	DEC 28	6° ♋
1918	JUN 8	17° ♊ 10' South	JUN 24	2° ♑
	DEC 3	11° ♐ 11' North	DEC 17	25° ♊
1919	MAY 29	7° ♊ 11' South	MAY 15	23° ♏
	NOV 22	29° ♏ 12' North	NOV 7	15° ♉

Solar			Lunar	
1920	MAY 18	27° ♉ 12' South	MAY 3	12° ♏
	NOV 10	18° ♏ 13' North	OCT 27	4° ♉
1921	APR 8	18° ♈ 13' South	APR 22	2° ♏
	OCT 1	8° ♎ 14' North	OCT 16	23° ♈
1922	MAR 28	7° ♈ 14' South	MAR 13	22° ♍
	SEP 21	27° ♍ 15' North	OCT 6	12° ♈
1923	MAR 17	26° ♎ 15' South	MAR 3	12° ♍
	SEP 10	17° ♎ 16' North	AUG 26	2° ♓
1924	MAR 5	15° ♓ 16' South	FEB 20	1° ♍
	JUL 31	8° ♌ 17' Old North		
	AUG 30	7° ♍ 17' New North	AUG 14	22° ♒
1925	JAN 24	4° ♒ 17' South	FEB 8	20° ♌
	JUL 20	28° ♋ 18' North	AUG 4	12° ♒
1926	JAN 14	23° ♑ 18' South	JAN 28	8° ♌
	JUL 9	17° ♋ 19' North	JUL 25	2° ♒
1927	JAN 3	12° ♑ 19' South	DEC 19 ('26)	27° ♊
	JUN 29	7° ♋ 1' North	JUN 15	23° ♐
	DEC 24	1° ♑ 1' South	DEC 8	16° ♊
1928	MAY 19	28° ♉ 2' Old North	JUN 3	13° ♐
	JUN 17	26° ♊ 2' New North		
	NOV 12	20° ♏ 2' South	NOV 27	5° ♊

Solar			Lunar	
1929	MAY 9	18° ♉ 3′ North	MAY 23	2° ♐
	NOV 1	9° ♏ 3′ South	NOV 17	24° ♉
1930	APR 28	8° ♉ 4′ North	APR 13	23° ♎
	OCT 21	28° ♎ 4′ South	OCT 7	14° ♈
1931	APR 18	27° ♈ 5′ North	APR 2	12° ♎
	SEP 12	18° ♍ 5′ Old South	SEP 26	3° ♈
	OCT 11	17° ♎ 5′ New South		
1932	MAR 7	17° ♓ 6′ North	MAR 22	2° ♎
	AUG 31	8° ♍ 6′ South	SEP 14	22° ♓
1933	FEB 24	5° ♓ 7′ North	MAR 12	21° ♏
	AUG 21	28° ♌ 7′ South	SEP 4	11° ♓
1934	FEB 14	25° ♒ 8′ North	JAN 30	10° ♌
	AUG 10	17° ♌ 8′ South	JUL 26	3° ♒
1935	JAN 5	14° ♑ 9′ Old North	JAN 19	29° ♋
	FEB 3	14° ♒ 9′ New North		
	JUN 30	8° ♋ 9′ Old South	JUL 16	23° ♑
	JUL 30	6° ♌ 9′ New South		
	DEC 25	3° ♑ 10′ North	JAN 8 ('36)	17° ♋
1936	JUN 19	28° ♊ 10′ South	JUL 4	13° ♑
	DEC 13	22° ♐ 11′ North	DEC 28	6° ♋

Solar			Lunar	
1937	JUN 8	18° ♊ 11′ South	MAY 25	4° ♐
	DEC 2	10° ♐ 12′ North	NOV 18	26° ♉
1938	MAY 29	7° ♊ 12′ South	MAY 14	23° ♏
	NOV 22	29° ♏ 13′ North	NOV 7	15° ♉
1939	APR 19	29° ♈ 13′ South	MAY 3	12° ♏
	OCT 12	19° ♎ 14′ North	OCT 28	4° ♉
1940	APR 7	18° ♈ 14′ South	APR 22	2° ♏
	OCT 1	8° ♎ 15′ North	OCT 16	23° ♈
1941	MAR 27	7° ♈ 15′ South	MAR 13	23° ♍
	SEP 21	28° ♍ 16′ North	SEP 5	13° ♓
1942	MAR 16	26° ♓ 16′ South	MAR 3	12° ♏
	AUG 12	19° ♌ 17′ Old North	AUG 26	2° ♓
	SEP 10	17° ♍ 17′ New North		
1943	FEB 4	15° ♒ 17′ South	FEB 20	1° ♍
	AUG 1	8° ♌ 18′ North	AUG 15	22° ♒
1944	JAN 25	5° ♒ 18′ South	FEB 9	19° ♌
	JUL 20	27° ♋ 19′ North	AUG 4	12° ♒
1945	JAN 14	24° ♑ 19′ South	DEC 29 (′44)	8° ♋
	JUL 9	17° ♋ 1′ North	JUN 25	4° ♑

Solar			Lunar	
1946	JAN 3	13° ♑ 1' South	DEC 19 ('45)	27° ♊
	MAY 30	9° ♊ 2' Old North	JUN 14	23° ♐
	JUN 29	7° ♋ 2' New North		
	NOV 23	1° ♐ 2' South	DEC 8	16° ♊
1947	MAY 20	29° ♉ 3' North	JUN 3	12° ♐
	NOV 12	20° ♏ 3' South	NOV 28	5° ♊
1948	MAY 9	18° ♉ 4' North	APR 23	3° ♏
	NOV 1	9° ♏ 4' South	OCT 18	25° ♈
1949	APR 28	8° ♉ 5' North	APR 13	23° ♎
	OCT 21	28° ♎ 5' South	OCT 7	13° ♈
1950	MAR 18	27° ♓ 6' North	FEB 2	12° ♎
	SEP 12	19° ♍ 6' South	SEP 26	3° ♈
1951	MAR 7	16° ♓ 7' North	FEB 21	2° ♍
			MAR 23	2° ♎
	SEP 1	8° ♍ 7' South	AUG 17	23° ♒
			SEP 15	22° ♓
1952	FEB 25	6° ♓ 8' North	FEB 11	21° ♌
	AUG 20	28° ♌ 8' South	AUG 5	13° ♒
1953	FEB 14	25° ♒ 9' New North	JAN 29	10° ♌
	JUL 11	18° ♋ 9' Old South	JUL 26	3° ♒
	AUG 9	17° ♌ 9' New South		

Solar			Lunar	
1954	JAN 5	14° ♑ 10′ North	JAN 19	28° ♋
	JUN 30	8° ♋ 10′ South	JUL 16	23° ♑
	DEC 25	3° ♑ 11′ North	JAN 8 ('55)	17° ♋
1955	JUN 20	28° ♊ 11′ South	JUN 5	14° ♐
	DEC 14	22° ♐ 12′ North	NOV 29	7° ♊
1956	JUN 8	18° ♊ 12′ South	MAY 24	3° ♐
	DEC 2	10° ♐ 13′ North	NOV 18	26° ♉
1957	APR 29	9° ♉ 13′ South	MAY 13	23° ♏
	OCT 23	30° ♎ 14′ North	NOV 7	15° ♉
1958	APR 19	29° ♈ 14′ South	MAY 3	13° ♏
	OCT 12	19° ♎ 15′ North	OCT 27	4° ♉
1959	APR 8	18° ♈ 15′ South	MAR 24	3° ♎
	OCT 2	9° ♎ 16′ North	SEP 17	23° ♓
1960	MAR 27	7° ♈ 16′ South	MAR 13	23° ♍
	SEP 20	28° ♍ 17′ New North	SEP 5	13° ♓
1961	FEB 15	26° ♒ 17′ South	MAR 2	12° ♍
	AUG 11	19° ♌ 18′ North	AUG 26	3° ♓
1962	FEB 5	16° ♒ 18′ South	FEB 19	0° ♍
	JUL 31	8° ♌ 19′ North	JUL 17	24° ♑

Solar			Lunar	
1963	JAN 25	5° ♒ 19' South	JAN 9	19° ♋
	JUL 20	27° ♋ 1' North	JUL 6	14° ♑
1964	JAN 14	24° ♑ 1' South	DEC 30 ('63)	8° ♋
	JUN 10	19° ♊ 2' Old North	JUN 25	3° ♑
	JUL 9	17° ♋ 2' New North		
	DEC 4	12° ♐ 2' South	DEC 19	27° ♊
1965	MAY 30	9° ♊ 3' North	JUN 14	23° ♐
	NOV 23	1° ♐ 3' South	DEC 8	16° ♊
1966	MAY 20	29° ♉ 4' North	MAY 4	14° ♏
	NOV 12	20° ♏ 4' South	OCT 29	6° ♉
1967	MAY 9	18° ♉ 5' North	APR 24	4° ♏
	NOV 2	9° ♏ 5' South	OCT 18	24° ♈
1968	MAR 28	8° ♈ 6' North	APR 13	23° ♎
	SEP 22	29° ♍ 6 South	OCT 6	13° ♈
1969	MAR 18	27° ♓ 7' North	APR 2	13° ♎
	SEP 11	19° ♍ 7 South	AUG 27	4° ♓
1970	MAR 7	17° ♓ 8' North	FEB 21	2° ♏
	AUG 31	8° ♍ 8' South	AUG 17	24° ♒
			SEP 15	22° ♓

Solar			Lunar	
1971	FEB 25	6° ♓ 9′ New North	FEB 10	21° ♌
	JUL 22	29° ♋ 9′ Old South (ends)	AUG 6	14° ♒
	AUG 20	27° ♌ 9′ New South		
1972	JAN 16	25° ♑ 10′ North	JAN 30	10° ♌
	JUL 10	19° ♋ 10′ South	JUL 26	3° ♒
1973	JAN 4	14° ♑ 11′ North	JAN 18	29° ♋
	JUN 30	9° ♋ 11′ South	JUN 15	25° ♐
			JUL 15	23° ♑
	DEC 24	3° ♑ 12′ North	DEC 10	18° ♊
1974	JUN 20	28° ♊ 12′ South	JUN 4	14° ♐
	DEC 13	21° ♐ 13′ North	NOV 29	7° ♊
1975	MAY 11	20° ♉ 13′ South	MAY 25	3° ♐
	NOV 3	10° ♏ 14′ North	NOV 18	26° ♉
1976	APR 29	9° ♉ 14′ South	MAY 13	23° ♏
	OCT 23	30° ♎ 15′ North	NOV 6	15° ♉
1977	APR 18	28° ♈ 15′ South	APR 4	14° ♎
	OCT 12	19° ♎ 16′ North	SEP 27	4° ♈
1978	APR 7	17° ♈ 16′ South	MAR 24	4° ♎
	OCT 2	9° ♎ 17′ New North	SEP 16	24° ♓

Solar			Lunar	
1979	FEB 26	7° ♓ 17' South	MAR 13	23° ♍
	AUG 22	29° ♌ 18' North	SEP 6	13° ♓
1980	FEB 16	27° ♒ 18' South	MAR 1	11° ♍
	AUG 10	18° ♌ 19' North	JUL 27	5° ♒
1981	FEB 4	16° ♒ 19' South	JAN 20	0° ♌
	JUL 31	8° ♌ 1' North	JUL 17	25° ♑
1982	JAN 25	5° ♒ 1' South	JAN 9	19° ♋
	JUN 21	30° ♊ 2' Old North	JUL 6	14° ♑
	JUL 20	28° ♋ 2' New North		
	DEC 15	23° ♐ 2' South	DEC 30	8° ♋
1983	JUN 11	20° ♊ 3' North	JUN 25	3° ♐
	DEC 4	12° ♐ 3' South	DEC 20	28° ♊
1984	MAY 30	9° ♊ 4' North	MAY 15	24° ♏
			JUN 13	23° ♐
	NOV 22	1° ♐ 4' South	NOV 8	16° ♉
1985	MAY 19	29° ♉ 5' North	MAY 4	14° ♏
	NOV 12	20° ♏ 5' South	OCT 28	5° ♉
1986	APR 9	19° ♈ 6' North	APR 24	4° ♏
	OCT 3	10° ♎ 6' South	OCT 17	24° ♈

Solar			Lunar	
1987	MAR 29	8° ♈ 7′ North	APR 14	24° ♎
	SEP 23	30° ♍ 7′ South	OCT 7	13° ♈
1988	MAR 18	28° ♓ 8′ North	MAR 3	13° ♍
	SEP 11	19° ♍ 8′ South	AUG 27	4° ♓
1989	MAR 7	17° ♓ 9′ New North	FEB 20	2° ♍
	AUG 31	8° ♍ 9′ New South	AUG 17	24° ♒
1990	JAN 26	7° ♒ 10′ North	FEB 9	21° ♌
	JUL 22	29° ♋ 10′ South	AUG 6	14° ♒
1991	JAN 15	26° ♑ 11′ North	JAN 30	10° ♌
	JUL 11	19° ♋ 11′ South	JUN 27	5° ♑
			JUL 26	3° ♒
1992	JAN 4	14° ♑ 12′ North	DEC 21 ('91)	29° ♊
	JUN 30	9° ♋ 12′ South	JUN 15	24° ♐
	DEC 24	2° ♑ 13′ North	DEC 9	18° ♊
1993	MAY 21	1° ♊ 13′ South	JUN 4	14° ♐
	NOV 13	22° ♏ 14′ North	NOV 29	7° ♊
1994	MAY 10	20° ♉ 14′ South	MAY 25	4° ♐
	NOV 3	11° ♏ 15′ North	NOV 18	26° ♉
1995	APR 29	9° ♉ 15′ South	APR 15	25° ♎
	OCT 24	0° ♏ 16′ North	OCT 8	15° ♈

Solar			Lunar	
1996	APR 17	28° ♈ 16′ South	APR 4	15° ♎
	OCT 12	20° ♎ 17′ New North	SEP 27	4° ♈
1997	MAR 9	19° ♓ 17′ South	MAR 24	4° ♎
	SEP 1	10° ♍ 18′ North	SEP 16	24° ♓
1998	FEB 26	8° ♓ 18′ South	MAR 13	22° ♍
	AUG 22	29° ♌ 19′ North	AUG 8	15° ♒
			SEP 6	14° ♓
1999	FEB 16	27° ♒ 19′ South	JAN 31	11° ♌
	AUG 11	18° ♌ 1′ North	JUL 28	5° ♒
2000	FEB 5	16° ♒ 1′ South	JAN 21	1° ♌
	JUL 1	10° ♋ 2′ Old North	JUL 16	24° ♑
	JUL 31	8° ♌ 2′ New North		
	DEC 25	4° ♑ 2′ South	JAN 9 ('01)	20° ♋
2001	JUN 21	0° ♋ 3′ North	JUL 5	14° ♑
	DEC 14	23° ♐ 3′ South	DEC 30	9° ♋
2002	JUN 10	20° ♊ 4′ North	MAY 26	5° ♐
			JUN 24	3° ♑
	DEC 4	12° ♐ 4′ South	NOV 20	28° ♉
2003	MAY 31	9° ♊ 5′ North	MAY 16	25° ♏
	NOV 23	1° ♐ 5′ South	NOV 9	16° ♉

Solar			Lunar	
2004	APR 19	30° ♈ 6′ North	MAY 4	15° ♏
	OCT 14	21° ♎ 6′ South	OCT 28	5° ♉
2005	APR 8	19° ♈ 7′ North	APR 24	4° ♏
	OCT 3	10° ♎ 7′ South	OCT 17	24° ♈
2006	MAR 29	8° ♈ 8′ North	MAR 14	24° ♍
	SEP 22	29° ♍ 8′ South	SEP 7	15° ♓
2007	MAR 19	28° ♓ 9′ New North	MAR 3	13° ♍
	SEP 11	18° ♍ 9′ New South	AUG 28	5° ♓
2008	FEB 7	18° ♒ 10′ North	FEB 21	2° ♍
	AUG 1	10° ♌ 10′ South	AUG 16	24° ♒
2009	JAN 26	6° ♒ 11′ North	FEB 9	21° ♌
	JUL 22	29° ♋ 11′ South	JUL 7	15° ♑
			AUG 6	14° ♒
2010	JAN 15	25° ♑ 12′ North	DEC 31 ('09)	10° ♋
	JUL 11	19° ♋ 12′ South	JUN 26	5° ♑
2011	JAN 4	14° ♑ 13′ North	DEC 21 ('10)	29° ♊
	JUN 1	11° ♊ 13′ Old South	JUN 15	24° ♐
	JUL 1	9° ♋ 13′ New South		
	NOV 25	2° ♐ 14′ North	DEC 10	18° ♊

Solar			Lunar	
2012	MAY 20	0° ♊ 14′ South	JUN 4	14° ♐
	NOV 13	22° ♏ 15′ North	NOV 28	7° ♊
2013	MAY 10	20° ♉ 15′ South	APR 25	6° ♏
			MAY 25	4° ♐
	NOV 3	11° ♏ 16′ North	OCT 8	26° ♈
2014	APR 29	9° ♉ 16′ South	APR 15	25° ♎
	OCT 23	1° ♏ 17′ New North	OCT 8	15° ♈
2015	MAR 20	29° ♓ 17′ South	APR 4	14° ♎
	SEP 13	20° ♍ 18′ North	SEP 28	5° ♈
2016	MAR 9	19° ♓ 18′ South	MAR 23	3° ♎
	SEP 1	9° ♍ 19′ North	SEP 16	24° ♓
2017	FEB 26	8° ♓ 19′ South	FEB 11	22° ♌
	AUG 21	29° ♌ 1′ North	AUG 7	15° ♒
2018	FEB 15	27° ♒ 1′ South	JAN 31	12° ♌
	JUL 13	21° ♋ 2′ Old North	JUL 27	5° ♒
	AUG 11	19° ♌ 2′ New North		
2019	JAN 6	15° ♑ 2′ South	JAN 21	1° ♌
	JUL 2	11° ♋ 3′ North	JUL 16	24° ♑
	DEC 26	4° ♑ 3′ South	JAN 10 (’20)	20° ♋

Solar			Lunar	
2020	JUN 21	0° ♋ 4′ North	JUN 5	16° ♐
			JUL 5	14° ♑
	DEC 14	23° ♐ 4′ South	NOV 30	9° ♊
2021	JUN 10	20° ♊ 5′ North	MAY 26	5° ♐
	DEC 4	12° ♐ 5′ South	NOV 19	27° ♉
2022	APR 30	10° ♉ 6′ North	MAY 16	25° ♏
	OCT 25	2° ♏ 6′ South	NOV 8	16° ♉
2023	APR 20	30° ♈ 7′ North	MAY 5	15° ♏
	OCT 14	21° ♎ 7′ South	OCT 28	5° ♉
2024	APR 8	19° ♈ 8′ North	MAR 25	5° ♎
	OCT 2	10° ♎ 8′ South	SEP 18	26° ♓
2025	MAR 29	9° ♈ 9′ New North	MAR 14	24° ♍
	SEP 21	29° ♍ 9′ New South	SEP 7	15° ♓
2026	FEB 17	29° ♒ 10′ North	MAR 3	13° ♏
	AUG 12	20° ♌ 10′ South	AUG 28	5° ♓
2027	FEB 6	18° ♒ 11′ North	FEB 20	2° ♍
	AUG 2	10° ♌ 11′ South	JUL 18	26° ♑
			AUG 17	24° ♒

Solar			Lunar	
2028	JAN 26	6° ≈ 12′ North	JAN 12	21° ♋
	JUL 22	30° ♋ 12′ South	JUL 6	15° ♑
2029	JAN 14	25° ♑ 13′ North	DEC 31 ('28)	11° ♋
	JUN 12	21° ♊ 13′ Old South	JUN 26	5° ♑
	JUL 11	20° ♋ 13′ New South		
	DEC 5	14° ♐ 14′ North	DEC 20	29° ♊
2030	JUN 1	11° ♊ 14′ South	JUN 15	25° ♐
	NOV 25	3° ♐ 15′ North	DEC 9	18° ♊
2031	MAY 21	0° ♊ 15′ South	MAY 7	16° ♏
			JUN 5	15° ♐
	NOV 14	22° ♏ 16′ North	OCT 30	7° ♉
2032	MAY 9	19° ♉ 16′ South	APR 25	6° ♏
	NOV 3	11° ♏ 17′ New North	OCT 18	26° ♈
2033	MAR 30	10° ♈ 17′ South	APR 14	25° ♎
	SEP 23	1° ♎ 18′ North	OCT 8	15° ♈
2034	MAR 20	30° ♓ 18′ South	APR 3	14° ♎
	SEP 12	20° ♍ 19′ North	SEP 28	5° ♈
2035	MAR 9	19° ♓ 19′ South	FEB 22	4° ♍
	SEP 2	9° ♍ 1′ North	AUG 19	26° ≈

Solar			Lunar	
2036	FEB 27	8° ♓ 1' South	FEB 11	23° ♌
	JUL 23	1° ♌ 2' New North	AUG 7	15° ♒
	AUG 21	29° ♌ 2' Old North (ends)		
2037	JAN 16	27° ♑ 2' South	JAN 31	12° ♌
	JUL 13	21° ♋ 3' North	JUL 27	4° ♒
2038	JAN 5	15° ♑ 3' South	JAN 21	1° ♌
	JUL 2	11° ♋ 4' North	JUN 17	26° ♐
			JUL 16	24° ♑
	DEC 26	4° ♑ 4' South	DEC 11	20° ♊
2039	JUN 21	0° ♋ 5' North	JUN 6	16° ♐
	DEC 15	23° ♐ 5' South	NOV 30	8° ♊
2040	MAY 11	21° ♉ 6' North	MAY 26	6° ♐
	NOV 4	13° ♏ 6' South	NOV 18	27° ♉
2041	APR 30	10° ♉ 7' North	MAY 16	26° ♏
	OCT 25	2° ♏ 7' South	NOV 8	16° ♉
2042	APR 20	0° ♉ 8' North	APR 5	16° ♎
	OCT 14	21° ♎ 8' South	SEP 29	6° ♈
2043	APR 9	20° ♈ 9' New North	MAR 25	5° ♎
	OCT 3	10° ♎ 9' New South	SEP 19	26° ♓

Solar			Lunar	
2044	FEB 28	10° ♓ 10′ North	MAR 13	24° ♍
	AUG 23	1° ♍ 10′ South	SEP 7	15° ♓
2045	FEB 16	29° ♒ 11′ North	MAR 3	13° ♍
	AUG 12	20° ♌ 11′ South	AUG 27	5° ♓
2046	FEB 5	17° ♒ 12′ North	JAN 22	3° ♌
	AUG 2	10° ♌ 12′ South	JUL 18	26° ♑
2047	JAN 26	6° ♒ 13′ North	JAN 12	22° ♋
	JUN 23	2° ♋ 13′ Old South	JUL 7	15° ♑
	JUL 22	0° ♌ 13′ New South		
	DEC 16	25° ♐ 14′ North	JAN 1 ('48)	11° ♋
2048	JUN 11	21° ♊ 14′ South	JUN 26	5° ♑
	DEC 5	14° ♐ 15′ North	DEC 20	29° ♊
2049	MAY 31	11° ♊ 15′ South	MAY 17	27° ♏
			JUN 15	25° ♐
	NOV 25	3° ♐ 16′ North	NOV 9	18° ♉
2050	MAY 20	0° ♊ 16′ South	MAY 6	17° ♏
	NOV 14	22° ♏ 17′ New North	OCT 30	7° ♉

Appendix 8

Eclipses in Zodiacal Order

This section is for research purposes. Every Solar and Lunar eclipse of the years 1900 to 2050 has been listed in order of the degree of zodiacal longitude in which it occurred. At the same time, the year is given, and the type of eclipse and the Saros Series is stated.

For example, in considering 20° Gemini, the following list provides these figures:

1983 SOL 3N: 2002 SOL 4N: 2021 SOL 5N: 2038 LUN (4S)

This means that at 20° Gemini, the following eclipses have occurred, or are going to occur:

1983 Solar eclipse Saros Series 3 North;

2002 Solar eclipse Saros Series 4 North;

2021 Solar eclipse Saros Series 5 North;

2038 Lunar eclipse belonging to the Solar Eclipse of Saros Series 4 South.

For the precise date of the eclipses, the years should be looked up in Appendix 7 on page 296.

This table of Solar and Lunar eclipses is an interesting table to browse through, as it shows how some particular zodiacal degrees receive no eclipses over the 150-year period while others receive quite a lot of activity.

Thus, by the use of the following sections, a forthcoming eclipse can be identified in terms of its Saros Series. The Series birth chart can be examined for the type of expression that the eclipse should produce and, additionally, you can check to see if any other eclipses have affected that natal point. This could be by conjunction, looking up the actual zodiacal longitude position; or by opposition, looking up the opposite zodiacal position; or by square; and so on.

ARIES

1°   1904 lun (15N)

3°   1912 lun (4S): 1931 lun (5 old or new S): 1950 lun (6S)

4°   1977 lun (16N): 1996 lun (17 new N)

5°   2015 lun (18N): 2034 lun (19N)

6°   2042 lun (8S)

7°   1903 sol 13S: 1922 sol 14S: 1941 sol 15S: 1960 sol 16S

8°   1968 sol 6N: 1987 sol 7N: 2006 sol 8N

9°   2025 sol 9 new N

10° 2033 sol 17S

12° 1922 lun (15N)

13° 1949 lun (5S): 1968 lun (6S): 1987 lun (7S)

14° 1930 lun (4S)

15° 1995 lun (16N): 2014 lun (17 new N): 2033 lun (18N)

16° 1913 sol 5N

17° 1978 sol 16S

18° 1902 sol 12 old S: 1921 sol 13S: 1940 sol 14S: 1959 sol 15S

19° 1986 sol 6N: 2005 sol 7N: 2024 sol 8N

20° 2043 sol 9 new N

23° 1902 lun (13N): 1921 lun (14N): 1940 lun (15N)

24° 1967 lun (5S): 1986 lun (6S): 2005 lun (7S)

25° 1948 lun (4S)

26° 2013 lun (16N): 2032 lun (17 new N)

27°   1912 sol 5N: 1931 sol 5N

28°   1977 sol 15S: 1996 sol 16S

29°   1939 sol 13S: 1958 sol 14S

30°   2004 sol 6N: 2023 sol 7N

TAURUS

0°   2042 sol 8N

3°   1901 lun (12N)

4°   1920 lun (13N): 1939 lun (14N): 1958 lun (15N)

5°   1985 lun (5S): 2004 lun (6S): 2023 lun (7S)

6°   1966 lun (4S)

7°   1911 sol 3N: 2031 lun (16N): 2050 lun (17 new N)

8°   1930 sol 4N: 1949 sol 5N

9°   1957 sol 13S: 1976 sol 14S: 1995 sol 15S: 2014 sol 16S

10°   2022 sol 6N: 2041 sol 7N

13°   1911 lun (3S)

15°   1919 lun (12N): 1938 lun (13N): 1957 lun (14N): 1976 lun (15N)

16°   1902 sol 12 new S: 1984 lun (4S): 2003 lun (5S): 2022 lun (6S): 2041 lun (7S)

18°   1910 sol 2 old N: 1929 sol 3N: 1948 sol 4N: 1967 sol 5N: 2049 lun (16N)

19°   2032 sol 16S

20°   1975 sol 13S: 1994 sol 14S: 2013 sol 15S

21°   2040 sol 6N

24°   1910 lun (2S): 1929 lun (3S)

26°   1937 lun (12N): 1956 lun (13N): 1975 lun (14N): 1994 lun (15N)

27°   1901 sol 11S: 1920 sol 12S: 2021 lun (5S): 2040 lun (6S)

28°   1928 sol 2 old N: 2002 lun (4S)

29°   1947 sol 3N: 1966 sol 4N: 1985 sol 5N

GEMINI

0°   2012 sol 14S: 2031 sol 15S: 2050 sol 16S

1°   1993 sol 13S

4°   1909 lun (1S)

5°   1928 lun (2S): 1947 lun (3S)

7°   1900 sol 10S: 1919 sol 11S: 1938 sol 12S: 1955 lun (12N): 1974 lun (13N): 1993 lun (14N): 2012 lun (15N)

8°   2039 lun (5S)

9°   1946 sol 2 old N: 1965 sol 3N: 1984 sol 4N: 2003 sol 5N: 2020 lun (4S)

11°   2011 sol 13S: 2030 sol 14S: 2049 sol 15S

14°   1900 lun (11N)

16°   1927 lun (1S): 1946 lun (2S): 1965 lun (3S)

17°   1918 sol 10S

18°   1937 sol 11S: 1956 sol 12S: 1973 lun (12N): 1992 lun (13N): 2011 lun (14N): 2030 lun (15N)

19°   1964 sol 2N

20°   1983 sol 3N: 2002 sol 4N: 2021 sol 5N: 2038 lun (4S)

21°   2029 sol 13S: 2048 sol 14S

25°   1918 lun (11N)

26°   1909 sol 1N: 1928 sol 2 new N:

27° 1926 lun (19N): 1945 lun (1S): 1964 lun (2S)

28° 1917 sol 9 old S: 1936 sol 10S: 1955 sol 11S: 1974 sol 12S: 1983 lun (3S)

29° 1991 lun (12N): 2010 lun (13N): 2029 lun (14N): 2048 lun (15N)

30° 1982 sol 2N

CANCER

0° 2001 sol 3N: 2020 sol 4N: 2039 sol 5N

2° 2047 sol 13S

6° 1917 lun (10N): 1936 lun (11N)

7° 1908 sol 19N: 1946 sol 2 new N

8° 1935 sol 9 old S: 1944 lun (19S): 1954 sol 10S: 1963 lun (1S): 1982 lun (2S)

9° 1973 sol 11S: 1992 sol 12S: 2001 lun (3S): 2011 sol 13 new N

10° 2000 sol 2N: 2009 lun (12N)

11° 2019 sol 3N: 2028 lun (13N): 2038 sol 4N: 2048 lun (14N)

17° 1907 sol 18N: 1917 lun (9 new N): 1926 sol 19N: 1936 lun (10N): 1945 sol 1N: 1955 lun (11N): 1964 sol 2 new N

18° 1953 sol 9S

19° 1963 lun (19S): 1972 sol 10S: 1982 lun (1S): 1991 sol 11S: 2010 sol 12S

20° 2001 lun (2S): 2020 lun (3S): 2029 sol 13 new S

21° 2018 sol 2N: 2028 lun (12N): 2037 sol 3N

22° 2047 lun (13N)

26° 1917 sol 9 new S

27° 1908 lun (18S): 1927 sol 1N: 1944 sol 19N: 1963 sol 1N

28° 1906 sol 17 old N: 1925 sol 18N: 1954 lun (10N): 1982 sol 2 new
N

29° 1916 lun (8N): 1935 lun (9 old or new N): 1971 sol 9S: 1973 lun
(11N): 1990 sol 10S: 2009 sol 11S

30° 2028 sol 12S

LEO

0°   1981 lun (19S): 2047 sol 13 new S

1°   2000 lun (1S): 2019 lun (2S): 2036 sol 2N: 2038 lun (3S)

3°   2046 lun (12N)

6°   1935 sol 9 new S

7°   1916 sol 8S

8°   1924 sol 17 old N: 1926 lun (18S): 1943 sol 18N: 1962 sol 19N:
1981 sol 1N: 2000 sol 2 new N

9°   1907 lun (17S)

10° 1934 lun (8N): 1953 lun (9 new N): 1972 lun (10N): 1991 lun
(11N): 2008 sol 10S: 2027 sol 11S: 2046 sol 12S

11° 1999 lun (19S)

12° 2018 lun (1S): 2037 lun (2S)

17° 1915 sol 7S: 1934 sol 8S: 1953 sol 9 new S

18° 1980 sol 19N: 1999 sol 1N

19° 1942 sol 17 old N: 1944 lun (18S): 1961 sol 18N: 2018 sol 2 new
N

20° 1906 lun (16S): 1925 lun (17S): 2026 sol 10S: 2045 sol 11S

21° 1952 lun (8N): 1971 lun (9 new N): 1990 lun (10N): 2009 lun
(11N)

22° 2017 lun (19S)

23° 2036 lun (1S)

26°   1906 sol 17 new N

27°   1971 sol 9 new S

28°   1914 sol 6S: 1933 sol 7S: 1952 sol 8S

29°   1979 sol 18N: 1998 sol 19N: 2017 sol 1N: 2036 sol 2 new N

VIRGO

0°   1905 lun (15S): 1962 lun (18S)

1°   1924 lun (16S): 1943 lun (17S): 2044 sol 10S

2°   1951 lun (7N): 1970 lun (8N): 1989 lun (9 new N): 2008 lun (10N): 2027 lun (11N)

4°   2035 lun (19S)

6°   1905 sol 16N

7°   1924 sol 17 new N

8°   1913 sol 5 old S: 1932 sol 6S: 1951 sol 7S: 1970 sol 8S: 1989 sol 9 new S

9°   2016 sol 19N: 2035 sol 1N

10°   1915 lun (7N): 1997 sol 18N

11°   1980 lun (18S)

12°   1923 lun (15S): 1942 lun (16S): 1961 lun (17S)

13°   1988 lun (8N): 2007 lun (9 new N): 2026 lun (10N): 2045 lun (11N)

17°   1904 sol 15N: 1923 sol 16N: 1942 sol 17 new N

18°   1931 sol 5 old S: 2007 sol 9 new N

19°   1950 sol 6S: 1969 sol 7S: 1988 sol 8S

20°   2015 sol 18N: 2034 sol 19N

21°   1914 lun (6N): 1933 lun (7N)

22°   1922 lun (14S): 1998 lun (18S)

23°   1941 lun (15S): 1960 lun (16S): 1979 lun (17S)

24°   2006 lun (8N): 2025 lun (9 new N): 2044 lun (10N)

27°   1903 sol 14N: 1922 sol 15N

28°   1941 sol 16N: 1960 sol 17 new N

29°   1968 sol 6S: 2006 sol 8S: 2025 sol 9 new S

30°   1987 sol 7S

LIBRA

1°   1913 lun (5N): 2033 sol 18N

2°   1932 lun (6N): 1951 lun (7N)

3°   1959 lun (15S): 2016 lun (18S)

4°   1978 lun (16S): 1997 lun (17S)

5°   2024 lun (8N): 2043 lun (9 new N)

6°   1913 sol 5 new S

8°   1921 sol 14N: 1940 sol (15N)

9°   1959 sol 16N: 1978 sol 17 new N

10°   1904 lun (14S): 1986 sol 6S: 2005 sol 7S: 2024 sol 8S: 2043 sol 9 new S

12°   1912 lun (4N): 1931 lun (5N): 1950 lun (6N)

13°   1969 lun (7N)

14°   1958 lun (14S): 1977 lun (15S): 2015 lun (17S): 2034 lun (18S)

15°   1996 lun (16S)

16°   2042 lun (8N)

17°   1912 sol 4S: 1931 sol 5 new S

19°   1939 sol 14N: 1958 sol 15N: 1977 sol 16N

20°   1996 sol 17 new N

21°   1903 lun (13S): 2004 sol 6S: 2023 sol 7S: 2042 sol 8S

23°   1930 lun (4N): 1949 lun (5N): 1968 lun (6N)

24°   1987 lun (7N)

25°   1995 lun (15S): 2014 lun (16S): 2033 lun (17S)

26°   1903 lun (14N)

28°   1911 sol 3S: 1930 sol 4S: 1949 sol 5S

30°   1957 sol 14N: 1976 sol 15N

SCORPIO

0°   1995 sol 16N

1°   2014 sol 17 new N

2°   1902 lun (12 old S): 1921 lun (13S): 1940 lun (14S): 2022 sol 6S: 2041 sol 7S

3°   1948 lun (4N)

4°   1967 lun (5N): 1986 lun (6N): 2005 lun (7N)

7°   1902 sol 13N

6°   2013 lun (15S): 2032 lun (16S)

9°   1910 sol 2S: 1929 sol 3S: 1948 sol 4S: 1967 sol 5S

10°   1975 sol 14N

11°   1994 sol 15N: 2013 sol 16N: 2032 sol 17 new N

12°   1920 lun (12S): 1939 lun (13S)

13°   1901 lun (11S): 1958 lun (14S): 2040 sol 6S

14°   1966 lun (4N): 1985 lun (5N)

15°   2004 lun (6N): 2023 lun (7N)

16°   2031 lun (15S)

17°   2050 lun (16S)

18°   1901 sol 12N: 1920 sol 13N

20°   1928 sol 2S: 1947 sol (3S): 1966 sol 5S: 1985 sol 5S

21°   1911 lun (3N)

22°   1993 sol 14N: 2012 sol 15N: 2031 sol 16N: 2050 sol 17 new N

23°   1919 lun (11S): 1938 lun (12S): 1957 lun (13S): 1976 lun (14S)

24°   1984 lun (4N)

25°   2003 lun (5N): 2022 lun (6N)

26°   2041 lun (7N)

27°   2049 lun (15S)

29°   1919 sol 12N: 1938 sol 13N

SAGITTARIUS

0°   1900 sol 11N

1°   1946 lun (2S): 1965 sol 3S: 1984 sol 4S: 2003 sol 5S

2°   1910 lun (2 old N): 1929 lun (3N): 2011 sol 14N

3°   1956 lun (12S): 1975 lun (13S): 2030 sol 15N: 2049 sol 16N

4°   1937 lun (11S): 1994 lun (14S): 2013 lun (15S)

5°   2002 lun (4N): 2021 lun (5N)

6°   2040 lun (6N)

10°   1937 sol 12N: 1956 sol 13N

11°   1918 sol 11N

12°   1947 lun (3N): 1964 sol 2S: 1983 sol 3S: 2002 sol 4S: 2021 sol 5S

13°   1909 lun (1N): 1928 lun (2 old N)

14°   1955 lun (11S): 1974 lun (12S): 1993 lun (13S): 2012 lun (14S):
      2029 sol 14N: 2048 sol 15N

15°   2031 lun (15S)

16° 2020 lun (4N): 2039 lun (5N)

20° 1909 sol 1S

21° 1974 sol 13N

22° 1900 lun (10S): 1917 sol 10N: 1936 sol 11N: 1955 sol 12N

23° 1908 lun (19N): 1927 lun (1N): 1946 lun (2 old N): 1965 lun
(3N): 1982 sol 2S: 1984 lun (4N): 2001 sol 3S: 2020 sol 4S: 2039
sol 5S

24° 1992 lun (12S): 2011 lun (13S or 13 new S)

25° 1973 lun (11S): 2030 lun (14S): 2047 sol 14N: 2049 lun (15S):
2038 lun (4N)

CAPRICORN

1° 1908 sol 19S: 1927 sol 1S

2° 1918 lun (10S): 1992 sol 13N

3° 1916 sol 9 old N: 1935 sol 10N: 1954 sol 11N: 1964 lun (2N or 2
new N): 1973 sol 12N: 1983 lun (3N): 2002 lun (4N)

4° 1945 lun (1N): 2000 sol 2S: 2018 sol 3S: 2038 sol 4S

5° 1991 lun (11S): 2010 lun (12S): 2029 lun (13S or 13 new S): 2048
lun (14S)

12° 1908 sol 18S: 1917 lun (9 new or old S): 1927 sol 19S

13° 1936 lun (10S): 1946 sol 1S

14° 1935 sol 9 old N: 1954 sol 10N: 1963 lun (1N): 1973 sol 11N:
1982 lun (2N or 2 new N): 1992 sol 12N: 2001 lun (3N): 2011 sol
13N: 2020 lun (4N)

15° 2009 lun (11S): 2010 sol 12N: 2019 sol 2S: 2028 lun (12S): 2038
sol 3S: 2047 lun (13S or 13 new S)

22° 1916 lun (8S)

23° 1907 sol 17S: 1926 sol 18S: 1935 lun (9 old or new S): 1954 lun
(10S): 1973 lun (11S)

24°   1945 sol (19S): 1962 lun (19N): 1964 sol 1S: 2000 lun (2 new N or 2N): 2019 lun (3N): 2038 lun (4N)

25°   1972 sol 10N: 1981 lun (1N): 2029 sol 13N

26°   1991 sol 11N: 2027 lun (11S): 2046 lun (12S)

27°   2037 sol 2S

AQUARIUS

1°   1907 lun (18N)

2°   1926 lun (19N)

3°   1917 sol 9 new N: 1934 lun (8S): 1953 lun (9S or 9 new S): 1972 lun (10S): 1991 lun (11S)

4°   1925 sol 17S: 2037 lun (3N)

5°   1944 sol 18S: 1963 sol 19S: 1980 lun (19N): 1982 sol 1S: 1999 lun (1N): 2018 lun (2N or 2 new N)

6°   2009 sol 11N: 2028 sol 12N: 2047 sol 13N

7°   1990 sol 10N

11°   1906 lun (17 old or new N)

12°   1925 lun (18N): 1944 lun (19N)

13°   1952 lun (8S)

14°   1916 sol 8N: 1935 sol 9 new N: 1971 lun (9S or 9 new S): 1990 lun (10S): 2009 lun (11S)

15°   1943 sol 17S: 1998 lun (19N): 2017 lun (1N): 2036 lun (2N or 2 new N)

16°   1962 sol 18S: 1981 sol 19S: 2000 sol 1S

17°   2046 sol 12N

18°   2008 sol 10N: 2027 sol 11N

22°   1905 lun (16N): 1924 lun (17 old or new N): 1943 lun (18N): 1962 lun (19N)

23°   1951 lun (7S)

24°   1915 sol 7N: 1970 lun (8S): 1989 lun (9 new S): 2008 lun (10S): 2027 lun (11S)

25°   1934 sol 8N: 1953 sol 9 new N

26°   1961 sol 17S: 2035 lun (1N)

27°   1980 sol 18S: 1999 sol 19S: 2018 sol 1S

29°   2026 sol 10N: 2045 sol 11N

PISCES

1°   1915 lun (7S)

2°   1923 lun (16N): 1942 lun (17 old or new N)

3°   1961 lun (18N)

4°   1906 sol 16S: 1969 lun (7S): 1988 lun (8S)

5°   1933 sol 7N: 2007 lun (9 new S): 2026 lun (10S): 2045 lun (11S)

6°   1914 sol 6N: 1952 sol 8N: 1971 sol 9 new N

7°   1979 sol 17S

8°   1998 sol 18S: 2017 sol 19S: 2036 sol 1S

10°   2044 sol 10N

11°   1914 lun (6S): 1933 lun (7S)

13°   1941 lun (16N): 1960 lun (17 new N): 1979 lun (18N)

14°   1998 lun (19N)

15°   1905 sol 15S: 1924 sol 16S: 2006 lun (8S): 2025 lun (9 new S): 2044 lun (10S)

16°   1951 sol 7N

17°   1932 sol 6N: 1970 sol 8N: 1989 sol 9 new N

19°   1997 sol 17S: 2016 sol 18S: 2035 sol 19S

22° 1913 lun (5 old or new S): 1932 lun (6S): 1951 lun (7S): 1970 lun
(8S)

23° 1959 lun (16N)

24° 1978 lun (17 new N): 1997 lun (18N): 2016 lun (19N)

26° 1942 sol 16S: 1904 sol 14S: 1923 sol 16N: 2024 lun (8S): 2043 lun
(9 new S)

27° 1950 sol 6N: 1969 sol 7N

28° 1988 sol 8N: 2007 sol 9 new N

29° 2015 sol 17S

30° 2034 sol 18S

Bibliography

Bradley, D. A., *Solar and Lunar Returns*. St. Paul, MN: Llewellyn Publications, 1974.

Braha, J. T., *Ancient Hindu Astrology for the Modern Western Astrologer*. Hollywood, FL: Hermetican Press, 1986.

Bram, J. R. (translator), *Ancient Astrology Theory and Practice: The Mathesis of Firmicus Maternus*. Park Ridge, NJ: Noyes Press, 1975.

Bulfinch, T., *Myths of Greece and Rome*. New York: Penguin Books, 1985.

Chinen, A. B., *In the Ever After: Fairy Tales and the Second Half of Life*. Wilmette, IL: Chiron Publications, 1989.

Cooper, J. C., *Fairy Tales: Allegories of the Inner Life*. London: Aquarian Press, 1985.

Ebertin, R., *The Combination of Stellar Influences*. Tempe, AZ: American Federation of Astrologers, 1972.

Encyclopedia Britannica. 15th edition, 1989.

Erlewine, S., *The Circle Book of Charts*. Big Rapids, MI: Circle Books, 1972.

Gibbs-Smith, C., *The Inventions of Leonardo da Vinci*. Oxford: Phaidon Press, 1978.

Grey, E., *Presidents of the United States*. New York: Gallery Books, 1988.

Harrison, J. M., *Fowler's Compendium of Nativities*. Romford, UK: L. N. Fowler & Co., 1980.

Hawking, S., *A Brief History of Time*. London: Transworld Publishers, 1988.

Lilly, W., *Christian Astrology*. London: Regulus Publishing Co., 1985.

Mann, A. T., *The Round Art*. New York: Galley Press (imprint of W. H. Smith), 1979.

Michelsen, N. F., *The American Ephemeris for the 20th Century: 1900 to 2000 at Midnight*. San Diego, CA: ACS Publications, 1983.

———. *Tables of Planetary Phenomena*. San Diego, CA: ACS Publications, 1990.

Rodden, L. M., *Profiles of Women*. Tempe, AZ: American Federation of Astrologers, 1979.

————. *The American Book of Charts.* San Diego, CA: ACS Publications, 1980.

————. *Astro-Data III.* Tempe, AZ: American Federation of Astrologers, 1986.

Sepharial, *Directional Astrology.* London: Regulus Publishing Co., 1986.

Walker, B. G., *The Women's Encyclopedia of Myths and Secrets.* San Francisco: HarperCollins, 1983.

Index

Also in Weiser Classics

The Alchemist's Handbook: A Practical Manual, by Frater Albertus,
with a new foreword by Robert Allen Bartlett

The Druidry Handbook: Spiritual Practice Rooted in the Living Earth,
by John Michael Greer, with a new foreword by Dana O'Driscoll

Futhark: A Handbook of Rune Magic, by Edred Thorsson,
newly revised and updated by the author

The Handbook of Yoruba Religious Concepts, by Baba Ifa Karade,
newly revised and updated by the author

*The Herbal Alchemist's Handbook: A Complete Guide to Magickal Herbs
and How to Use Them,* by Karen Harrison, with a new foreword
by Arin Murphy-Hiscock

Liber Null and Psychonaut: The Practice of Chaos Magic, by Peter J. Carroll,
newly revised and updated by the author, with a new foreword
by Ronald Hutton

The Mystical Qabalah, by Dion Fortune, with a new foreword
by Judika Illes and a new afterword by Stuart R. Harrop

*Psychic Self-Defense: The Definitive Manual for Protecting Yourself Against
Paranormal Attack,* by Dion Fortune, with a new foreword by
Mary K. Greer and a new afterword by Christian Gilson

Pure Magic: A Complete Course in Spellcasting, by Judika Illes, with a new
introduction by the author and a new foreword by Mat Auryn

Saturn: A New Look at an Old Devil, by Liz Greene,
with a new foreword by Juliana McCarthy

Spiritual Cleansing: A Handbook of Psychic Protection,
by Draja Mickaharic, with a new foreword by Lilith Dorsey

Taking Up the Runes: A Complete Guide to Using Runes in Spells,
Rituals, Divination, and Magic, by Diana L. Paxson,
with new material by the author

Yoga Sutras of Patanjali, by Mukunda Stiles,
with a new foreword by Mark Whitwell